*"I AM NOT A COURTESAN OR A PRO-
MISCUOUS WOMAN, BUT I NEED TO
LOVE AND TO BE LOVED . . . I CANNOT
FUNCTION WITHOUT IT!"*

Britt Ekland is one of the screen's most successful sex goddesses—the object of countless
men's fantasies.

But for many men, Britt Ekland has been far
more than a fantasy—as she rode a dizzying,
dazzling merry-go-round of love with some of
the most famous partners in the world.

The story Britt Ekland has to tell is incredible,
fascinating, fantastic—but it is quite simply the
naked truth.

TRUE BRITT

TRUE BRITT
by
BRITT EKLAND

BERKLEY BOOKS, NEW YORK

This Berkley book contains the complete
text of the original hardcover edition.
It has been completely reset in a type face
designed for easy reading, and was printed
from new film.

TRUE BRITT

A Berkley Book / published by arrangement with
Prentice-Hall, Inc.

PRINTING HISTORY
Prentice-Hall edition published 1980
Berkley edition / June 1982

ISBN: 0–425–05341–5

A BERKLEY BOOK ® TM 757,375
Berkley Books are published by Berkley Publishing Corporation,
200 Madison Avenue, New York, New York 10016.
The name ''BERKLEY'' and the stylized ''B'' with design
are trademarks belonging to Berkley Publishing Corporation.
PRINTED IN THE UNITED STATES OF AMERICA

For Victoria, who has been the only permanency in my life, and who, unwittingly, kept me sane.

And for Nicholai who, since his arrival, has given nothing but love and affection.

And for Lou, just for giving.

Mother and Father too, of course.

—Britt, Los Angeles
May 1979

— *one* —

WHEN my daughter Victoria was thirteen I sat her down and spelt out the vagaries of my life to her as a warning.

"You have to understand I am an actress. I'm divorced. I've lived with men without being married. I've had a child out of wedlock. I've got everything stacked against me and if you do anything wrong it will reflect, not on you, but on me," I told her. "And the world will say, 'Well, what do you expect with a mother like that?' "

I fear the world may already have judged me, but I do not want Victoria, or my son Nicholai, ever to have to answer for my sins. If sins they are.

I am not a courtesan or a promiscuous woman, but I need to love and to be loved. My work, my whole way of being, cannot function without emotional nourishment.

Over the years I have resisted the blandishments of Hollywood to mold me as a sex symbol because I would sooner acquire the status of an actress with bona fide credentials.

Unfortunately, my personal life has frequently impeded that desire.

I am famous, but not for the reasons I still hold sacred.

The statistics of the celluloid industry show that I have made twenty-five movies but none, alas, has borne such scrutiny or provoked so much conversation and controversy, as my private life. Forbid this should be my epitaph.

In affairs of the heart I am frail and vulnerable and often irrational. When I give myself to a man it is a total commitment that imprisons me. For better, for worse.

I have been accused of being capricious; of shielding behind the trappings of the rich and the distinguished. This may well be a fair judgment, but in what circumstances would I meet a factory worker, a clerk or an engineer?

We are all domiciled in our own professions.

It is true that most of my lovers have been wealthy, but I have always managed to retain my independence.

I can say "No" to any man at any time. I cannot be bought.

Should testimony be required, I am sure that Patrick Lichfield, Warren Beatty, George Hamilton and Ryan O'Neal, all of whom have figured in my life, would subscribe to it.

I have loved many men and I have lost many men.

Some have come to chip rough edges smooth, others to provide a broad shoulder to cry on and there are those who have led me helplessly into blind alleys.

Three men only have shaped my destiny.

I was a young naïve, impressionable Swedish starlet when I married actor Peter Sellers in 1964. New horizons opened for me. I was whisked into the heady provinces of princes and palaces; I played hostess to a procession of celebrities and stars I only knew as legends from my youth.

Sellers smothered me with so much love in the first month of our marriage, that I should have guessed that like a fractured wine cask, it would soon run dry, but our moments of real happiness, like in the days surrounding the birth of our daughter Victoria, were rare and far apart.

The man who made millions laugh on screen and radio was unhappy on the blind side of the cameras and microphones, while in public he presented himself as my affectionate husband.

It was not always easy to bear, but I did not want to

be the one to destroy his image.

Ultimately, I could no longer stand the strain of this relationship. I swallowed a handful of sleeping pills, not in a deliberate attempt to commit suicide, but unperturbed whether I woke or not to see another dawn.

I survived. Divorce was the only logical step.

Even now I cannot bring myself to refer to my former husband by his Christian name. The pain hurts that much.

Sellers may have held similar feelings about me. He always prefaced his letters, "Dear Miss Ekland" . . . when he wrote to me on matters affecting our daughter.

We were distant even when he was alive, though Victoria was always a bond between us.

How different a man is Lou Adler, the American film director in whose love I once basked. He is compassionate and caring, the proudest of fathers to our son Nicholai.

Of all the men who have played a part in my life, I hold the most respect for Lou. He remains uncontaminated by the glamour and glitter of Hollywood, in which he picks his living.

A maverick of Tinsel Town, Lou is able to view things in perspective. He is a pillar of quiet wisdom.

I worshiped Lou through our live-in relationship. Ours was not an instant, burning love, but one that grew steadily in the passing days when those early passions had subsided.

Sadly our love expired when Lou cheated on me. In the end, neither of us could live with deception.

I was more frenetically in love with Rod Stewart, the rock star, than with any other man, past or present.

Our relationship was a fantasy from the beginning, like a comet in the sky, but one which I never thought would burn to earth.

We jetted the world in our peacock finery, a couple so much in love and with so much to live for.

Our love nest was a cloistered mansion in California

into which we poured our hearts, our dreams and a million dollars' worth of art nouveau.

My career came to a halt. I sacrificed everything for the man I would have gladly died for.

Rod, the tartan terror among an infectious camaraderie of musicians, treated me like a goddess but one he passed off as the "missus."

Alas, somewhere along the line I slipped from my pedestal. I deceived myself into believing that Rod would never stray back to the environmental hazards of the pop world.

When it happened, it was as though the tide had reclaimed him.

I clung to the threads of our relationship with bare, shattered fingernails.

In my sheer and utter desperation I turned to drugs, snorting cocaine, in the crazed belief that it would help me through the crisis.

Eventually, like a simpering, tortured freak, I surrendered myself to a psychiatrist's couch.

Obediently accepting my lawyers' advice, I filed a 12,500,000 dollar lawsuit against Rod.

It was the biggest mistake of my life. By my own hand I had painted a portrait of myself as a vengeful, grasping and materialistic woman—characteristics which I feel are alien to my true nature.

The real motive was lost. All I wanted back was my man, my pride and my dignity.

— *two* —

THE year 1942 was dawning. The world was at war. Most of Europe was under the heel of the jackboot.

But life in Sweden, preserving its traditional neutrality, remained remarkably untouched by the mayhem beyond its borders.

My father was recruited to the Army reserves, their role being a precautionary measure, and he kept his gray uniform in his wardrobe, along with a gas mask which was occasionally produced as a party piece. As a toddler that was all I knew of the war.

Through those dark years Sweden was inundated by protected citizens from other countries, and, as a result, our society instinctively put up class barriers.

I was born in the Allmänna B.B., a maternity hospital in Stockholm on 6 October, a true Libran at least. My early childhood had been extremely happy, even though my parents were strict and I was unnecessarily sheltered and cosseted.

There were times, which, when I think back, seem like one long summer's day. These memories still bring me pleasure. I can see the wheat fields, where I picnicked with my mother and three brothers Bo, Bengt and Kalle; I can recall gathering berries from the rambling briars and climbing the green hills. And at season's end, wrapping up for the bitterly cold black winters, running to and from school by six-foot-high snow walls, our breath nearly turning to icicles.

There was no shortage of money and we were all pam-

pered as children. Whatever we asked for we usually
got, whether it was a new toy or perhaps in my case a
new dress.

Our home was an apartment on Sturegatan in the
center of bustling Stockholm. It was bright and roomy
with tasteful antique furnishings, ornate fireplaces and
stucco ceilings and walls.

My mother's artistic talents surrounded us in the decorative porcelain figurines that she spent hours paint-
ing, while my father collected modern art.

My father Sven Axel Eklund, was a true Viking. A
tall, blond and handsome man, curiously resembling
Britain's Prince Philip, to whom I was to be presented
in the years ahead.

As a young man my father's ambitions were to become a commercial artist, and he traveled extensively,
studying in Vienna and Bucharest.

However, his energies were somewhat wasted since it
was always apparent to the rest of the family that one
day he and his younger brother would inherit the family
business.

My grandfather, a truly remarkable figure, had
founded a store specializing in women's fashions in
Boras, which was later transferred to Stockholm. On his
retirement, it was handed down to my father. It was
then a very flourishing concern, importing designs from
London and Milan.

Father, now with a family to support, realized it was
impractical to continue his pursuits to become an artist.

The role of merchant suited him well. The social
gateway opened to him, although he was already a
popular figure in sporting circles.

Sport was his big love. As a yachtsman he narrowly
missed an Olympic place in Sweden's 1948 team.

He played golf, he went bowling and when he wasn't
skiing during the winter months he was to be found on
the ice rinks playing the traditional game of curling of
which he was a champion.

My father possessed a certain lust for high living. He
touched life where he could with humor, and at parties

he was always surrounded by admirers who sought out his sparkling wit and conversation.

My mother was very different. She was content to be a housewife, happy to stay at home and look after her children.

As a young woman she had been very beautiful. She had long dark hair and soft feminine features. She had come from the North but her ancestry was always thought to be Flemish.

She was the youngest of fourteen children but the family was beset by tragedy and only eight of them survived.

She was only a year old when her parents were divorced. She never knew her father at all.

Her mother went out to work to make ends meet. Grandmother was a deeply religious woman and I can see her even today reclining in her chair as she read passages from the Bible to me.

The years of hardship were etched on her face.

Single-handed she had made a home that was simple, but spotless. It was a far cry from the luxury that was to be found in the home of my father's parents.

But my paternal grandmother had not had an easy life either.

She had left home when she was sixteen and had gone to America, which was a precarious trip to contemplate in the early years of the century.

Qualifying as a physiotherapist she worked in a hospital, arming her bodice with safety pins to discourage lecherous patients from fondling her breasts.

Her marriage brought her back to Sweden where she was able to enjoy her life more fully, and close to retirement she moved into a seventh floor apartment block with my grandfather which would only become disorganized on the arrival of their spirited grandchildren.

In the ominous view of butler-cum-chauffeur, we would play catch ball from the balcony to the street below, and when retrieving the ball we would compete with the elevator by taking the staircase and the clatter of our feet would echo round the building.

My grandfather's proudest possession was a huge maroon car, an Oldsmobile, which I believe was the only American car on the streets of Stockholm at that period.

It was kept in immaculate condition and I would be given long Sunday afternoon rides in the car, sometimes to the seaside and on other occasions into the countryside, although I secretly dreaded these outings because I was invariably car sick.

It was at an all-girls State-aided private school, the Nya Elementar För Flickor, only a mile from my doorstep, where I learned that life is truly a compromise.

Those who have labored with words to describe my beauty and appeal in adult years would not have recognized me in childhood, for I was the original ugly duckling.

It wasn't surprising that I suffered from so many complexes. For a start I was grossly overweight, and because of my size my mother dressed me in gray Cashmere twin sets. With a cloak on top I resembled a sailing barge and my friends would tease, "You'll take off in the wind."

My hair was an unfortunate mousey brown and father insisted that I should wear it swept up in a French "twirl" which I hated.

Only a certain breed of girl wore her hair down, he told me, and "You don't want to be a bad girl, do you?"

But that was not the worst of it. My upswept hair meant my protruding ears were also visible for ridicule and although I tried taping them down with adhesive strips they always popped out again. Then there were my buck teeth. My friends watched fascinated as I gnawed at my food like a rabbit. My forehead also bore a scar—it is still faintly visible today—which I collected when slipping up on the parquet floor at home.

I disguised the hurt and pain of the taunts by pretending to be the "funny" girl. By making the other girls laugh I was accepted into their classroom cliques.

The energy I put into this deception was clearly at the expense of my academic studies.

Britt-Marie Eklund was never destined to win many school honors or degrees, but she trod a safe, middle-of-the-road course through her curriculum.

There was one significant experience which came at the age of twelve. I was cast in a school play and on stage I remember taking the limelight for the first time from the prettier girls who sat in the audience watching me. I tingled inside with excitement and although I hardly realized it then, the seeds of the acting profession were surely sown.

Yet I still thought I might become a vet. I loved animals and we kept a Siamese cat and a Dachshund. But my greater passion was for horses.

My father had friends who ran trotting horses and occasionally he took me to the races. I had also taken riding lessons, paid for by my grandmother, who bought me a helmet, suit and breeches and other accessories.

Again, my affinity with animals was probably an escape measure from my physical unattractiveness.

At home all four of us accepted my father's discipline which was suitably diluted by my mother.

My father reminded us that he had been brought up more strictly and he had always addressed his father as "Sir." We were similarly groomed into observing certain formalities. Whenever my brothers were introduced to a visitor to our home, they were expected to bow and I would have to curtsey. We would also have to shake hands firmly, rather than limply, and always look the visitor straight in the eye and respond, "How do you do?" Our manners were polished to impeccable standards for the correct occasions.

There were no exemptions from Sunday School. We were expected to attend every class. We were Protestants as a family and from the age of seven I believed in God and in miracles.

My mother once lost a pearl necklace just as she was going out to a party with my father. I knelt down inside a clothes cupboard and prayed and the necklace was found behind a chest in the hall.

My parents moved in a tight bourgeois circle where certain conventions and regulations existed. A wife had not arrived in society until she had at least one fur coat in her wardrobe and one diamond ring in her jewelry case, while her husband would be expected to boast an English car. One obligatory evening a week was spent playing bridge.

My mother, on her rare occasions out, would wear an elegant Balmain gown and my father would favor a reefer jacket and gray flannels, a casual contrast to his working-day gray suit, camel hair coat and Humphrey Bogart style hat.

These conventional standards, I am sure, influenced us considerably as children, but I don't think we suffered too much as a result.

In the constant company of three brothers I was unwittingly molded into something of a tomboy and I took delight in dressing as they did because slacks also helped to disguise my weight problem.

My favorite outfit about the house was the "cowboy" look with check shirt and cords and I would always tag along as one of the "gang."

The boys, once out of parental sight, would smoke cigarettes and they trusted me sufficiently not to spill the beans. When I was accidentally shot in the leg by one of their pellet guns, it was more than my life was worth to tell my parents. So the wound was left to heal naturally under my socks. I am convinced that the stray pellet is still lodged in my leg today.

Several times, I collected a spanking from my father because of my rebellious nature. Once for playing among the logs in the wood cellars from which we were barred because of the dirt and the danger.

The unconscious changes that come to a girl passing through puberty created a rift in the home as I began to retaliate against my father's discipline. Other aspects also emerged in his character that I was to see for the first time.

Whenever I had worn lipstick or make-up my father had ordered me to wash it off immediately, but when I peroxided my hair at a friend's home I knew that it could not be washed out. I just had to face the music.

My mother, as well as my father, was aghast, but there was nothing they could do about this. I had become a blond—and a defiant blond I stayed.

My father did not accept defeat easily. When I dared to stay out until the early hours with successful end-of-term pupils who had gained their "White Hats," which in Sweden signify a student's graduation, he thrashed me. My mother climbed out of bed to intervene and my father, by then uncontrollable with rage, hit her, too, and accused her of having reared me as a "slut."

If I dated a boy, my father would lodge a broomstick against the front door so that it would collapse when I returned and rouse him from his slumbers in his living-room armchair. Life at home was becoming intolerable.

I first discovered love when I was seventeen and still at school.

Suddenly I had become aware of the opposite sex; or more likely they had become aware of me. The ugly duckling had undergone a remarkable transition.

I had lost my puppy fat and my figure had some shape to it. Out of school I let my hair down and for the first time I could face myself in the mirror without a trace of shame.

Kjell was a crew-cut boy from Stockholm. I had met him at a party. He was also seventeen but had already left school and worked as a used car salesman while playing as a drummer in a local band at nights.

Unfortunately, my parents did not approve of him because he had left school without any degrees and they were not happy about his background, although his father was a famous musician.

We wanted to get engaged and Kjell bought two rings which we exchanged. But I did not dare tell my parents.

I kept the ring hidden, slipping it under my pillow at

night. I had also started smoking, but I dared not light a cigarette in my room. It seemed that I was living under a veil of secrecy.

After going out with Kjell for more than a year, my schoolfriends were shocked to learn that I was still a virgin, so rather than suffer further embarrassment I surrendered to Kjell's continued persuasion.

I yielded my virginity at Kjell's home when his parents were out one Saturday afternoon. It was all carefully planned.

We were with another couple of friends who had been sleeping together for some time. We tossed coins for which couple should have the best room and alas, they won. We were left to make love on a single pull-down bed in the kitchenette.

We were so excited that we kept on most of our clothes and Kjell could not contain himself.

There was little of the pain of which my friends had warned me and in five minutes precisely my virginity was no longer precious.

We immediately straightened the bed before breathlessly bowling into the other bedroom to tell our friends of our wonderful achievement. They were hardly interested—they were still in the throes of their own encounter.

It was strange. I felt no sexual awareness even after that first experience. The first time, with any man, is always a disappointment. So much is expected; unfortunately the anticipation is always greater than the reward.

Young love is essentially innocent and selfish, and Kjell never considered that a girl needed to be satisfied too.

Our secret engagement lasted almost a year before I realized that we had grown apart and that I was maturing faster than Kjell.

Instinct told me that my future could not be with a boy whose ambitions were so limited. Anyway, I wasn't at all sure that he had given any thought to sharing his life permanently with a woman.

There were no tears or "Dear John" letters. I simply told him that I did not feel it would work out and handed back the ring.

Seeing me alone, my father gradually eased me into his social world. Suddenly I was taking my mother's place with him at cocktail parties and sporting events and he bought me dresses for all occasions.

Deep down I felt quite guilty because he did not buy my mother similar presents, but although this must have hurt her a great deal, she never allowed it to show.

Indeed she seemed happy for me. My father took pride in showing me off, and when we returned from one of father's outings, my mother would ask me without any sign of jealousy, "Did you have a good time?"

My father needed to have someone glamorous at his side: it bolstered his ego.

I did not realize then the stresses and strains that mother had secretly suffered to make her marriage work.

Slowly, it dawned on me that my father really was a playboy and a flirt. I felt sure he had been disloyal to my mother. I was even more certain when I spotted his car in the parking lot with another woman in the passenger seat.

I was appalled. I was positive that my mother had never been unfaithful to him.

This discovery led to fresh friction between us and I found myself defending my mother in arguments. The rows became more frequent as my father stayed out late at night. I suspected that the evenings were not always entirely spent on a "game of cards" with the boys.

By now, it had become all too clear to me that my parents' marriage was far from happy; that they had probably lived in pretense for many years and that mother had only held on because of us, the children.

I often became caught in their quarrels. On one occasion when I could suffer no more, I moved to my grandparents' home for three weeks.

Fortunately my three brothers escaped the ordeal as

the rows usually broke out well after they were in bed.

Normally I would have stayed at school until I was eighteen, but all this upheaval made me impatient to make my own way in life.

My previously held ambitions to become a veterinary surgeon I am afraid had waned in the knowledge that I would have to undertake a seven-year course.

I wanted my independence, my freedom, much sooner than that.

I decided to become an actress.

My parents objected strongly to the idea and thought it was a phase I would quickly pass through. They directed me to a commercial school to take up typing and stenography, so that I would always have something solid "to fall back on" as they stressed repeatedly.

Needless to say I was quite hopeless and seventeen successive typing lessons did little to persuade me that I would ever qualify as a secretary.

My horizons were much broader than that.

After all, what was so wrong with the life of Brigitte Bardot whose daily activities were so vividly documented in the glossy magazines?

It was contagious to me.

— *three* —

IMITATING Brigitte Bardot led to my debut as an actress. I was fifteen when the bug first took me and still at school. Bardot was the reigning sex symbol of the day and I got the classroom vote for bearing the most striking resemblance to her.

One of my closest school friends thought so, too, and told this to her sister who worked for a woman who was a television producer. Fortuitously, she was in the process of filming a program on the trends of the modern teenager and she could not ignore the influence that Bardot exerted on us all at that time.

Obtaining the consent of my parents and the school headmistress, she selected me to play in a small cameo of the program where a teenaged boy was to remark how much I looked like the famous French actress.

There were another twenty teenage girls on the program but I remember being very nervous about my trivial little part.

However, once the television company's make-up department had dolled me up, I could quite easily have won a Bardot clone contest with my yellow hair tumbling about my heart-shaped face.

The success of the production meant that I was invited to appear in other Swedish television shows in walk-on parts.

I was also asked to model in photographic commercials and cinema advertising films, including those for chewing gum, toothpaste and soda water.

My parents continued to nurse doubts at my desire to

be an actress, but after much pleading and cajoling they sent me on a short holiday to stay with a friend whose name was distinguished in Swedish theatrical circles.

I must have impressed her because, to my surprise, father agreed to pay for my first year at a recognized drama school, the Kalle Flygare, in Stockholm.

It was more than I dared hope for.

My studies in drama school proved far less rigorous than I imagined. There were readings from Shakespeare, Keats and other masters; there were long and laborious productions, and we did excerpts from musicals like *No, No, Nanette* and *Oklahoma*.

Everything else centered on the social life.

Sometimes I thought that drama school was only a means to wear black leotards, tights and turtle neck sweaters and to go to wine cellar parties where we all looked alike in the glow of a candle stuck into an empty Chianti bottle.

My ambitions, however, were accelerating rapidly. I also took ballet lessons which subsequently resulted in an affair with a handsomely sculptured Russian tutor I called Boris. He was like Nureyev in looks and his life was just as enigmatic.

No one knew how he came to be in Stockholm, or anything about his family background. It made him all the more mysterious.

We would make love on the hard wooden benches in the ballet school's changing rooms, because Boris, who was living in digs with the school's principal, the aging Madame Karina, could never take me home.

I knew that my parents would not approve of Boris, who eventually left Madame Karina to form his own jazz ballet classes. His aim was to open branches all over Sweden. Then, strangely, he disappeared.

My father got a phone call from the police asking whether he could help trace the missing Russian "as he is known to be a close friend of your daughter's."

Father erupted with predictable fury and I was forbidden to see Boris, who eventually reappeared at the stage door of the drama school sobbing like a child when I tried to shrug free of him.

A holiday in St. Moritz was the remedy to cure my broken heart—or so my father thought. And off I went with my father as chaperone.

Boris did not dare to follow and our affair was over. But I had not heard the last of him.

Sometime later I received a dramatic call from him late at night. He said he was ill and needed help. I hurried to him, and found him sprawled out on the floor of a high-rise apartment. He asked me to get him a drink into which I was to stir six spoonfuls of sugar. In later years I learned that this was a drink used by drug addicts going into cold turkey. I left him recovering in a chair: he said he had another girl friend who was pregnant and he imagined they would marry.

"I just had to call you Britt to see you again. I was in a bad way," he said.

When next I heard from the Russian ballet dancer I was married to Sellers: Boris pleaded on the telephone to see me but by then my future was determined. I could not go back.

My stage school days were of profound experience to me. Most of the students came from poorer homes than mine and I was so embarrassed by my well-to-do background that I didn't dare to take any of my new friends home. I pretended that I was starving and broke, just to be one of them, but the guise did not fool anyone for very long.

My sheltered, comfortable upbringing was soon exposed and I felt fragile in my brittle surroundings. My fellow students, most of whom were truly adept at fending for themselves, hammered out my green edges. Their armory of defense relied on a barrage of four letter words, the meaning of which was never lost on me.

Sooner than I anticipated I also had to fend for myself. My father withdrew his financial support in my second year at drama school. He was putting me to the test. Just how much did I want to be an actress?

My monthly fee at school was 250 kroner, so I took a part-time job in a Stockholm theater, the Kar De Mumma Revue, as a hat-check girl.

My best friend in school Mari Goranson, today a very well known stage actress in Sweden, also worked with me. It was more like slave labor for the slender wages we received. Not only did we check all the coats and hats and sell ice cream, soft drinks and peanuts during the interval, but we also had to clean the sales kiosk afterwards.

We relied heavily on tips and a "tronc" system operated so that the spoils should be equally divided among the staff. We were too naïve to realize that the "dragon" who supervised us had perfected a unique method of cooking the books.

My first job out of stage school was with Knapp Upp (Button-Up), a touring revue company famous in Scandinavia for its musicals and variety shows.

We would work in the provinces performing under our own tent, which was the largest in Europe.

We were like a traveling circus! Our show was a kaleidoscope of comedy and burlesque with all the song-and-dance favorites of the day. There were three stars of the show, four shapely chorus girls and a couple of hopeful protégées of which I was one.

We all wore an identical Bunny-club style costume: a gaudy, silver-buttoned swimsuit creation which was so heavily boned that in order to slither into it we had to inhale deeply while another member of the cast buttoned it up. No wonder they called it the Button-up company!

Our top hats were decorated with silver buttons and, of course, we wore the statutory fishnet stockings and high-heeled shoes.

As the newcomer, I paraded the placard announcing the acts and then dived backstage to help with the props. Sometimes I even found myself playing the rear half of a donkey!

The main dressing room—only the stars had their own—was a communal affair with heavy curtains dividing the boys from the girls and if, in the backstage pandemonium, the makeshift partition fell down—it was just too bad! Even caught half-naked we were all too busy to re-hang the wretched thing.

I was twenty and this was my first real glimpse into the glittering world of show business. Out front it was all gloss and glamour, but backstage things were really threadbare.

In my first month I earned 800 kroner together with an allowance of 40 kroner expenses per day. To me, it seemed a fortune. I was even able to send some money home for my mother.

I made swift strides. Within a few months I was playing in the sketches and my big opportunity came when one of the stars fell sick. I took her place and my heart thumped so loudly that I'm sure the front row of the audience could hear . . .

We traveled from town to town by coach across Sweden. The stars had their own cars, like Birgitta Anderson who was to Sweden what a young Phyllis Diller is to America today—a very fine comedienne.

I had become a close friend of Birgitta's and we shared long hours at the driving wheel of her Volkswagen beetle. We timed our exits and entrances to the split second, changing in the car and keeping our makeup in the glove compartment, dabbing on our greasepaint at the traffic lights.

We did such wonderful scatty things and got away with them!

Each touring company has a "Mr. Casanova," the macho man who thinks he can persuade every girl he meets to climb into the sack with him.

We had our own muscular version whose favorite ploy, once rejected, was to burst into the girl's hotel room stark naked in the middle of the night, presuming she would give in at the mere sight of him. We treated him as a joke and Mr. Casanova was often repelled by ashtrays, table lamps and pillows.

One night two of us thought we would teach him a lesson. We raided his room and reversed the procedure. Our sexy friend took cover as we stripped off. His much vaunted sexual prowess deserted him in his moment of need and his image was shattered instantly.

My own sex life was being conducted with some degree of caution. The theater owner's daughter was in love with the pianist, a handsome boy whose hands would stretch out beyond the keyboard—to me, if possible.

I didn't object. Affection on a lonely road is as necessary as drink, food and sleep.

We slept together whenever his true love was absent from the party and he said I kindled the genius within him, although I would be reluctant to take the credit for his fame today.

I was terrified that the theater owner, Povel Ramel, upon whom we all relied for our living, would rumble us. But the young, lustful pianist orchestrated the two affairs with meticulous timing and I don't think his "true love" ever suspected that I was part of his reprise.

Sure, it would have been a very different matter if they had been married. I would not have contemplated the affair in the first place.

I would like to say that I don't sleep with married men, but perhaps it would be more prudent and correct to say that I don't sleep with married men who are *happily married*. After all, those men who swear to a blissful marital life, just don't need to stray, do they?

My first fulfilled affair was with the Italian film director Igi Polodori whose interest in me was to mark a change in the whole direction of my career.

I first met Igi in Stockholm when he was shooting a semi-documentary with Alberto Sordi under the ambiguous title, *To Bed or Not to Bed*. The screenplay revolved round the life of an Italian living in cosmopolitan Sweden. I appeared in a tiny segment of the film as the goodbye-girl on a platform at Grand Central Station.

I had contributed quite a lot to the script, relating to Igi and his writers the more intimate details of day-to-day life among Sweden's trendies.

Young life in Stockholm, like the other major cities in the world, congregated in the coffee bars.

Igi was fascinated by my revelations: but even more fascinated by my potential as an actress after seeing me in one of the "Button-Up" matinees.

When he returned home to Rome, we wrote to one another.

I did not think any more of our relationship until I received a call one night from Igi's associate, the writer Rudolfo Sonego, whose voice shrilled with excitement as he told me of plans to film *Il Commandante* with the Italian star, Toto.

I was told by Rudolfo that I could appear in the film as the Commandant's secretary, witnessing his decline into retirement after his heroic military life.

It all seemed a fairly simple role but I was completely overwhelmed. For a fleeting moment I was in a state of headiness as I imagined that the film gates of the world would now open for me.

However, gathering my senses, I recognized that my first loyalties were to the "Button-Up" company. After all, I had risen to star billing and with another ten days of the summer season to go I could not ditch them overnight.

I need not have worried. Povel had become something of a mentor to me and he regarded the Italian film as an opportunity that I could not afford to miss.

I found a replacement for my part in the show and then Povel's production manager drove me to Stockholm to catch the next plane to Rome.

My return air ticket awaited me at the check-in desk and for the movie I was to get 800 dollars and all my expenses, which I learned I could save on Igi's budget plan!

"Why spend your expenses on a hotel?" he asked when he greeted me at the airport. "Why not stay with me? I have a spare room at my house which you can have."

Igi was elegant and educated and he spoke perfect English: I could offer no sensible objections to his offer, while realizing that the inevitable would occur.

In the past I had never known the meaning of sexual satisfaction. With Igi it was different. I had found someone who was to care about me more than he was to worry about himself.

He was patient and unselfish and possessed a rare tenderness that set him apart from the kind of man who is obsessed by the macho-type image.

I responded to Igi's love-making with a passion that I had not experienced before, and in my first sexual fulfillment I felt I had become a woman.

Perhaps with Igi I turned-on because sex was not forced on me and no demands were made. He had not deceived me at the airport: there *was* a spare room at his apartment and he did not intrude on my privacy.

He waited on my love without persuasion or inducement.

Igi's understanding and protection were extended beyond the confines of the boudoir, and it was as well. The whole atmosphere of Rome is intoxicating. Life on the Via Veneto, after a day's work in the film studios, became the ritual highlight among a throng of playboys, princes and pimps in the bustling bistros.

Igi had the good sense to guide me in the right directions. Once it is known you are an actress, there is no escape in Rome. Every Italian, whether he is a cab driver or a window cleaner, becomes a producer, or a producer's friend.

After *Il Commandante* was completed I stayed on in Rome, where I had warmed to the life. By now I had a good smattering of Italian and as well as my native tongue I could speak English, French and German all of which I had studied at school.

When Igi was away, I lived in his mother's flat, and somehow, by careful pruning, I managed to stretch my savings from the movie.

It was when Igi was away from Rome for a week, and I felt an incredible loneliness, that I fell prey to one of the very men he had always warned me to avoid.

Gio was more than just an Italian playboy. He was the gigolo to an Italian contessa who had installed him in one of Rome's smartest apartments, given him a Mercedes and tailored him in silk and gold.

Cuff links, medallion, bracelets and buckles gleamed on that bronzed frame. When I first caught sight of him I was breathless. I had never seen a more gorgeous man and I melted with one glance from his dark brown, flashing eyes.

When he asked me out the temptation was too much. Why shouldn't I taste "la dolce vita" that Igi had guarded me from? I felt secure enough to cope with any situation.

There were no preliminaries.

We went back to his apartment and straight to bed. Sadly, his performance fell below par and had I been the Contessa I would have despatched her gigolo elsewhere!

To my eternal shame I heard Gio telephone a friend as I was dressing claiming that he had won his bet in bedding me down! How I wished I had listened to Igi's warning.

I hadn't intended to tell Igi, but I underestimated the Via Veneto grapevine, fueled by Gio's consuming ego.

Igi forgave me for my little indiscretion and if he appeared upset at all, then it was for my sake, not his. He knew that my conscience was sadly stricken.

From that experience I was on my guard not to succumb to "la dolce vita" again and I might well have slapped the face of a small, rotund greasy-haired Italian who propositioned me a few days later, but just in time I realized that he was an agent who was offering me a film contract.

He was adamant that I should dye my blonde hair black so that I wouldn't be conspicuous amongst the Italians.

My funds were at a low ebb and I was grateful when he got me a small part in a Vittorio Gassman film. Thankfully, the director did not object to my blonde looks.

Through the entire film my new Italian agent waited stealthily in the wings on my signature to a contract that would have practically ensured my services on breadline terms for life.

It was lucky for me that I did not sign. Less than a week later two Hollywood talent scouts from 20th Century-Fox literally plucked me from my seat in a coffee bar on the Via Veneto and persuaded me to go with them to the Excelsior Hotel where, I was informed,

Darryl F. Zanuck was holding auditions.

Zanuck's name hung like a rhapsody on their lips and I guessed that he must have been very important, but I had never heard of him.

In his suite Mr. Zanuck, gray-suited and benevolent-looking, talked with me for the best part of an hour.

He stroked his chin thoughtfully and said, "I have got to see some other people while I am here, but would you be available to go to New York for screen tests if necessary? If you are successful we will be able to offer you a seven-year exclusive contract."

My heart missed a beat. A seven-year contract with 20th Century-Fox! I telephoned my parents unable to contain my excitement.

My flight from Rome to New York met with a storm and I didn't think any of us aboard would make it alive but for the prayers of a priest on board.

The skyscrapers rose starkly against the gray autumn skies and the trees on Central Park were already stripped of their leaves. It was bitterly cold and everything seemed so bleak until darkness, when suddenly the whole city was magically lit up in neon lights.

My blood boiled with expectation. I was checked into the Drake Hotel and every day a fresh posse of Fox executives were fêting me before the all-important screen tests which were conducted by a German director.

I thought I did reasonably well until the director told me I would have to lose weight. "You have been eating too much spaghetti," he said. He guessed right.

I started to diet immediately. Nothing was going to stop me from becoming an actress.

I returned home to Sweden to spend Christmas with my family but I was so restless waiting for 20th Century-Fox's decision that I decided to go to St. Moritz with a girl friend for the skiing season.

A spontaneous romantic excursion with an American student was abruptly interrupted by a call from my parents. I had received a cable saying I had landed the Fox contract.

My bewildered American student friend pleaded with me to stay but I hung my ski boots round his neck, kissed him goodbye and took the first plane to Stockholm.

Instructions were awaiting me. I had to fly to London to start my first film, the first of fourteen movies under the contract and through which I would earn 250,000 dollars.

That clinched it. I was convinced I was a star!

So on to London, a city that had never held any particular appeal for me. I knew so many Swedish au pairs who had quit London because of the weather and the stodgy food. Much they complained of was true. The English capital was gray and foggy.

I was booked into a large London hotel. And, for two days wearing thick tweeds and fur coats loaned by the studio, I was whizzed from Big Ben to the Tower of London, from Westminster Abbey to Piccadilly Circus, and photographed with Beefeaters, busby helmeted guardsmen and pigeons. All for publicity.

My co-star on my first picture, *Guns at Batasi*, was to be Michael Caine and Fox laid on cocktails for us to meet at their Soho Square offices.

I was given a running brief on Caine, who had just completed *Zulu*, the most ambitious role of his career.

From the Cockney actor's exhilarating mood on our introduction I gathered he was very, very sure of himself. We had barely begun a conversation before he threw out an invitation to join him at dinner on the Monday night.

"I will ring you at your hotel," he said. I could hardly dent his pride by saying that I did not fancy blue-eyed blonds, so I let his invitation slip past, thinking he would review the situation when the time came.

Monday was an eventful day for me. Fox were to unveil me, almost gift-wrapped in a white angora dress, my ribboned hair in a chignon, at a Press conference staged in one of the banqueting rooms of the hotel.

My name also had a different ring about it. Instead of Britt-Marie Eklund I was to become Britt Ekland, the film company determined. Not only was it more slick, but it was a name less likely to be mispronounced, they said.

There must have been thirty photographers and journalists present: it wasn't every day that 20th Century-Fox launched a new star.

By the afternoon my pictures were on the front pages of the London evening papers and I could hardly believe all that was happening to me.

Suddenly, in the hotel foyer everyone recognized me. I was conscious for the first time of curious eyes all leveled in my direction. I tingled inside. It was a feeling I had never experienced before. Could I really be famous?

I glanced at my watch. It was 5:00 p.m.

Michael Caine had not called. Maybe I had missed him, but there were no messages other than those from newspapers.

I was sure he would call and I started to get ready for dinner. I turned on the shower and stepped in. The doorbell rang.

"Oh dear," I thought. Surely Michael Caine would have rung first before venturing to my room? But one of the film men had warned me that Cockneys were not always well mannered.

I wrapped a bath towel round me and with my wet feet leaving imprints on the carpet opened the door while first ensuring that it was still on the chain.

Outside stood a tall stranger in tweed trousers and waistcoat who said that his employer wished me to join him for dinner.

"He's staying along the corridor, miss, and he would like to do some photographs of you as well."

I looked blank.

"Who is your employer?" I asked nervously.

— *four* —

"PETER Sellers," he replied.

I could wait no longer for Michael Caine's call.

The curiosity was stifling. Just who was this man who sent his valet off with a dinner invitation? And what *kind* of photographs did he want to take of me?

I discovered the valet's name was Bert Mortimer and he was very persistent. I only managed to get rid of him by promising to look by for drinks after dinner.

I checked my wardrobe. The one evening gown I had brought with me was too seductive and I decided against it. I didn't want to give him any ideas. I only vaguely knew him by reputation as an actor: I did not know him as a photographer at all.

I chose something thick and tweedy, with a pair of lace-up boots which came to the knees. All very prim and proper.

I rang the bell of the Oliver Messel suite and Bert opened the door, at the same time addressing a man standing in the center of the room.

"May I introduce you to Mr. Sellers, miss," said Bert.

Peter smiled and shook hands with me.

"I saw your photographs in the evening newspaper and when I discovered we were neighbors I thought we should get together," he beamed.

Sellers was slim, dark and suave. He wore horn-rimmed glasses and he was dressed in a conservative dark gray suit. He poured out a whisky for me and beckoned me to join him at the dining table. He was halfway through a Chinese meal. There was a familiar record playing "Desifinado," a bosanova by Stan Getz.

"Are you sure you have eaten?" he asked, "there is plenty here . . ."

I was trembling and nervously I said, "Yes, thank you, I have."

With growing fascination I watched him tackle the mound of beanshoots and sweet and sour pork with chopsticks. He seemed quite skilled with them.

"You know, you are very beautiful," he said, sparing me a quick glance, "and when you see the photographs I will do of you . . . Tell me, who has photographed you in the past?"

Bert brought in a huge leather case of photographic equipment and started hauling out all sorts of cameras.

Sellers quickly finished his meal and beckoned me to stand against one of the pretty walls of the suite which was designed with the scenes of an 18th-century English garden.

I thought he might suggest unbuttoning a few things, but he didn't. My outfit was fine, he said.

He picked up a Nikon, unswivelled the lens and put on a fresh one. Then he started clicking away. He asked me to turn profile, look demure, grow petulant, throw back my head in laughter . . . until the camera shutters almost broke into a symphony.

When he had finished he poured me another drink and then glanced at his watch.

"You know, Britt," he said, "we could go and see my new movie *The Pink Panther*. It has just opened here. Would you like to see it?"

Bert went for the American limousine, a maroon Lincoln. We inched our way through the evening traffic to Leicester Square.

The Empire manager was surprised to see us, but in an instant he laid on the VIP treatment. Drinks appeared from the cocktail cabinet in his office and we were escorted into the theater after the house lights dimmed.

I was impressed. No one mentioned tickets or paying for them.

And seeing Peter on the big screen as the bungling Inspector Clouseau was enough to convince me of the magnitude of his stardom. He was marvelous and the kind of charisma he projected from the screen made my own impact on the media earlier that day quite insignificant by comparison.

Caviare and champagne were wheeled into his suite when we returned to the hotel.

Sellers impersonated his Clouseau character for my amusement, but this really wasn't what I would term the "funny" period of his life.

Strangely enough, he was rarely funny in private and, at this time, he seemed to prefer to project himself as the great lover.

Sellers was lonely. He had never recovered from the shock when his wife, former Australian actress Anne Hayes, had left him to marry the architect Elias Ted Levy who had designed their matrimonial home at Hampstead.

On Anne's part it was poetic retribution.

Sellers said it was revenge for his friendship with Sophia Loren while filming *The Millionairess*.

"I was in love with Sophia," Sellers confided, "and I know that she was very fond of me. Why me? She could have had Gregory Peck or Cary Grant, but she chose me . . ."

His words were not lost on me. I was impressed. I could not pretend otherwise.

Sellers had delivered me into the dream sanctuary of a Hollywood star's life and now he was pouring champagne and asking me what music I liked.

He had moved his own stereo equipment into the hotel suite which he had virtually made his home since the collapse of his marriage.

I remember thinking that it must have cost a fortune to stay there, but he obviously had money to burn. He was already filming a Pink Panther sequel, *Shot in the Dark*.

I was sitting comfortably on the settee and he asked if I smoked. When I said "Yes" he added, "Would you like to try a special brand?"

I had not heard of marijuana before, but I was about to try my first joint. I was instructed on how I should inhale.

"It will make you feel really good," he promised.

I took one or two puffs and I felt a strange feeling in my stomach and then my head started floating.

Suddenly I caught sight of Bert across the room clearing the drinks tray. I remember thinking that he was a wicked, evil man and I kept staring at him. I was frightened of him; Bert had such strange eyes.

Sellers grasped my hand and took me out on to the balcony. It was a freezing winter's night but I didn't notice. I was in Sellers's arms and he was kissing me.

I woke the next morning in my own room along the corridor. I was fully clothed. My recollections of the previous night were scant. My head throbbed and then I heard someone knocking at the door.

It was the maid who brought in a huge bouquet of flowers which she put by my bedside. I looked for a card, but could not see one. I closed the door but the maid reappeared with more flowers. And more flowers. My room was like a florist's shop. Orchids and freesias, lilies and roses, daffodils and carnations . . . there were so many.

I imagined 20th Century-Fox must have sent them; that this was the way they looked after their stars. And some of the flowers might have come from fans who had seen my picture in the newspapers. I was so childish.

But one card on the very last bouquet explained all. It read simply "Hope you slept well—Jacques Clouseau."

All those flowers from one man! I could not believe it.

Sellers called me from Shepperton Studios where he was finishing *Shot in the Dark*. It took little persuasion for me to have dinner with him that night.

At Trader Vic's beneath the Hilton we shared an exotic Caribbean drink with a gardenia floating on its surface. Two straws—and two hearts beating as one! On to Annabel's where we danced until the early hours.

My emotions ran fast in the wake of the unquenchable passions generated by Sellers.

We were, in the space of forty-eight hours, already pledging our undying love to one another.

The Sellers charm oozed like an oil well and he did not hesitate to express his love with sentimental notes and presents.

One of Sellers's great joys in life was evident then: he simply loved to give presents. I was overwhelmed when I unwrapped a leather box containing a diamond studded gold nugget brooch he brought from Aspreys.

So much thought went into everything he did. He even gave me a protector. Someone he could trust with me when he wasn't around. His name was Pepe, a Dachshund puppy who was an adorable ball of fun.

Sellers's fountain of love swept me away. I was his woman.

It was our third night together and it was pointless to delay the impossible. I knew in my heart that I was going to sleep with him and I wasn't going to win any points by keeping him waiting.

I told him I wasn't a virgin and Sellers said I didn't have to account for anything, as he could not plead innocence either, being the father of two children from his marriage to Anne.

In some ways it was quite funny. Sellers could unwittingly have been playing his Clouseau role.

He would have preferred to have kept the bedside lights on. But I turned them off and kept my petticoat intact: I was still reticent about sex and embarrassed about nudity.

We finally got into bed, but it was hardly an awe-inspiring moment. More of a rehearsal as Sellers said. The more satisfying performances were to come.

Sellers didn't propose marriage to me: he just assumed that this was the next logical step.

I remember telephoning my mother and saying, "I think we are going to get married."

"Yes," she replied with astonishment ringing in her voice, "but who did you say you were marrying?"

In graphic detail I explained the whole episode to her and emphasized that Sellers was a famous film star.

Perhaps typical of any mother, she asked cautiously, "How old is he?"

That jolted me a bit. It was a question I had never considered.

Sellers was 38 and I was only 21, but not once had it crossed my mind that there was a seventeen year age gap between us.

It made no difference, although I could tell from my mother's voice that she was apprehensive, particularly after I told her that Sellers had been married once before.

By then I knew a lot more about Sellers. He poured out his whole family history to me. Although born in Portsmouth he had come from a London vaudeville family. His mother Peg had been a music-hall artist and his father, Bill Sellers, a pianist.

Sellers also related with pride that his great-great-grandfather Daniel Mendoza had been a famous Portuguese-Jewish bare fisted prize-fighter from Aldgate in London's East End who became the heavyweight champion of England and who later gave lessons to the Prince of Wales.

My 20th Century-Fox contract took me to New York within the first week of meeting Sellers. In fact we had only known each other for five days and trying to steady myself I questioned my own judgment in even thinking about marriage.

Sellers was desperate when I took off and once he knew that I had arrived in New York he frantically burned up the transatlantic telephone lines.

One morning I was in the middle of a photographic session for publicity pictures when Sellers came on the line once more.

"I've told everyone in London we're going to marry," he said, "is that all right by you?"

It was an odd way of making a proposal, but I gulped, "Yes, I guess so."

In actual fact Sellers had done an interview with Roderick Mann, the distinguished London *Sunday Express* columnist saying he had fallen madly in love with a Swedish starlet and he was to marry.

Said Sellers in the interview: "It's just as my clairvoyant predicted. He said I would marry someone with the initials of B.E."

Sellers, I was to learn in the not-too-distant future, was obsessed by the occult and he would seek advice from Maurice Woodruff, then a famous clairvoyant who practiced in London.

It was said that Sellers consulted him before making any decision or signing any contract. This wasn't strictly true. Sellers would "live out" any advice, whether it was given by Maurice or a funfair crystal ball gazer for that matter.

Maybe Maurice did say that Sellers would marry again. It was hardly a bold prediction as Sellers was an isolated figure when I met him who needed marriage and was steering inexorably towards it.

But looking back I refuse to believe that Maurice uttered the initials "B.E.": I think they could quite easily have been "F.R." or "Y.Z." or any other initials because Sellers, so mesmerized by these kind of revelations, would only have put his own interpretation on them.

There were wild suggestions that Woodruff had "planted" me deliberately in the Dorchester so that his predictions to Sellers would materialize.

I had never heard of Maurice Woodruff until then and I was amused by such speculation.

But all of this was beyond me. There I was on the end of a telephone line in New York and Sellers pressing me for a more definite answer.

"Of course I will marry you," I said, too dazed to think of anything else to say.

When I got back to the Drake Hotel, mayhem descended with the roar of an avalanche. Newsmen, television cameras and photographers were waiting for me. The ticker tape machine had broken the news.

Sellers wanted me to return to London immediately. There was an unexpected hitch. I had no work permit to return. The immigration people made it clear that they would not let me through at Heathrow.

My husband-to-be protested vehemently, "Why is

there a problem? This lady is going to be my wife."

That still didn't move the immigration department. Only when Sellers took out the marriage license did they agree, reluctantly, to bend the rules.

The blushing bride flew into London wearing a second-hand, moth-eaten leopard skin coat she had bought from a Swedish friend in Rome for 200 dollars. It was my first fur and I was proud of it.

Sellers was at the airport to meet me, along with hundreds of Pressmen, television cameras and fans. I was truly petrified.

Someone in the crowd yelled, "Where's your engagement ring, Britt?" And Sellers, like an absent-minded professor, slapped his forehead, tugged me into a cleaner's washroom where brooms and buckets were stored and dug from his small pocket a small red box from which he produced the most incredible ring. It was a triple banded Victorian ring of emeralds, diamonds and rubies which he had brought from Garrards the Crown jewelers.

My eyes were moist as he slipped it on my finger, pecked my cheek and said, "Didn't I tell you we were going to marry?" He pressed me closer to him and we cried tears of joy.

We emerged from the cubicle into a conclave of cameras and my engagement ring, sparkling in the dazzling television arc lights, went under microscopic inspection.

Our marriage was planned for the following Wednesday, 19 February 1964, giving me just sufficient time to establish residency, but leaving a thousand and one things to do. There were guests to be invited, the cake and the food to be organized and the dress to be made.

Sellers hired the Queen's couturier, Norman Hartnell, to design my wedding gown and the newspapers predictably spent the week trying to sabotage his drawings.

Like every bride I nursed fairytale dreams about my wedding day. I wanted it to be a candlelit ceremony and Sellers ensured it would be, even though we were going to marry in a register office in the Surrey market town of Guildford, only a few miles from "Brookfield" the beautiful, 15th-century English home in the pretty village of Elstead that Sellers had bought the previous autumn.

I loved the house. It was so quaint. It had stone floors, lattice windows, inglenooks and beamed ceilings, some so low that we had to duck beneath them.

When it came to my wedding eve I suddenly developed an old-fashioned notion that I could not sleep with the bridegroom on that particular night.

Sellers, always wary of superstition, understood and he put me into a four-poster in the guest room. When the bedside lights were extinguished the house became spooky. Every few minutes I heard a different noise and I began to believe that the house was haunted as Sellers had mentioned in passing.

I threw on the lights and the oak beams seemed to descend almost on top of me. Claustrophobia set in.

With the jitters getting the better of me, I sped back to join Sellers in the master bedroom. He merely chuckled as I gasped, "I can't sleep in that four-poster. All sorts of things keep coming at me and I keep hearing things."

He put a comforting arm round me. "You are right, darling, you're much safer with me," he said.

We laughed and made love before falling asleep.

My parents and family had flown over from Sweden for the wedding and with snow showers descending from the bleak winter sky it was as if my fairytale dreams had been fulfilled.

The somber Guildford register office had been transformed to a chamber of spiritual beauty by burning candles and bowls of white flowers everywhere.

There were thousands of people gathered in the forecourt, more fans than there were guests. Ecstatic cries greeted my arrival in my Hartnell gown which was fairly classical, with a scooped neckline, fitted waist and the skirt embroidered with white flowers to match my white hat.

Over my shoulders I wore a black diamond mink coat—my wedding present from Sellers.

I was so nervous during the actual ceremony that I

lost my grasp of English and couldn't understand everything the Registrar said.

Our wedding rings were platinum, a preference I made to yellow gold.

Outside a wave of cheers erupted when we emerged as man and wife. Sellers, a carnation in the buttonhole of his gray suit, waved to the fans but their cheers turned to fright for us when the crowd stampeded forward to block our car. Bert, who was behind the wheel, could not even start before a path had been cleared by the police. Some of the fans threw themselves on to the bonnet of the car, others bludgeoned the roof and windows. I was scared.

The Lincoln was so badly damaged that Sellers later had to sell it.

I was relieved when we reached the safety of the house, where we had arranged an appetizing Swedish smorgasbord lunch for our guests.

My brother Kalle and Sellers's son Michael (he also had a daughter Sarah by his marriage to Anne Hayes) did quite a thriving business in selling slices of wedding cake and titbits of information to pressmen on the other side of the gates.

Our best men, actors Graham Stark and David Lodge, filmed our guests at the reception with a 16 mm camera, having already recorded the ceremony itself by secreting microphones in the flower vases of the register office.

At last I was able to relax and as the festivities bubbled in champagne, I found a quiet corner to open some of the letters that had arrived.

One letter was addressed to Mrs. Sellers. The handwriting was hardly legible. I was totally unprepared for its contents.

A tremor of shock passed like an electric wave through my body when I began to read,

"Dear Mrs. Sellers, I am the only woman that Peter loves and I think you should know that I am expecting his baby. You had no right to marry him."

There was no address or signature. I read it again. I was trembling; my tears flowed like glycerine drops. I was ready to believe every word. I was convinced that the letter revealed a secret from my husband's past.

Among all the guests in the room was a priest: Father John Hester whose Soho parish embodied the welfare of those in entertainment. He was the friend of many artists, in good times and in bad.

He saw me dabbing my eyes. "What is the matter?" he asked. "Is there anything wrong?"

I showed him the letter. He read it and said, "There are some evil people in the world who get a kick out of life denying others happiness."

I had never read a poison-pen letter before. I was stunned to think that anyone could express such malice.

Father Hester quietly tore the letter up and told me to forget the whole episode.

"Don't allow this to spoil your wedding day," he said. "Here, have a sip of your champagne. It will put some color back into your cheeks."

I tried to force a smile.

"Thank you," I said. "I will be all right now."

I rejoined the festivities, endeavoring to dismiss the incident from my mind.

Out of the corner of my eye I caught a glimpse of Sellers, clowning with David Lodge and I felt guilty that I could have even suspected that the contents of the letter were remotely true.

Sellers had never concealed the affairs he'd had in the past, but nothing like this had ever cropped up.

He was not a promiscuous man. His emotions needed to be channeled to one woman, making her the symbol for his affection and devotion.

I never mentioned the letter to him ever, and fortunately, the sadly misguided woman who penned it never pestered me again.

Our celebrations ended with a late dinner party at Sellers's favorite restaurant, the Tiberio in London's Mayfair. We made our excuses close to midnight telling our guests we had better things to do.

Our honeymoon night was spent at "Brookfield." I wore a white baby-doll nightie and I was so coy that I actually changed in the bathroom.

It seemed so romantic then. Sellers had his initials monogrammed on the pillows, sheets and towels and even on the pocket of his striped pajamas. And very soon, in scroll lettering, my initials were to join his . . .

Our marriage was just four days old when Sellers left for Hollywood. The wrench was unbearable for us both.

It was a moment of tears and frustration. Reality had come to replace the fantasy we had lived in for three unforgettable weeks.

Sellers was signed to start another comedy film *Kiss Me Stupid* with the talented Billy Wilder whom he greatly admired, while I had to remain in England for *Guns at Batasi* now ready to go before the cameras.

I could have stayed on at our home in Elstead but Sellers, never lacking in consideration, thought the journey would be too hazardous for me especially when studio calls meant setting out for Pinewood Studios at 5 o'clock in the morning.

So he installed me in a chintzy, dimly-lit flat in Royal Avenue, Chelsea, overlooking the crowded pavements of King's Road and although I did not immediately recognize it, this was to become my gilded cage.

My life had been turned upside down by Sellers. He encased me in such luxury and my wedding day mink was only the beginning. He gave me a red Lotus sports car, a diamond watch, crocodile handbag and shoes, a gold pen inscribed with my initials and many more gifts.

In return I symbolized his prize possession; untouchable to others and dedicated only to him.

No doubt the conquest of a very young wife at his mature age had fortified Sellers's image in the eyes of the world. An impressionable, golden-haired, fluffy pudding with a little nose sprinkled with freckles whose blue eyes were still so wide and innocent.

Now he had to protect me and the fact he was 6,000 miles away in California did not inhibit him.

The true character of Sellers began to emerge. His incredible affection soured rapidly into an habitual jealousy which filled the first few weeks of our marriage with despair.

Pepe, our Dachshund, was not my only watchdog in the Chelsea flat. Sellers insisted, before his departure, that I should have a secretary to live in and he appointed Elizabeth, a girl in her late twenties, to move in with me.

It was embarrassing, because while she was a qualified and competent secretary, I had no work to give her, except to take the occasional telephone message.

At Pinewood there were watchdogs too! Our best men Graham and David also had roles in my film *Guns at Batasi*, which was an Indian inspired war thriller of sorts, and Richard Attenborough and Flora Robson led the cast.

Michael Caine dropped out at a late hour and John Leyton took his place.

I was overjoyed to see Graham and David at Pinewood. I had friends to talk to and as old buddies of Sellers I felt secure in the knowledge that they would be around if any problems arose.

What I did not suspect was that Sellers was in communication with them and this was part of his inquisition that went on all through filming.

Sellers would ring me every night to ask how I got on and then the tack of his questioning would switch to who I talked to, who I dined with, what time did I get home and how well did I sleep? I would have to describe my day almost minute by minute.

I had not given Sellers anything to worry about, but he seemed worried.

"What about John Leyton? How do you get on with him?" he asked one night. John was a handsome blond-haired actor managed by Robert Stigwood at the time, and he was being groomed as a leading man.

"Has he asked you out?" Sellers probed on the transatlantic line. "He must have chatted you up by now . . . Tell me the truth, Britt."

"But Peter, I have only spoken to John Leyton once. We played in a scene together yesterday . . ."

"What kind of a scene?"

"Oh, it was nothing."

"Britt, just tell me. What kind of scene?" His voice became more agitated. "You didn't have to kiss him?"

"No. I only kissed him when I did the test and you know everything about that."

"Yes, all right Britt, but please be careful. Are you sure you don't fancy him?"

"Darling, don't be silly. I couldn't look at anyone else," I assured him.

Sellers wasn't convinced even then.

He had thrown a house party in Hollywood and screened several movies to entertain his guests. One of the movies *The Great Escape*, starred John Leyton, of all people.

An actor had told Sellers that when he worked with actresses he liked to get involved with them otherwise it didn't look "real enough."

Sellers described how he watched a Brigitte Bardot film earlier and imagined that I had played in the seduction scene and not "B.B."

Sellers explained how he would absorb himself totally into a role and could not always detach himself that easily from the character he played.

The letters and cables poured out. He sent three cables just to say, "I" "Love" "You."

Sellers didn't seem to realize that I felt lonelier than he did. Although I would go out for dinner with Graham and David and their wives, I had no other friends in London at all at that stage.

At least my husband knew people in Hollywood and English actors were then very much in vogue.

Sellers would tell me about all the fabulous Hollywood parties he went to alone. Once he told me how a famous film star's wife made a pass at him.

"But darling, she did not succeed," said Sellers.

The days slipped by and the phone calls, the cables and the letters increased in volume.

Finally, with Easter only a few days ahead, Sellers phoned me and said, "I can't stand being on my own any longer. You've got to come out for Easter.''

His children Michael and Sarah were already joining him for the holiday.

I longed to be with him to put his mind at rest. To convince him that I wasn't having an affair with John Leyton and that he had nothing to fear. I was loyal to him and I intended to stay that way.

I pleaded with the Pinewood production office into extending the four day Easter recess, but I met with a blunt refusal.

A crisis loomed.

Sellers was adamant that I should join him and I had to reassure him of my loyalties, even though I realized that I was putting my whole career at stake leaving without the studio's permission and certainly without any guarantee of my return date.

Surreptitiously, Sellers organized a limousine to pick me up from the studios on the Thursday night. He instructed me not to say anything or do anything to let anyone suspect that I was going to catch a plane from Heathrow.

''What about my luggage?'' I asked.

''You won't need any. Don't bring a thing,'' he replied. ''Just make sure your passport is in your handbag.''

So I left London without saying a word of my intentions to Dickie Attenborough or even our best men.

It was like playing truant from school, although I intended to be back in time for the Tuesday morning schedule.

Sellers devised other plans.

When I arrived in Los Angeles he kept remarking on my pallid appearance and when I said, ''Maybe I'm suffering from jet lag,'' he retorted, ''No, no. Darling, anyone can see you are suffering from nervous exhaustion.''

He summoned a doctor who examined me and left with the advice that I should ''rest for a long period.''

Sellers had no intention of letting me return and when I pleaded that I could not let the other members of the cast down, he ignored me and said firmly, "Britt, you are a sick girl. You don't want to crack up totally, do you?"

I began to think I actually was sick. I certainly felt fragile.

Maybe I had been under strain without realizing it.

The doctor said I needed a rest, that I was on the verge of a breakdown. Was it not wise to accept his advice and remain with my husband?

The Californian sunshine was enticing.

Sellers had rented a beautiful marble floored mansion in Beverly Hills with a stone flamingo reigning over the swimming pool.

In the king-size master bedroom Sellers took my hand and slid back the wardrobe door. I blinked. Inside were racks of clothes in my size—dresses, coats, casual wear and even lingerie—and bearing the labels of the best Parisian and Italian fashion houses.

"It's no good saying you have to go home to collect your clothes. You'll find you've got everything you want here," beamed Sellers. And I had. There were even lower racks of shoes, all in size 5½ and in my fitting.

Sellers had got his American secretary to go out and stock up an entire wardrobe ready for my arrival. The budget had been unlimited and her choice of clothes was immaculate, having ascertained from Sellers all my favorite colors and designs.

It was a fait accompli. I could not return to England now.

My absence at Pinewood on the Tuesday morning caused immense consternation. Eventually someone managed to obtain our ex-directory number and Sellers's secretary took one urgent message after another demanding my recall.

I was too scared to answer the telephone myself and the secretary was briefed to say that I was "not available"—a comment that does not engender too much goodwill.

After three or four days the constant telephone calls stopped, and just when we thought the whole incident was over, we faced fresh harassment.

The film company had issued writs against us both; mine presumably for breach of contract and the other accusing Sellers of conspiring with me.

A Los Angeles process server was assigned to hand us the writs but we gave him a very tough time. The wretched man waited outside the house when we refused to answer his knock. To get past him we had to drive out in our car at high speed.

We did our best to deceive him. On one occasion I hid in the boot and once I even disguised myself in a black wig while sending out the secretary wearing a blond wig to act as a decoy. There was one hilarious moment, as if it might have been a scene from a Keystone Kops movie.

The indefatigable process server discovered we were at Sam Goldwyn's studios one afternoon and arrived at the main gates just as we were leaving in a long wheel-base Cadillac. Sellers spotted him and tapped the driver on the shoulder to take off. The car lunged away at high speed leaving the poor man running vainly after us through a cloud of exhaust. Still in his hand was the unserved writ.

Eventually the writ was served formally at our front door when Sellers's legal advisers said there was no advantage in carrying on the charade. We had to give an answer to the case brought against us by 20th Century-Fox.

Ironically, the house we were renting belonged to 20th Century-Fox President Spyros Skouras, although he did not intervene in the legal proceedings against us.

He might have otherwise had reason to suspect that we were hostile tenants although an amicable solution to the problem was resolved when Sellers agreed to pay Fox a sum of 60,200 dollars to compensate for the discarded reels of film containing my three weeks' work.

In London a replacement for my role had been found. She was the young American actress Mia Farrow who was just as much a starlet on the treadmill of fame as I was at the time.

A fascinating sequel resulted. Mia's name was romantically linked with John Leyton.

Village life is often said to be incestuous and Hollywood had its own rules, as I was to discover.

Not that I realized it then. I was still green at the edges. There I was, plummeted in the film capital of the world, Sellers's new young wife, a small blond Swedish waif with faltering English who was rapidly losing her grip as Sturegatan's answer to Brigitte Bardot in the awesome retinue of celebrities who glided in and out of our home as my husband's friends.

Steve McQueen, who shared Sellers's passion for cars and gadgetry, Cary Grant who once employed my husband's valet and Bob Wagner—"R.J." to his chums—who worked with Sellers on the first *Pink Panther* movie would drop by for cocktails and barbecues.

Samantha Eggar, Capucine and Goldie Hawn became good friends. So did Shirley Maclaine who introduced herself to me at our front door when Sellers was in the bathtub! If only Shirley had known just how nervous I felt in holding a conversation with her, feeling so inadequate!

It was all a new world to me. And it didn't stop there. In later months we were to fly to Jamaica to spend a holiday with the charismatic Noel Coward and in Los Angeles we were presented to President Johnson and his wife Lady Bird.

I could easily have lost all grip of reality. Only in the face of tragedy did my feet bump back to earth again.

— *five* —

SELLERS believed that the essence of his masculinity relied on his ardor as a lover. He was always searching for what he liked to term as the "ultimate" orgasm and when he discovered that amyl nitrate assisted his physical endurance the tiny capsules of chemical became almost a routine component of our nightly love-making pattern.

He would produce the capsules from the bedside cabinet, snap one in half between a crumpled handkerchief and we would have to inhale the vapor.

My heart would instantly beat like a runaway pump, but my husband told me not to worry and to anticipate only the heightening of our sexual desire.

Shamefully, without admitting the fact to Sellers, the capsules did not have the desired effect on me, although he would plead his own physical stimulation was infinite.

I was genuinely scared of the capsules and their lingering toxic smell. My mind was transported back to my childhood when the doctors administered ether on the removal of my adenoids. I was only six but I never got over that smell. It hung for ages in my nostrils.

I had not known of the existence of amyl nitrate before and I was unaware that it was usually prescribed for patients with a heart condition. It was only later that I learned that its misuse would even cause the very condition it was meant to remedy.

We had used the "poppers" on the night when he had the first of a series of eight heart attacks which brought him to the periphery of death.

We had gone to bed early. We made love and the amyl nitrate came into play as usual and eventually reveling in our satisfaction we opened champagne. We took the bottle from its ice bucket at the side of the bed and Sellers uncorked it. The champagne cascaded over the bed and the sheets were saturated. We got out to change the covers around when Sellers suddenly crouched over the bed, his hands clasping his chest and he began fighting for breath.

I asked him what the matter was and he groaned. He said that his chest was on fire and that he felt a shooting pain down his left arm. He whispered, "Get me some brandy quickly." I tore out of the bedroom and went to find the brandy bottle. I also got some aspirin from the bathroom, thinking that he might need those too.

Sellers was lying propped up in bed. His face was ashen and contorted with pain.

"I know what it is. I've had a heart attack," he said, "quickly phone the doctor."

It was after midnight but Dr. Rex Kennamer, our physician, came over immediately and examined Sellers. He sedated him, making him comfortable for the night.

"He will have to go into hospital tomorrow for tests," the doctor told me as he left the house.

I accompanied Sellers to the Cedars of Lebanon hospital the next morning where he was detained for the tests. He was still feeling weak and confused.

"I am sure it was a heart attack," he kept muttering, "my father died from a heart attack . . ."

"Please don't think that way," I cried, knowing that his father had died only seventeen months earlier.

I telephoned the film studios to inform them of my husband's sudden illness and there was immediate concern, more perhaps for their own dilemma than my husband's.

Their multi-million pound movie *Kiss Me Stupid* was at a key stage of production.

"What can we do without Sellers?" groaned one of the executives, thinking only of his own predicament.

Their problem did not bother me. I knew they were well insured against events of this nature.

My only concern was for my husband, the man I loved. All day I was in and out of the hospital where he was given a cardiograph and other tests.

They decided to detain him overnight and I said to him, "Don't worry darling, I will be back to see you tomorrow."

I kissed him goodbye and returned home.

It was 5:00 a.m. in the morning when I woke to the telephone ringing. Then it stopped. Bert, the valet, had intercepted the call on his extension at the end of the corridor. I heard Bert's slippered feet shuffling along to my door. He knocked and came in. His face was flushed.

"It's Mr. Sellers," said Bert uneasily, "the hospital has just got through. They would like you to get over there as soon as possible. I'm afraid it looks very serious."

Bert got our agent Dick Shepherd on the line, who promised to collect me immediately.

We got to the Cedars of Lebanon thirty minutes later and a nurse came through to take me to the intensive care unit. I almost broke down in tears when I saw Sellers, enmeshed in tubes, drip feeds, oxygen equipment and the threads of his life hanging thinly to a Pacemaker machine. His weak heartbeats hardly flickered on the visual screen.

He was not conscious and a doctor came to comfort me. He shook his head at Dick Shepherd and I knew that they did not expect Sellers to live.

"There is nothing more we can do," the doctor whispered.

In a span of two hours Sellers had suffered seven consecutive heart attacks. Medically, his recovery seemed impossible. I did not believe that God could be that cruel. We had only been married 46 days.

I prayed. I had often prayed in my life before but

never in such a moment like this. I prayed to God that
my husband would live.

I gazed through the glass partition and thought only
of the man who had entrenched me in such affection
and who had kissed and cuddled me at all moments of
the day: the man who only forty-eight hours earlier had
been playing happily with Michael and Sarah on an
outing to Disneyland.

Just how could my husband die?

At the outset of the crisis I moved into the hospital. I
was given a room next to the intensive care unit and I
kept constant vigil at his bedside.

The newspapers were discreetly removed from my
gaze. Only much later did I read the somber headlines
that read: "Sellers: Doctors Fear For His Life" and
"Sellers—His Last Hours."

No one expected him to live. Bryan Forbes, the
producer and actor, and one of his closest friends was
asked to prepare an obituary and Sellers's business
manager tentatively began to wind up the estate and
liquidate all his assets.

I flew Michael and Sarah back to London, not happy
to let them see their father in this plight. I also kept my
husband's aging mother Peg, who remained in England,
in constant touch with the situation. It would have been
too risky for her to make the trip.

I prepared myself for the worst. I asked the doctors to
level with me.

"The truth is we just don't know whether he will live
or die," Dr. Kennamer told me, "I would not put his
chances any higher than ten per cent."

It was enough. While that chance existed I clung on to
it, willing Sellers to get better with every breath I took.

The medical team were anxious to establish the cause
of the heart attacks. Stress, strain and overwork were
regarded as the primary reasons but was there not
another factor?

"I don't suppose he has ever used stimulants?"
voiced one of the medics.

"Yes," I nodded, unable to disguise the guilt of my admission, "yes, he has . . ."

I felt that I had to be absolutely frank with them and offer any vestige of information, however embarrassing, if it would help to save my husband's life.

There was a murmur of enlightenment and one of the doctors said, "It's just possible that a stimulant could have caused this situation, Mrs. Sellers." I shuddered.

Sellers battled on. Every hour he survived aroused fresh hope within us all. Every morning I woke to find him still alive meant another day won.

After four days, through which his life hung desperately in the balance, signs came of his remarkable recovery. His heart bleep started to get louder and more stable.

For brief periods he was conscious of what was happening around him. He recognized me. If his eyes were momentarily forlorn I could still see the depths of his determination to pull through. I kissed him and squeezed his hand.

My own health was running into the ground. I lost a stone in weight, unable to eat any food during the crisis. It was insignificant in relation to my husband's recovery.

As Sellers improved the doctors were talking of a miracle. Medically they had exceeded their limitations.

On the fifth day Sellers was moved from intensive care into a private recuperation room. He lay in bed smiling faintly but he seemed unable to grasp how close to death he had been. In fact, it was not until weeks later that the truth hit him.

At that moment his whole preoccupation was his need to get back to work and if he had been strong enough I'm sure he would have dressed and gone to the studios.

He wanted to talk always with his agent, manager and accountants and demanded that business papers were brought to the hospital. The doctors occasionally had to sedate him and I would endeavour to divert his thoughts away from work.

His lead role in *Kiss Me Stupid* had been taken over by Ray Walston.

Sellers remained in the hospital for more than a month. My parents flew over from Sweden to stay with me in the house and during the crisis the Soho priest Father John Hester had flown over at his own expense to administer his spiritual blessings.

We made my husband's 65-dollar a day hospital suite as comfortable for him as possible. Color television and radio were inbuilt and we installed extra stereo equipment along with many of Sellers's favorite gadgets.

Sellers's final few days in the hospital found him intolerably impatient to be discharged. I was to be the target of his frustration and he would create petty squabbles, demanding to know where I spent my free time when I wasn't visiting him.

I had conversations in Swedish with my mother on the telephone. Sellers thought that we were saying something about him that he did not understand. As it was, my mother knew very little English but Sellers would not acknowledge this.

When Sellers was allowed home it was conditional that a nurse would be in attendance at all times. The nurse carried out her duties to the letter. She would remain in our bedroom even at night, in case Sellers should have another attack. This rather precluded any sexual activities and Sellers, having been incarcerated in hospital for five weeks, was feeling amorous.

There was only one place where the nurse would not follow us and that was into the bathroom. It was our only private sanctuary and we made love under the shower at the very first opportunity.

Again, the consequence might have snugly slotted into an Inspector Clouseau situation: Sellers reeled out of the shower clutching his chest, fearing the dreaded encore had come!

The nurse got the doctor on an emergency line and rather shamefully we had to confess that we had indulged.

"Your recuperation must come first," said the doctor, finding nothing wrong with Sellers other than an outbreak of paranoia, "and then, okay, sex, sport and everything else, only in moderation. You won't be able to get into any marathons."

Finally we persuaded the nurse to move into an adjoining room and normal marital relations were eventually resumed without the presence of a reluctant voyeur.

Within a matter of weeks I discovered I was pregnant and as neither of us had employed any protective measures other than withdrawal, the shock was merely a mild one.

The thought of having a child filled me with joy, but at the same time I was scared. I think most mothers-to-be must feel this way. Nine months to carry a child is a long term, so much can happen on the way. It is impossible not to worry.

Sellers conveyed his initial delight on my announcement. Of course the role of becoming a father was not unique to him and I suspected that in reality he found the responsibility of parenthood difficult to contend with. He would disguise this by swamping Michael and Sarah with expensive presents but seeming to me to be starving them of any real affection.

When he was well on the road to recovery we flew back to England and to "Brookfield." It was early summer and the trees were in leaf, the rhododendrons were out and I breathed in the happiness of the countryside. Not for long. Sellers was in contretemps with the might of Hollywood.

On his return Sellers unwisely made some disparaging remarks about Hollywood and he told Alexander Walker, the London *Evening Standard* film critic, "I've had Hollywood in a big way, luv." Sellers complained that sightseers were allowed on to the *Kiss Me Stupid* set when scenes were being shot, cutting his line of vision to the camera.

Billy Wilder who had already said that Sellers was as difficult to work with as Marilyn Monroe, now sent a cable saying, "Talk about unprofessional rat finks" which was signed not only by the director but by Dean Martin, Kim Novak and other members of the cast.

Sellers's immediate reaction was to take a £250 whole page advertisement in *Variety* to say that he had been misjudged.

"I have no criticism of Hollywood as a place, only a place to work in," he announced.

The advertisement went on to thank Dr. Rex Kennamer and the medical staff at the Cedars of Lebanon who had saved his life.

His London friends, at least, were glad to see Sellers back in fighting form. Spike Milligan thought that the experience might at least cure my husband's complex. He explained, "Years before he had this heart attack he always worried about it, was always searching for the bloody thing as if it were a letter that he knew had been posted and hadn't arrived."

I think that for the first time since leaving hospital Sellers realized how close to death he had been.

His reactions were natural for any human being who had survived such an ordeal. Suddenly he turned closer to religion, as if he wanted something to hang on to. Until that time he had never really expressed any religious beliefs at all and I think his conversion had always been the hope of Father Hester.

Sellers's mother was Jewish, his father had been Protestant. Sellers was caught twixt the two and he hedged his bets. A Bible with both old and new Testaments appeared at his bedside and on other occasions he would extol the Jewish faith.

His health and the preservance of it, became a bigger concern.

As well as his heart condition, Sellers was plagued by recurring back trouble.

Before our marriage he had slipped a disc when falling from the stage into the orchestra pit at a provincial theater. Periodically, the disc would spring out of place and cause him to reel over like a puppet severed from its strings.

I would then have to drive him to his physiotherapist

in London who would manipulate the disc back into place.

However, this mischievous disc was of less worry to Sellers than suffering a coronary. My sole function at this period was to convince him that he would never have another heart attack and help him back to peak health.

At regular moments through the day he had to swallow an assortment of multi-colored pills and we monitored the intake on a bathroom wall chart until the doctors phased out the supply.

Sellers also quit smoking during this period and he was placed on a salt-free diet.

Keeping trim was absolutely essential to him. In his determination to succeed he bought a whole range of keep-fit appliances, including a muscle-toner fly wheel, a rowing machine and other contraptions. He also contemplated taking up golf and tennis and he bought the most expensive equipment on the market.

My worries that he might overdo things were unfounded. He played very little of either sport.

We went for long walks and cycle rides into the countryside on bright sunny summer afternoons and our marriage at this point was mercifully mellow.

For Sellers, the whole slimming process was to become a permanent burden to him, realizing that any excess flab was a danger to his life. It was not a new situation to him. He had taken slimming pills in the past.

Not a month went by without him embarking on some fresh diet. Once he was on a Canadian wine and steak diet. Then he discovered an ancient Chinese diet of greenery that guaranteed a weight loss of at least half a pound a day. Then he experimented with a pure spaghetti diet, the theory being that if he only ate spaghetti and nothing else he would reduce the intake of carbohydrates. An all-banana diet was later tried before he got on to macrobiotic foods and yoga: but of course Sellers's weak discipline meant that he could never master any of them.

Sellers's weakness came from being a gourmet. He enjoyed the most exotic of cuisines. He loved Chinese and Polynesian foods and it was as well that we had an inventive chef at Elstead. I don't think I could have ever come up to his expectations. In those days I could only pass on a grilled steak or a boiled egg.

Wines were less of a problem for me. We bought crates of the stuff from Jackson's, although Sellers kept the cellars stocked with named French labels including Chateau Latour and other vintages, to serve to our friends when they called. One night when we were having a small dinner party a cat burglar climbed through into our upstairs rooms and stole £20,000 worth of our jewelry, furs, camera equipment and other belongings.

We discovered the theft only when we retired for the night. Sellers had the house burglar-proofed the next morning, with the most sophisticated of alarm systems. That a burglar had been prowling on our landing while we were actually in the house upset us both.

However, by the end of the summer Sellers was looking tanned and well, although he took no chances with his health. He slept for long periods, and I played the role of nurse, checking always on his pills, blood pressure and keeping syringes constantly sterilized for use in an emergency.

We flew to the Costa Brava for a short holiday and while dining with an aristocratic Spanish family I got a call from a London gossip columnist asking me to confirm the fact that we were expecting our first child.

We could not figure out how they managed to trace us that particular night, or how they had managed to establish the fact that I was pregnant. It hardly mattered. By then there was no way I could conceal the secret any longer!

I was nearly four months pregnant when a past incident in my life suddenly reared its head, putting unnecessary stress on our marriage.

It came when Hugh Hefner, the *Playboy* boss, phoned one night and said that he had acquired some racy pictures of me which he'd like to use. However, he would discard them if Sellers would take another set of photos of me in the nude. Some chance!

The next few days were impossible until Hefner's photographs arrived.

All they showed was my bare shoulder swivelled to the camera in the sexy kind of pose that was the cover girl's stock-in-trade in those days.

Sellers secretly yearned to get back to work but he was troubled that his talents and genius had deserted him. Indeed at one point he was convinced he would never work again and for several days he was gripped in the depths of moroseness.

It was insufferable. Every word we exchanged sparked fresh friction.

I was in tears on the night Sellers suddenly told me to get rid of our child.

In fact his attitude became paradoxical: Sellers began devising ways on how we would produce a superhuman babe! Sellers recalled a conversation with the director Stanley Kubrick when they were working on *Dr. Strangelove* together. Kubrick apparently knew of a remote African tribe who strapped their pregnant women to the back of a chair and placed them in an oxygen tent to ensure their infants were born with the most vigorous of mental and physical health.

I was quivering with nerves when Sellers actually began suggesting to me the merits of this experiment.

I said that I would get an opinion from Harley Street.

Good fortune was on my side. A call from our agent set my husband's mind racing in another direction.

There were two films on the immediate horizon for him: a New York documentary *Carol for Another Christmas* in aid of UNO and a major comedy feature film *What's New Pussycat?* co-starring Ursula Andress and Peter O'Toole.

Sellers signed for both and we left for New York for the UNO documentary in which I actually appeared playing the part of a pregnant girl!

We headed on to Paris for *Pussycat*. I was eight

months pregnant by then and like a walking barrel. I felt distinctly embarrassed about my condition, particularly when we ran into the super sexy Ursula Andress for the first time. We were in the Plaza Athenee foyer and Ursula was all wrapped up in a cheetah skin coat, boots and hat.

Discarding her coat she put on something of a fashion show for us and other unsuspecting guests collected in the vestibule.

"Look," said Ursula pulling up the hem of her sheath-tight dress, "no more old fashioned knickers." Sure enough Ursula wasn't wearing any but instead wore pantyhose, a brand new garment on the market, but one that was to cause a revolution in the lingerie trade.

"No more girdles and straps from now on," cried Ursula, although my expression may have been one of disbelief. With an eight-month girth I doubt if pantyhose would have stretched to those dimensions.

Victoria was born four weeks later on 20 January 1965. We had returned to England and checked into the Dorchester, conveniently situated for the Welbeck Street Clinic.

Sellers, having never mentioned the word "abortion" again, was as nervous as any father-to-be.

When my water went and I felt the first pangs, Sellers whisked me from the hotel to the clinic in a flash. My suitcase was already packed. Unceremoniously he dumped me on the steps of the Clinic and promptly disappeared without so much as taking one step inside the door. He retreated to the safety of our hotel, having no wish to witness the birth.

The next morning, after Victoria's arrival, Sellers was as proud as punch. He grasped her in his arms and said, "Thank God she is safely here." I knew what he meant: husbands are entitled to change their minds!

My room was full of flowers and congratulatory messages from all over the world. Some from people we just didn't know.

Nicole, the Duchess of Bedford, whom I had never

met, sent me a bed jacket and in later years, still not introduced, she wrote to me in the friendliest of terms enclosing a life membership card for Regine's night clubs.

In choosing Victoria for our baby's name I could not think of anything more English than the aura of Queen Victoria and Sellers agreed that the name was a perfect choice. We settled for Maria as her second Christian name as all women on my mother's lineage were christened.

At "Brookfield" the nursery was all prepared. I had taken no chance on the baby's sex. I had the room decorated in white, with beautiful white lacy curtains and a canopied cot. We also engaged a post-natal nurse whose assistance meant that I could dispense with the necessity of breast feeding, the thought of which was alien to my nature.

I am afraid the nurse was more efficient at her job than I cared to imagine. I came to rely on her almost entirely in domestic matters affecting Victoria's weaning and I hardly changed a diaper.

Through my confinement and in Victoria's infancy, I thought Sellers might have invited my mother to England to see me. It would have been reassuring to have had her support through that period.

However his own mother Peg was of course on hand. He never called her "Mum" it was always Peg. I suppose Christian names were the rule of the theater irrespective of relationship.

Peg was a typical old vaudeville star, living her past as though it was part of the present. She would wear the most garish clothes and make-up.

Small and slender, she liked to wear little-girl dresses and even flaunted mini-skirts although she was well past sixty. She also painted thick lashings of rouge on her face and bright, glossy lipstick.

She smoked and drank heavily, and Sellers admonished her on both counts. Peg hid the cigarette packets under the settee cushions and kept her supply of gin flowing by filtering it into empty medicine bottles so that her son would not guess. She was close to being an alcoholic but there was nothing I could do to prevent her from having her regular "tipple."

Peg did not like the role of Grannie and she would always refer to Victoria as "it." If "it" was in the garden I knew she meant Victoria.

Her relationship with Sellers was a love-hate affair typical of a Jewish mother whose dependant was an only son.

I got along with Peg well and I knew that as long as I didn't betray the secret of her gin reservoirs, I always would.

— six —

IN the gracefully elegant surroundings of Kensington Palace in London just a few days before our marriage, I stood frocked but braless in one of Lord Snowdon's borrowed white shirts, while he photographed me in seductive poses.

His wife, Princess Margaret, chuckled in the background and Sellers encouraged me to unbutton the shirt one degree lower.

"That will be fine. Hold it there. This is a great shot," cried Tony, clicking away on his camera and echoing the words that photographers preach like an Eleventh Commandment.

This, then, was my remarkable "induction" into Royal society, and one I shall never forget, because not only was it totally unexpected, but the circumstances were so bizarre.

Sellers, the superstar, I had come to terms with, but he was still a stranger to me and we were only just beginning to explore each other's lives.

I was completely unaware of his connections with the British monarchy. One afternoon before we married he had disappeared saying that he had to do something "important." I was to learn he had spent afternoon tea with the Queen Mother at Clarence House.

The Queen, Prince Philip and Prince Charles, in particular, were also devoted fans of the Goons in whose steam radio ranks Sellers rose to fame.

And his friendship with Tony and Princess Margaret was blossoming.

Both Tony and Sellers were camera freaks and they exchanged Leicas and Nikons like youngsters swapped cigarette cards.

They also shared a penchant for gadgetry and both had massive banks of stereo equipment with hi-fi speakers, dials and headphones.

The Princess regarded Sellers as the perfect foil to the dull, monotonous official duties which members of the British Royal family were required to fulfil. He was a "breath of fresh air" in the austere household: a figure upon whom they could rely as a means of escape from pomp and protocol.

Protocol was never entirely forgotten however. I was never to call Margaret by her Christian name and neither was Sellers or any of her friends. This was a prerogative that belonged only to her husband, the family and of course, her sister the Queen.

In fact, my introductory address to Princess Margaret was "Your Royal Highness" and Sellers instructed me to curtsey, which was rather reminiscent of my childhood.

I had curtsied before the Crown Prince of Sweden in Stockholm but less protocol surrounded the Swedish monarchy than that embracing the English sovereignty.

Naturally I was nervous, but the informality of Princess Margaret in Kensington Palace that day with Sellers did much to calm me.

Kensington Palace with its labyrinth of high ceilinged rooms and tall, beautiful windows, was indeed an august contemplation but I soon felt an intimate homeliness in its living quarters.

Family photographs, on the piano and mantelpiece, created an atmosphere of coziness and wellbeing. I could not help but notice some lovely snaps of their infant son Lord Linley who was still a toddler and was cared for by a nanny.

Tony and the Princess seemed a very loving couple in those surroundings on that particular day: we were to see a special set of pictures Tony had taken of his wife as milestones of their marriage, and on another of the walls was a framed collage of sentimental souvenirs . . . first night tickets, a restaurant bill, a blade of grass, a locket of hair, a matchbox . . . all signifying some special moment of happy memories for them.

We sat down to lunch in the dining room and although servants were on hand the meal was quite informal and the menu simple: consommé, roast beef and a bottle of Jackson's red wine.

I gathered that Tony was one of England's best photographers and when the brandies were being poured he suggested that I might like to pose for some glamour pictures.

"What a good idea!" exclaimed Princess Margaret, whose passion for music, games and charades was to become a familiar pattern of our friendship.

"He's actually quite good, Britt, if he remembers to put film in the camera!" she teased Tony.

The Princess showed me to her first-floor bedroom to change. They each had their own separate bedrooms and bathrooms and Tony came through and tossed me one of his shirts.

I was in a tweed costume and once the Royal couple had gone I slipped off my jacket and blouse and bra and exchanged it for the shirt.

I wanted to go to the loo but felt nervous about it. The loo was situated in the bathroom in a position unlike any other toilet I had seen before. It was located right in the middle of the bathroom like a throne.

Unsure of the door locks, and there were two doors, I had to take a chance that no one would walk in on me while nature paid its call.

I would have dearly liked to have asked why the loo was placed in such a position, but there was nothing I could say.

Sellers meanwhile had done a recce of the house with Tony and they had decided to use the natural light in the spacious hallway. Sellers assisted in the erection of the tripods.

Once in front of the camera I felt at ease in a way that any model does with a professional photographer, and I instinctively knew that Tony was highly experienced, as indeed the set of pictures he later produced were to show.

One of the shots he had mounted in a glass frame which he then decided to autograph, engraving the glass with Princess Margaret's diamond ring. The stone fell out of the ring to the amusement of everyone and Tony, handing the pieces back to the Princess, quipped, "So much for innovation!"

We became close friends of the Royal couple and Tony was a particularly well meaning, friendly and considerate person.

The Princess wasn't any less friendlier but I think we were always conscious of her position and sometimes she was to impose that if anyone upset her. On the other hand she was always extremely gracious and courteous to people she did not know and I think I learned a great deal from her as our friendship developed.

In the ensuing months I was to be presented to other members of the Royal family. I had already met Prince Philip at a Royal film première but meeting him at home at Windsor Castle was a very different experience, especially with the Queen at his side and the rest of the Royal family in force.

We were invited to join the pheasant and grouse shooting expeditions at Windsor and one Boxing Day we drove home with four pheasants from the morning's bag in the boot of the car.

Sellers would totally immerse himself into any new situation and he would always acquire the best possible equipment, even if its use was for a single function.

Pheasant shooting necessitated the immediate purchase of a £1200 twelve bore shotgun and ammunition from Purdey's, as well as the accepted attire: a padded hacking style jacket, breeches, boots and what I can only describe as a Sherlock Holmes deerstalker.

Sellers also engaged an instructor who would shadow him and cry "Fire" whenever a flock of pheasants passed overhead.

His success ratio increased with practice. Whenever a bird fell from the sky Sellers was ecstatic and he would

collect the odd word of congratulation from Prince
Philip, Angus Ogilvy and, on occasions, from Prince
Charles who was then accompanying the shoots.

The Queen and Princess Margaret, along with the
wives of all the other hunters in the party, trailed behind
in tweeds and furlined boots and head scarves fluttering, joining the men for "hot toddies" en route at
one of the lodges.

We were now becoming accustomed to the routine
but some of our visits to Windsor Castle were very
special.

We packed various changes of clothes and we were
given our own lovely quarters where a personal maid
and butler were assigned to look after all our needs.

The maid would unpack my clothes and lay out my
dresses, shoes and jewelry for me whenever we were invited to stay on for the day.

There was one afternoon tea I remember in the
drawing room when the Queen, her beloved Corgi dogs
scampering around her feet, and surrounded by the
members of her family, poured the afternoon tea from a
trolley like any mother in any ordinary home.

The Queen asked me if I would like sugar in my tea,
as she arranged the cups and saucers from the bone
china service on the lower shelving of the trolley.

"No thank you, Your Majesty," I replied, feeling
suddenly bewildered that this motherly woman who was
serving me tea was the English monarch.

Princess Margaret, Tony, Prince Charles, Princess
Anne, the Duke and Duchess of Kent and all the members of the Royal family were present.

Sellers and I were the only visitors that day, but the
Queen made us so welcome.

We talked about Sweden and Stockholm and the
Queen's visits there, and we talked too of the Swedish
Royal family. Our conversation turned to the countryside, to horses and of course to the morning's
pheasant shoot.

After tea we played charades and all the Royal family
joined in. By now I was so beetroot faced that in por-
traying a "lobster" in the game Prince Philip had no

difficulty in guessing my disguise, while Sellers warmed to the occasion throwing in Goon-like animations to confuse everyone.

It is often said that couples who remain happily married gradually begin to resemble one another and I remember thinking that about the Queen and Prince Philip whose comfortable rapport reflected their love for each other.

The Queen and Prince Philip remained however on a different platform to other members of the Royal family who could afford to be more outgoing.

Tony and Princess Margaret, like Charles and Anne in time, could let their hair down, not having to live up to the same exacting responsibilities of the Queen.

We were now very much part of the Royal social whirl: hardly a week went by without contact somewhere. Princess Margaret became simply PM in the orbit we moved in and we threw dinner parties at our home at Elstead for the Royals, relying heavily on the superb cuisine of our chef.

Another of PM's friends Janie Stevens, later to be lady-in-waiting and who was the wife of newspaper baron Jocelyn Stevens, would also host high spirited parties at their Kent countryside home and Sellers filmed one boisterous shindig when we all had to "star" in the action.

PM impersonated Queen Victoria, Tony hopped along as "The One Legged Golfer," Sellers captured some "Goodness Gracious Me" moments as the Indian doctor he portrayed in *The Millionairess* and I posed as an old movies' screen vamp, but on the final curtain we were all linking arms together for Ralph Reader's "anthem" "We're Riding Along On The Crest of A Wave" in the best Gang Show traditions!

Sellers paid out £6,000 to dub a musical score to the film and to have it edited and it was given its première at Kensington Palace on the night of the Queen's 39th birthday party.

PM had taken a party of us to see Spike Milligan in the stage play *Son of Oblomov* and with Harry Secombe and Michael Bentine in tow, the Goons were assembled to put on an impromptu cabaret to end the festivities at the Palace that night.

PM loved these moments and all our outings. We made up a party to see the French singer Francoise Hardy in her season at the Savoy and when it came to high jinks PM was usually in the forefront of the revelry. We organized a "seance" once at Janie's home and managed to raise the table a foot from the ground only to discover that the electricity from our out-stretched hands was not quite so remarkable as Jocelyn's ability to manuever the table top with the butt of his knee which rather upset Sellers who was on the verge of declaring a phenomenon.

Another dinner at the Stevens's was wildly funny. Some stuffy social climbing neighbors, always pushing for an invitation when the Royals were expected, finally got their wish.

They were advised to wear evening dress, when the rest of us including Tony and PM were in casual clothes.

When the couple were due to arrive we took our places at the dining room table, the men stripped to the waist but with bow ties that Jocelyn distributed.

As the doorbell rang we went through the motions of conducting a perfectly normal conversation until the butler ushered the unfortunate couple in. They stood in the frameway of the door, mesmerized, thinking that our menfolk were sitting at the table naked.

The poor couple just did not know what to do. With PM sitting at the table they could hardly turn and run.

At that point we could no longer control our mirth. One outburst from PM was sufficient for the room to collapse in an outbreak of hysteria and our victims, having paid the penalty for their social climbing, took it all in good spirit.

Social climbing is a human disease. I fear we are all culpable to a degree but nowhere is it more prevalent than in England. It is however a small price to pay for the good of its Monarchy.

Unfortunately, our association with the Royals did cause considerable antipathy among our other friends. The grapevine whisperings insinuated that Sellers was secretly canvassing the Royals for his knighthood.

Many stars at that period made no secret of the fact that a title was a much more rewarding accolade than an Academy Award.

One of our friends, John Mills, got both and Richard Attenborough collected a title.

There could be no doubting the genius of Sellers. Long before I married him he was a British Institution. Much loved by the public, he had worked earlier in his career at the famous Windmill Theater and he established his name in a string of domestic comedy films including *The Lady Killers, I'm All Right Jack*, and *Only Two Can Play*.

However it was in his role as a Goon that he was truly idolized—by public and Royalty alike.

The Goons invoked a new satirical comedy style on the masses through an insane breed of animated characters impersonated by Sellers and his three "accomplices" Spike Milligan, Harry Secombe and Michael Bentine. Their weekly radio show was plugged into millions of homes and became something of a cult.

Eventually the radio program ran out of steam but the legend lived on and when I came into Sellers's life, one could still buy their long playing albums, occasionally hear nostalgic "repeats" while the quartet themselves would hold buoyant reunions.

Some were staged in public, or for the benefit of the television cameras, but most were conducted in private.

This meant that Spike, Harry and Michael were frequent visitors to the house and once I remember Prince Charles joined in for an evening's goonery, while I discreetly stayed in the background so that they would not have to censor their script.

On other occasions we threw the reunion parties in the old barn in the grounds when the wives were invited too and if I lacked any knowledge of the Goons it was soon remedied.

Sometimes, at the height of the babbling mimickry, I wondered if I was not actually married to a shameless Indian Army officer named Major Bloodnok, a cretin known as Henry Crun, a villain who answered to the unlikely title of Grytpype Thynne or Bluebottle, a schoolboyish Walter Mitty of sorts.

These were just a few of the weird characters into whose identity Sellers would transcend whenever in the company of his fellow Goons or at any other time as a party piece.

The Goons got their name from an obscure character in the old Popeye cartoons loved by Spike whose identities in the series were divided between the antics of the lovable, toothless dimwit known to listeners as Eccles, or those of the twittering Abdul, the vague hen-like Minnie Bannister or the seedy Count Jim Moriarty.

Harry Secombe played the pivotal figure of the plot, Neddy Seagoon, a pioneer of the British Empire whose explorations always ran into trouble. And Michael Bentine was a willing assailant to it all.

Together they were incorrigible.

Dinner parties would mean a revival of all their old scripts and we, the patient wives, would provide them with a ready-made audience.

We would punctuate our laughter on cue and this, I found, was one of the penalties in being married to a comic. A wife has to suffer the same anecdotes over and over again because there is always someone who hasn't heard a joke, and pleads for it to be recited.

Sellers would never hesitate to relate Goon snippings and he would also indulge in anecdotes gleaned from his movies.

Milligan was the real eccentric of the quartet and it was hard for the others to compete against him. When he was in a "creative" mood he would lock himself away from the world in his attic as though it was a prison cell and not even his wife Paddy would be allowed to talk to him. When he wanted a bite to eat, or a cup of coffee, he picked up the telephone and dictated a telegram to be delivered to Paddy in the kitchen below by a confused postman.

"Don't you mind?" I asked Paddy on one occasion.

She sighed.

But it was here that there existed the fundamental difference between the two Goons. Milligan always said that he *was* mad and took periodic rest cures in a clinic whenever he felt shades of insanity threatening his genius!

As a human being Spike was hard to define. Even when he was laughing he never seemed absolutely happy. He would stalk around with his hair sticking from his head like blades of grass and his mind locked in thought. It appears he was driven by an unseen force over which he had no apparent control.

Paddy, who sadly died from cancer in 1978, spent most of her married life trying to analyze Spike. As I did with my husband but in Sellers's case he refused to admit he was ever over the edge although he once wrote to me saying that he was a raving idiot and that he ought to have his head examined. Yet when I timidly suggested that he should see a psychiatrist he retorted, "Are you saying I'm crackers?"

Maybe it was their absurd eccentricities that made Milligan and Sellers the catalysts of the Goons' brand of humor, but they were always threatened by the super brilliance of Michael Bentine, whose intellect flattened them. The Eton-educated Bentine was the son of a Peruvian scientist.

Bentine earned only contempt because he was also able to apply his talents in a practical sense. He was a marvelous cordon bleu chef and a do-it-yourself expert to boot.

He also studied medicine and had delivered one of his own children much to the delight of Janine his lovely delicate wife.

Sellers and Milligan could barely disguise their jealousy. They spent much time fathoming out things that Bentine couldn't possibly do and they played tricks on him. Invariably they backfired like the time they matched Bentine at fencing with a former British champion. Bentine outfenced the champion!

They were even more mortified when the Bentines invited us to a celebratory dinner. Michael not only cooked and served the meal, but also mentioned having caught the fine Scotch salmon that was the centerpiece of the decorative table.

Bentine really rattled Milligan and Sellers in the stakes of oneupmanship. Not so the round and cuddly Harry Secombe, quite the loveliest member of the quartet in whose mirthful life there was no place for intrigue.

Harry was the only comedian I knew who was as funny off stage as he was on and his falsetto laugh is infectious. His wife Myra was equally warm and jovial and whenever we met up with them I always wished my marriage to Sellers could have been just one grain as happy as theirs.

Somehow I had to try to separate Sellers's private life from his professional one. They were totally different lives, but as his wife I was to witness both at close quarters and there could be no compromise between the two.

If the Goons established Sellers as a national hero then the *Pink Panther* films were to glorify his name on the screen. And if an "Oscar" wasn't forthcoming Sellers took solace from the invitation to cast his footprints in cement alongside those of the Hollywood colony, Bogart, Gary Cooper and Spencer Tracy among others, on the pavements outside the Chinese Graumann theater.

Ironically Sellers only got the Inspector Clouseau role as second choice. Peter Ustinov turned it down in order to shoot *Topkapi*.

Blake Edwards, who wrote, produced and directed the *Pink Panther* movies, had a running feud with Sellers for some time before they were able to bury the hatchet.

My husband once vowed that he would never work with Blake again and I remember going to one dinner with Blake and his wife Julie Andrews when the atmosphere was distinctly chilly. Julie didn't contribute too much. I thought she lacked any real warmth, while still clinging on to her English rose image.

I am sure Blake recognized moments when Sellers actually despised him but somehow he accepted it and with the success of the *Pink Panther* line assured, the acrimony that existed began to heal.

Sellers loved to recount a marvelous story about Blake which occurred when both were given honorary

judo black belts after training for karate scenes in the
original *Pink Panther* movie.

On his way home from the studios Blake was in
collision at traffic lights with another motorist who
adopted a threatening, hostile attitude.

Blake apparently warned him, "I shouldn't try anything. I am a judo black belt and I'll kill you with one
chop." Poor Blake. While pausing to release his safety
belt he was knocked out cold by the other motorist's
first punch. Sellers thought they might reconstruct the
incident as a scene for the next *Pink Panther* sequel.

I could never criticize Sellers's creative output.
Whenever filming allowed he would explore every
avenue to energize his talents in the pop music field.

With Sophia Loren he had recorded a novel chart
record after their success in *The Millionairess* and he
made his own recording of the Beatles' song "It's A
Hard Day's Night" which he mimicked in the majestic,
stentorian tones of Richard III as played by Lord
Olivier.

Sellers's love for jazz and Latin music was well
known but he also admired the Beatles and Simon and
Garfunkel.

He was not without his screen idols either. The
irascible Lee Marvin was one of them. We were in
Ronnie Scott's club in London one night and Sellers
suddenly spotted Lee Marvin sitting at a corner table.
Sellers was ecstatic.

"I must go over and pay my respects to him," said
Sellers, leaving me with my drink.

Moments later Sellers was back at our table, feeling
totally destroyed. The great Lee Marvin had apparently
failed to acknowledge him and Sellers said, "From now
on legends shall remain legends. Never make them
people."

Sellers was a man of many idiosyncrasies and deeply
rooted superstitions, bred no doubt by the music hall
background of his parents. The theater had always
thrived on superstition.

Like so many other artists, Sellers refused to allow

anyone to whistle in his dressing room for fear of bad
luck.

If we crossed on the stairs he would order me to
retrace my steps and count to ten before descending further.

When we were in California the rains brought down
our bedroom ceiling when we were in bed and although
we escaped injury, Sellers regarded it as a bad omen.

In these areas, Sellers was totally credulous and
gullible.

Someone once told him that the color of purple was
unlucky and that it was only associated with death.

He instantly tossed out a purple chair from our living
room.

In Rome, a secretary appeared on the set wearing a
purple sweater. Sellers immediately called a halt until
the girl had been shepherded off the floor.

I searched my wardrobe and disposed of any gar-
ments with even a semblance of purple.

Zodiac signs would also influence Sellers, whose
moods could be determined by the horoscopes of the
morning newspapers.

If one prediction was disheartening he would discard
it for another reading that promised more optimistic
things.

Sellers was a Virgo and a very finicky one at that
which made life intolerable for the artistic, home-
making Libran that I truly am.

Every two or three months my husband would consult
with the British clairvoyant, Maurice Woodruff, and he
would return home brimming with expectancy of fresh
triumphs likely to emerge in his career.

I am sure that Woodruff knew my husband well
enough to know that the only predictions he could pass
on were those that would flatter him. Sellers could not
have coped with anything detrimental.

He persuaded me to see Woodruff when I felt apprehensive about starring in a play that the West End
entrepreneur Michael White offered me.

"If you can't make up your mind about it, why don't

you go and see Maurice?'' said Sellers, making an appointment for me.

I went to Woodruff's Hampstead home and paid my 25 guinea fee. He seemed a very plausible fortune teller but still I was in quandary.

Feeling that I should not go into a production where I harbored so many doubts, I finally rejected the stage play. Others may have considered that I flunked it and perhaps I did, but the decision was fateful. The production burned itself out on its provincial run and did not come into the West End, while I signed for a major feature movie that I could not have possibly accepted if I had gone into the play.

Woodruff wasn't Sellers's only guru. Shamelessly he consulted with many other soothsayers, astrologers and cranks throughout our marriage. Even tea-leaf readings he held in awe and he would visit the well-known medium Estelle Roberts whose predictions would lift him when his horizons were indefinable.

Later, Sellers moved on to yoga, having been introduced by the Beatles to the Indian sitar player Ravi Shankar.

Ravi would come to our house and give concerts, and as a token of his gratitude Sellers gave him a gold Piaget wristwatch.

Sometimes I worried for my husband. He placed so much trust in the powers of spiritualist mediums, faith healers and others with knowledge of the occult.

It was so hard for me to tell him that he just might have been taken as a sucker.

Two years after getting over the terrible tribulations of Sellers's heart attack, I was plunged back into the depths of despair by the sudden and desperate illness of my mother. She had cancer.

My father telephoned me early one evening, fearing that she might not last the night after being rushed into hospital for immediate surgery.

I had not seen my mother for a year.

I was grief stricken. I should have kept a closer eye on her.

The vision of his own life-or-death ordeal clearly flashed back through his mind and Sellers was galvanized into sympathetic action.

Canceling my booking on the *QE2* for New York, he got me out on the next plane to Stockholm and was the caring and consoling husband.

My mother, Maj-Britt, was 49 and the irony of her illness was that she had always tried to keep fit. She kept rigidly to a diet of yogurt, cheese and molasses. She took long walks every day and had regular massage sessions. She'd never smoked and she didn't drink.

I hardly recognized her in the intensive care unit. The sickly yellow face that peered at me from the pillow was almost as hollow as a skeleton's. A doctor conveyed little hope. "We are in God's hands," he said.

My brothers and I were in tears and for the next few days her life hung on a thread. One afternoon, when the immediate crisis was over I flew to Paris and bought my mother three Christian Dior nightgowns, some sheets and in Stockholm a diamond and ruby ring. In the back of my mind I kept thinking that if these were her last hours then she should know how much we all loved her. I also felt that if I kept buying things for her, it might make her live.

I could not think of her dying. I asked the surgeons, after two major operations, if there was any advantage in transferring my mother to the Mayo Clinic in New York or to the Royal Marsden in London where I knew cancer research was carried out. They advised against it. One replied, "We have the best equipment available in the world here. Your mother is getting all possible attention."

Every day I kept a vigil at her bedside, just as I had done with my husband.

Sellers was very kind. He had taken Victoria to Hollywood where he had to start a new movie but he kept in constant touch, telling me that if there was anything my mother wanted I was to buy it for her. He also sent roses and cassette tapes with loving messages for her. One that gave her a lot of happiness was a recording he made with Victoria on a trip to Disneyland.

Slowly, mother improved and she began to talk and smile when earlier she had been barely conscious of my presence.

I thought that if she gained sufficient strength I intended to take her to Lourdes, but a miracle was already on its way.

In the sixth week, the Senior surgeon told me, "Your mother is making an incredible recovery. We have arrested the cancer, but as it is malignant it could return in five or ten years. On the other hand it may never reappear. But the fact your mother has pulled through this present crisis is a miracle beyond explanation. One thing is for certain. She had a great will to live."

My mother's recovery was all the more significant when assessed against the added emotional sufferings of her crumbling marriage to my father. After twenty-five years they were heading irretrievably for divorce.

When our old home had been pulled down they had moved into a much more spacious flat that had served as an Embassy, but there my parents occupied separate bedrooms.

Exerting increased pressure on the marriage was the collapse of my father's business. The women's fashion store which had been a private family enterprise for two generations had fallen victim to the big conglomerates that changed the shopping face of Stockholm. My father had been forced into bankruptcy and his only income as far as I knew was from his administrative and secretarial work with the Swedish curling team.

But typical of my father's flamboyance was his reluctance to trim back on any of his extravagant ways. He maintained his nightly social life, going out to cocktail parties and playing golf and bowling whenever he fancied doing so.

My poor mother, in order to keep the household going, had become a full-time worker as a football pools checker, a job that she once did on a part time basis and more or less as a hobby. I could remember working there with her as a teenager during school holidays earning 20 dollars a week.

Through my mother's illness, my father rarely surfaced, not wishing to face up to the worry or responsibility. When my mother came out of hospital I sent her into a convalescent home for several months and I paid the 15,000 dollar fees for her room and treatment.

My two elder brothers had left home but my youngest brother was still living at home and I knew that my father would not be able to cope with him on his own while my mother was convalescing.

I thought it would be in Kalle's interests to get him into boarding school and I settled for an expensive academy in Sigtuna because I wanted to give my brother the best possible opportunity in life.

I told the Principal that I would pay all his fees and that I would be responsible for him.

My mother was grateful for all the arrangements I had made and when she was well enough she instigated divorce proceedings against my father. It was sad. They had been married 25 years. But my mother had the entire sympathy of the family. None of us tried to talk her out of it; she had been more like a servant to my father than a wife.

The home was eventually sold up and property divided. My parents took their own apartments and for several years I didn't talk to my father. Neither did my brothers on whom he had been particularly harsh when they were small and who could not forgive him for the selfish way in which he had led his life.

My mother, having licked Big C., was able to weather the divorce, knowing it was the last hurdle before finding her own happiness.

— *seven* —

SELLERS gave me a word of advice. "If you do the *right* films at the *right* times then you could be bigger than Loren," he said.

By now I was getting quite accustomed to the comparisons he liked to draw between me and the Italian superstar he was once so very fond of.

There was a time when Sellers, examining a new set of photographs of me taken in New York, remarked that I was "alarmingly more beautiful than any other woman."

I was flattered, of course, but I must admit that over the months I grew curious about Sophia Loren from all the references that my husband made to her.

Quietly I wondered what she was really like.

An opportunity to meet Sophia unexpectedly came at a private preview screening in London of Charlie Chaplin's movie *The Countess from Hong Kong*, his first picture in nine years.

It was a big occasion. Sellers and I were both invited to go but at that point Sellers did not want to face Sophia again.

Many stars and celebrities had been invited to the screening and when I walked in I tried to disguise my overwhelming nervousness at venturing to such an occasion on my own.

I still lived in total awe of the screen legends I had known as a child.

Now one of them stood before me: Charlie Chaplin, the face instantly recognizable beneath his whitening hair. He was smiling and extending his hand of welcome to me.

I felt other unseen eyes on me as I turned to be introduced by a film company executive to Sophia Loren and Carlo Ponti.

They asked after Sellers and expressed their condolences when I conveyed to them that he was feeling unwell. Sophia recalled moments when she had worked with Sellers on *The Millionairess* and we made polite conversation over the cocktails that were served before the screening of the film.

Women are able to communicate the unspoken word so much more easily than men and it wasn't difficult to read our transmission of thoughts.

I was thinking, "So this is the woman Sellers went crazy about" and I'm sure that she was musing herself with the notion, "So this is the little Swedish mouse Sellers got to marry."

But for all of that Sophia was pleasant and friendly and so was Carlo whose whole persona was one of charm.

The evening passed pleasantly enough but the film, unfortunately, was tedious and was not saved by Chaplin's ingenious idea to hire an organist to play the theme music during the actual showing because the print we were seeing had not been dubbed with the musical score.

When I got home Sellers was still sullen but his mood was mercifully lifting and he was only too keen to listen to my account of my meeting with Sophia and Carlo.

Sellers must have thought that the ice was broken. Facing Sophia and Carlo would not be the ordeal he feared and when we found ourselves in Italy a few months later we were inevitably to meet them.

In fact, we were to go out as a foursome on many social occasions and we dined once at the Pontis' home at Frascati just outside Rome. It was a beautiful red tiled villa with tall conifers towering over the patio and swimming pool.

Sophia could not have been a more considerate hostess, but it became increasingly clear to me that she was always conscious of her sex symbol image.

Every appearance she made, even within her own household, meant that she had to be properly dressed and made-up. Not a hair, not an eyelash, could be out of place. I did not see her once in anything casual, even so much as a pair of jeans.

As a woman I could not find her attractive. Bodily she was overpowering and I had no desire to compete with her in those areas.

Strangely, all through our friendship, I never regarded her as a threat or challenge, and I must have instilled this thought within Sellers because the subject of Loren became a diminishing one.

My confidence may have fired Sellers into thinking that I could successfully emulate Sophia on the screen. He genuinely wanted me to succeed and the reason for our presence in Italy was to make the first of two films together.

Sellers shrugged aside any accusations of nepotism, which today is pretty rampant in the industry. Charles Bronson wouldn't dream of making a movie without the casting of his wife Jill Ireland and Richard Harris and Ann Turkel are among many other husband and wife screen pairings.

But at that period Sellers was ready to pass on the skills of his genius to me, illustrating the subtleties involved in the timing and delivery of dialogue and expounding on editing and dubbing techniques employed in the studios.

I had to believe that Sellers wanted me to be a star, although I could not rid myself of the lurking suspicion that he involved me in his films only so that he could keep his clutches on me.

Indicatively, whenever I was offered a script from an outside source, he found fault with it or said it was unsuitable for me and he would turn it down without telling me.

Sellers had formed a new film company, Brookfield Productions one of whose directors, John Bryan, was credited as the producer of *After the Fox* which began shooting in Rome.

Sellers's role in the movie was that of a master Italian criminal who breaks jail to organize a gold bullion robbery, while saving his wayward sister from a life of shame.

It was unique enough to play Sellers's screen sister but in order to resemble an Italian girl I had to wear a black wig over my blond hair.

We rented a beautiful villa in Rome on the ancient Appian Way, living almost opposite Neil Simon and his then wife Joan.

Neil, a well-known American playwright, renowned for his Broadway comedy successes, had written the screenplay for *After the Fox* and a mutual respect existed between Sellers and Neil for their own particular categories of humor.

I wanted to feel that my marriage to Sellers had turned the corner, that our problems were over and in working together we could face the future on a more solid footing.

To the outside world we still appeared as the affectionate, loving couple and dining with Richard Burton and Liz Taylor one night I wondered if they saw through our guise.

In many respects I was not worried. Elizabeth Taylor was my heroine and I knew that she had come through a lot of mental anguish in her own life. Unlike Sophia she had no predilections about preserving her star image. She was candid, gutsy and to the point.

I told Liz about my part in *After the Fox* and she said, "Don't think of Sellers as your husband when you are on set with him. Regard him only as an actor and Britt—play it for real."

I wanted to put my heart into my work but our disagreements grew by the day.

Once a row broke out between us after we had gone to bed. I ran, still in my nightgown, in an hysterical state and sought refuge at Neil Simon's home opposite.

Neil and his wife were bewildered. They had genuinely believed I was happily married to Sellers. They had been deceived by the impeccable front which he falsely purveyed.

We moved on to the beautiful island of Ischia for six weeks' location work. I invited my mother and two of my brothers to join us, but I was so intimidated by Sellers that I checked them into a different hotel.

We had a suite at the Hotel Regina Isabella, and our nanny cared for Victoria in an adjoining room.

It was a marvelous setting for the location. Oh, how happy we could have been there!

Our only free day was Sunday. Most of the cast and crew would take the opportunity to sunbathe by the pool or on the beach: it was the natural thing to do. But Sellers would stay in our hotel suite all day and refuse to budge.

I didn't dare to go down to the pool without him otherwise he would have accused me of disloyalty. He did not want to see me enjoy myself. He was even suspicious if I went out to check on Victoria, who would be taken down to the beach by the nanny who was so often embarrassed by the atmosphere in our suite.

My mother and family saw little of me as they were never invited to our suite, and the only two occasions Sellers ventured out of the hotel on a Sunday was when some of his friends, Quentin Crewe and Angela Huth visited us from England.

Of course he created the impression that our marriage was idyllic and I went along with the façade in order not to let him down.

I tried so hard to understand Sellers. I related his "dark moods" to the pressures and ambiguities of his genius. Where was the warmth, humor and humanity he generated on the screen?

There were interludes when he was truly a loving, gentle and generous human being, but these moments were like flashes of sunshine.

Sellers's whole demeanor gravitated between the highs and lows of a barometer. If only he could have set the arrow to "Fair" life might have been a lot easier.

There were sighs of relief when shooting finally wrapped up on *After the Fox*. Sellers hadn't been too complimentary about the way Vittorio de Sica directed the movie and later commented that he wasn't the right choice as a director.

Sellers had reached the stage when he felt that he was better qualified to direct a movie than most established directors.

Real trouble occurred on *Casino Royale* when Joe McGrath who originally had Sellers's backing as director was replaced by a whole collection of directors, including John Huston.

There was also an insurance hitch. Because of Sellers's heart condition, none of the big insurance companies would provide adequate cover on the movie. So producer Charles Feldman had to step in and underwrite the liability himself.

These harassments apart, Sellers was getting a million dollars for his role as the bogus James Bond in this movie spoof of Ian Fleming's fictional agent, and he regarded the film as a major milestone in his career. Alas, Sellers played the role straight, when the producers wanted him to be funny.

My husband was also strangely disturbed by the presence in the cast of the gargantuan Orson Welles, secretly believing that Welles might ''steal'' the key scenes. Sellers avoided filming with Orson on days when they were supposed to be on call together and with chaos descending over the whole studio, someone's head had to roll. It was the unfortunate Joe McGrath's.

Sellers quit on his own account and we went to Switzerland. Feldman pleaded with me to placate my husband by any means possible.

I think everyone knew that *Casino Royale* was heading for disaster and the operation of decorating the movie with thirty glamour girls could not save it from bombing out.

I still have one memory of the episode. I got a bouquet of flowers on our wedding anniversary and a card signed ''from James Bond.''

After this débâcle Sellers went to the sunshine of the South of France. I was offered a major part in the spy thriller *The Double Man* and even before I started work on it in England it was suggested that I intended to have an affair with the movie's leading man, Yul Brynner.

I said that this was totally ridiculous.

Our dissension grew. There were times when I crossed oceans with just a toothbrush to patch things up between us.

We were in a situation of stalemate just prior to filming *The Bobo* which was our second film in harness together although the reins snapped on more than one occasion.

Sellers left for Italy in a huff and I got a letter from his lawyers telling me that he was instigating divorce proceedings and that I should take separate accommodation. The letter said, "He intends to work with you in the same manner as he would with any other actress and he trusts you will reciprocate his intentions."

I was so devastated by the letter that I caught the next plane out to Rome without packing a thing except my toiletries, humble enough once more to try and reconcile our differences.

Our reunion was one of tears and joy in the villa that Sellers rented on the Appia Antica.

The reconciliation saw us through to dawn but from that point on the marriage was still under duress.

Sellers didn't cease to remind me that he had engineered my part in the movie against more likely candidates of Brigitte Bardot, Ursula Andress and Virna Lisi.

He could sack me whenever he wished, he threatened.

There were perpetual rows and sometimes our precious furniture got broken.

In one row I chipped one of my front teeth. The flaw is still visible today.

After another stormy episode my husband stalked out of the villa and told our servants, Massimo the butler, Vera the maid and Assunta the cook, that I would be paying their wages in future.

Sellers moved into a local hotel, but a few nights later he was back. Inexplicably, we still managed to find some common ground on which to repair our marriage!

My husband wasn't happy about the way the movie was developing, either.

It was a very funny script but Sellers didn't feel we were getting things right. His role was that of a singing matador and I was cast as his seductress Olimpia, the most enchanting of Barcelona's women.

I think that Sellers was unnecessarily anxious about the direction and this put all sorts of pressures on Bob Parrish.

Right in the middle of things we received a call from London to tell us that Sellers's mother Peg had suffered a coronary.

I anticipated our immediate departure to London, but I was astounded when Sellers apparently regarded the completion of the movie more important than his own mother's plight.

Bob Parrish pleaded with Sellers to return, but he insisted on staying in Rome. My husband's answer was contained in author Peter Evans's subsequent biography in which Sellers was quoted as saying, "Peg is going to be fine. I know everything about heart attacks, don't forget Bob. I'm the expert."

A week later, on 29 January 1967, Peg died. It was too late to do anything at all. We flew back for the funeral and Sellers was beside himself for not having seen his mother before she died.

Like most sons in such an hour, he thought he could have done much more to have made his mother's life happier, although I doubt if Peg would have had any real grumbles.

In her twilight years, Sellers had ensured she was comfortable. He paid the rent of her conveniently-situated Primrose Hill apartment and provided a chauffeur-driven Bentley so that she always had transport. He also took care of all her bills.

Peg had done much to encourage Sellers into the profession and she'd had a hard, but good life. And I was sad to see her go. In many respects I had lost a friend.

In my relationship with Sellers, I could always be sure that Peg would take my side. She took care of me and I took care of her, never breathing a word to Sellers about her hidden gin bottles.

When we got back to Rome filming on *The Bobo* was resumed but a flashpoint was reached when Sellers insisted on taking the director's credit from Bob Parrish.

There were sighs of relief when the last shot was canned and the movie was completed.

Our only light relief during filming was a trip to Genoa when Sellers suddenly decided to buy a yacht.

He commissioned its structure in a mariner's yard just along the coastline from the Italian seaport.

Later in the summer the *Bobo* was launched, Sellers naming the 50ft. long motor vessel after our film, rashly believing we could overcome turbulence at sea even though we failed to achieve it on land.

Sellers incorporated every modern navigational aid in the £150,000 yacht including radar, air conditioning, automatic pilot and radio, as well as television, stereo and the rest of his gadgetry.

The yacht, duly launched with its decks awash in champagne, was registered in Panama for tax reasons.

Sellers liked to play the role of the Captain at the helm as the *Bobo* took to sea.

It was a thrilling moment and for a time there were no squalls at sea or on deck. For once we were on friendly terms as Sellers explored the joys of his new, if expensive, "toy."

With a yacht we soon found we were never short of guests, especially at our mooring in Monte Carlo.

Kirk and Anne Douglas stayed aboard with us and later we sailed to Sardinia to link up with PM and Tony who were then holidaying with the Aga Khan at his luxurious Hotel Pitrizza.

The Royals must have thought that their holiday would have been rather dull without Sellers who gooned his way through countless cocktail parties.

During the daytime we ran tenders from the yacht and skied. I admired the techniques of the Royal couple on water skis, particularly Tony whose right leg was weakened by the effects of polio as a child.

I skied with them and so did Sellers whose constant

duckings only added to Royal amusement. Like all other sports Sellers only "dabbled"—and water skiing needs serious application, so his interest flagged.

Sellers was always careful to keep on good relations with the Royals.

However, his alliance with John Bryan, convened on a six-film deal, ended abruptly once *After the Fox* was finished.

Other similar partnerships had gone sour for Sellers in earlier years and before our marriage he had backed out on a partnership with playwright Wolf Mankowitz on the very morning their new company was to be financed.

Wolf didn't forgive Sellers for this rebuttal, as he was to relate to me over dinner one night.

What transpired I cannot recall because my entire mental and physical energies were weighed down by the atrocious sham that my marriage had become.

Delayed at Elstree studios one night my homecoming was a doorstep confrontation with Sellers demanding to know where I had been. We had a dreadful row and the next morning, when I was dressing, I could not find my Cartier gold watch, only to discover that it had been smashed into particles on the floor, presumably with the heel of a shoe, and an attempt had been made to flush the remains down the loo.

When I saw the broken pieces of the watch lying in the bottom of the porcelain pan I could not believe it was possible.

When Sellers's blinding anger receded, he would experience the most painful remorse and to win back my affection he would smother me with trinkets. After one altercation he gave me a red garnet and diamond ring delivered on an imitation Egyptian mummy's hand.

Sellers would invite me to participate on "treasure trove" trails, hiding gifts about the house and inviting me to find them. One "treasure trove" expedition he arranged in the Oliver Messel suite at the Dorchester. He set me on the track of a gold watch, cigarette lighter and case, a pen, silk scarf, perfume and boxes of fragrant soap.

"There Britvic," he purred when I successfully recovered the booty distributed beneath armchairs, cushions and vases, "now do you see how much I love you?"

It was hard not to forgive him in those moments and at least it meant that peace would be restored for two or three days and that was more highly prized than any of the gifts.

Of course these interludes were brief.

At nights I would take refuge on the sofa in the study.

At the same time I was anxious to conceal our slanging matches from the ears of Michael and Sarah who no doubt recounted them word by word to their mother.

Our friends rallied to our assistance. I burdened my friend Nanette Newman Forbes with our troubles.

Nanette was sympathetic. "You have no alternative Britt. You've got to leave him," she said.

Nanette and Bryan were able to see for themselves how badly our marriage had fallen.

I sought refuge with them one day at their home at Wentworth and poured out my heart to them. Sadly, they listened to my unhappiness and they tried to console me.

Eventually, they telephoned Sellers to assure him that I was safe, because I had not told him where I was going when I marched out of the house.

Sure enough, Sellers came to pick me up.

For the benefit of Bryan and Nanette, my husband gave the impression that I was tired and depressed and that we had had no more than a small tiff.

We drove home in silence but the next day he telephoned his lawyers about a divorce, for reasons he didn't share with me.

It was always baffling to me, but the trigger spot for our quarrels was invariably at weekends or holiday periods.

There was one Christmas when the hostility was so unbearable that the only relief I could find was scrubbing the kitchen floor. I was so beaten down and so unhappy that I could no longer defend myself against his tyranny.

In his presence I could never relax.

Our incessant travels did little to soothe Sellers's temperament either. In America so as to keep in shape, I had an aging Swedish physiotherapist come to the house to massage me.

Sellers insisted I keep my clothes on.

"How can anyone have a massage and keep their clothes on?" I said. "A physiotherapist regards someone's body in the same way as a doctor does. It doesn't mean anything more to them than a typewriter to a secretary."

He was upset about anyone else seeing me in the nude and it wasn't only the masseur he was worried about.

When I signed to play New York's first music hall stripper in *The Night They Raided Minsky's* he vetted the screenplay from beginning to end.

"If you're going to have to strip then they will have to get a stand-in to do it," he said.

I had to reassure him that I would not play the one nude scene and that they were in fact bringing in a stand-in.

As much as the role was a provocative one, it was also rather poignant as the screenplay traced the stripper's life to her origins as a Quaker girl who ran away from home and her family.

It had all the bearing of being a film classic.

An amusing incident precipitated filming. Frank Sinatra sent a note to my agent saying, "Jeezers baby, if I'd known you were going to cast a broad like Britt Ekland I would have done the movie . . ."

Sellers went along with the spirit of things and on the first day of shooting in New York I got at least twenty "good luck" telegrams from Sellers signed in bogus names but they all had a certain ring about them . . . "Elizabeth and Philip," "Margaret and Tony," "John, Paul, George and Ringo," "Richard and Elizabeth," "Maharishi Yogi," "Juan Batista" and the "Yorkshire Terriers Quarantine Committee"—the latter being a reference to my three little doggies, Scruff, Pucci and Fred.

My co-stars Jason Robards, Elliott Gould and Norman Wisdom were in hysterics when I pinned them up in my dressing room trailer.

I think it was Norman who said, "It must be a laugh a minute being married to Peter, Britt."

I would have liked to have told him the truth, but I doubt if he would have believed me, being a comic himself.

Sometimes I came to the conclusion that it would have been easier to have been the wife of an alcoholic. At least with an alcoholic he finally lies down and goes to sleep. You get some rest.

With Sellers, even though Los Angeles and New York separated us, I could never rest. That he was confined in Hollywood filming *I Love You Alice B. Toklas* only served to make him more insistent.

The telephone never stopped ringing. I could not move in New York without my exact whereabouts being relayed to him hour by hour.

I went to a party thrown for Paul Newman. Half way through the hostess came and told me there was a phone call from my husband.

"You should be home by now. It's 11:00 p.m. Why aren't you there?" said Sellers.

I said meekly that I was just leaving, even though I had gone to the party under the wing of David and Lee Begelman who were his friends. Indeed David was our agent.

Jason Robards threw a dinner party and I went along. Jason was then married to Humphrey Bogart's widow, the legendary Lauren Bacall. She had something of a bitchy reputation in the trade, but I found her an extraordinarily friendly person, having joined the party late night from her Broadway-running stage show *Applause*.

So much happened during the filming of *Minsky's* but the one note of sadness that hung over the production was the sudden death of the American vaudeville comedian Bert Lahr who was cast as a narrator in the movie. He died from cancer midway through the schedule.

Our director William Friedkin used what footage they had already shot of Bert and a "double" was found to complete the movie.

The one hardship that faced me at weekends was the prospect of an arduous round trip back to Los Angeles. I missed my plane on one occasion, which meant that I traveled all night to get to the studios in time for the dawn start.

Fortunately, there were times when I had company on the regular voyage. Elliott Gould would frequently travel with me, as he was then married to Barbra Streisand and they lived only three blocks from us on Bedford Drive.

Elliott and Barbra, who was filming *Funny Girl* at the time, would throw dinner parties for us and we would reciprocate a week or two later. They were an entertaining couple and I remember one evening when we all got stoned on grass. We pursued a harmless game of inventing new flavors for ice cream . . . declaring avocado, peanut and cucumber top of the list!

I welcomed our evenings with Elliott and Barbra, if only as a respite from my running marital battles.

Although Sellers regarded us as "tax exiles" which meant that our days at Elstead were strictly limited, we somehow acquired a four bedroom town apartment in Clarges Street in the heart of Mayfair. We spent 125,000 dollars on its redesign and furnishings. Its elegance and flair caught the interest of the glossy magazines. We had an L-shaped living room paneled and stained in pale turquoise which Sellers pronounced was "sympathetic to Britt's persona."

We had a four poster in the master bedroom and in our dining area we bought a suite of white tulip style chairs and a table designed by Eero Saarinen. The apartment also boasted a collection of abstract paintings by Michael Tain that Sellers liked.

We were naturally excited about our new home but the one requisite we needed most we could not obtain. It was impossible to buy happiness.

One of the gossip columns observed this peculiarity after one of our abrupt partings.

Sellers said, "I am working on a new film at Pinewood and as I don't want to disturb my wife at the crack of dawn I thought it would be better if I moved into the hotel."

When I was asked to comment I'm sure that everyone drew their own conclusions as to the real truth of the situation. "Our separation is great fun," I said ambiguously. "It's just like dating all over again."

I'm sure we fooled no one.

Sellers always made me feel the blameful partner. Until now we had never come to blows but in an embittered exchange a few weeks later Sellers slapped my face and I took a crack at his.

Unfortunately, my flailing arm caught the sacred framed picture of Peg, and it smashed to the floor along with Sellers's horn-rimmed specs. Both were lying shattered on the carpet and Sellers burst into tears.

"That's the only picture I've got of my mother," he wailed like a child who had just lost his marbles.

I was made to feel conscience stricken.

"I'm sorry," I said. "I'll get the picture repaired and framed again."

I was genuinely sorry, but there was nothing more I could say.

My health deteriorated under the strain of our matrimonial discord. I developed sinus troubles and tonsilitis and on one occasion I collapsed with an ailment that the doctor at first thought was thrombosis. Later, he blamed the Pill as much as personal stress.

Luckily it was not thrombosis, but I saw the illness as a warning and stopped taking the contraceptive pill.

I could not, however, contain the stress. Our marriage lurched crazily on like a doomed ship seeking navigation in uncharted waters.

We were not alone. It seemed our friends PM and Tony had also run into heavy marital squalls and when word reached Sellers he enlisted with rallying friends hoping to fortify the Royal couple's marriage.

The Stevens offered their villa in the Bahamas and

Sellers put his yacht the *Bobo* at their disposal. His gesture was sincere.

It is said that sharing one's heartaches can often relieve the burden, but I hesitated to contact PM to tell her that, we too, were having problems. Although I guessed she knew.

I sensed that PM's situation would be more delicate than my own. She was in an invidious position, with the Queen and the protocol of the Court to consider. I felt really sorry for her as well as for Tony.

My only preoccupation at that time however was the task of holding my own marriage together.

Nothing improved.

Our disagreements were occurring almost daily.

There was a night we were staying in the Royal Garden Hotel in London. Things just got too much for me. I swallowed a handful of sleeping pills. Maybe six or seven. It wasn't a deliberate attempt to commit suicide, but I wanted to find oblivion.

I went into a deep sleep for two days. When he had been unable to wake me, Sellers had summoned a doctor who virtually stayed in attendance in the hotel suite until I woke.

Sellers was scared. He knew that I might have died and his eyes moistened as he pledged his love for me once more.

No other marriage could have run so hot and so cold. I began to wonder if we were not a pair of masochists.

As always the bribes would follow the rows. I remember how Sellers promised me a new Ferrari car and thrust the brochures and color samples into my hands.

The car was delivered on the day I flew into St. Moritz, where ostensibly for tax reasons we were to live for a short spell. But it was obvious that Sellers had bought the car for himself—not me. He kept the car in his name and he declined to hand over the keys.

To show him that I was still independent I bought my own Lotus sports car in peacock blue.

It was in St. Moritz that I threw a birthday party for Sellers's son Michael. He must have been eleven. Spike Milligan's wife Paddy and their children were over with us and everyone was in high spirits. Except Sellers. He could not disguise his lack of interest and he went to bed.

In London the depression that gradually encased Sellers led him to believe he was ill. He checked into the London Clinic for three days but nothing wrong could be found.

I began to wonder how much longer we could salvage the remnants of our marriage. God knows how. But I was still in love with him!

Sellers flew off alone to Venice and I think I realized we had reached the final curtain.

Two weeks later I joined him in what was to be our last attempt at a reconciliation. We were going to embark on a spring cruise from Venice down the Yugoslavian coastline and I took along my three Yorkshire terriers.

Quiet, placid waters were beguiling to the tempest ahead. On our return we moored up at Brindisi and Sellers thought we might break the monotony of life aboard by taking the plane up to Rome for the night.

Alas, the journey did not please his palate.

We had a tiff on the plane because Sellers accused me of not listening to one of his jokes. He said Bert his valet was more interested in his jokes than I was.

When we disembarked he deliberately kept all the other passengers waiting before boarding the bus to take us to the terminal. "They can all wait for us," said Sellers.

In Rome we checked into the Excelsior Hotel. The one or two things I traveled with I had put into Sellers's case.

We went out for dinner and Sellers drank more wine than usual. When we came out of the restaurant it was to the flashbulbs of the paparazzi. Sellers didn't like it, and while I smiled for the benefit of the cameras he started sulking, blaming me for the presence of the photographers.

Back in our hotel suite I stood petrified as he paced up and down, gesticulating like a militant union leader.

My clothes became torn and my cassette radio

smashed in the ensuing contretemps.

Other hotel guests telephoned the night porter to complain. Meekly the night porter came to have words with us, only to find Sellers attired in his pajamas and kimono dressing gown.

When he opened the door he gave the performance of a lifetime and would have surely won his much longed for Oscar.

"Noise? Disturbance? Obviously you've got the wrong room. There's some noise coming from along the corridor. I think they must have a party going," he said airily, glancing at his watch to remind the porter that it was well past midnight and that he was just retiring for the night.

I crept into the bathroom and took a couple of valium. All I wanted to do was sleep and lose consciousness so that I might escape from my husband's virulence.

But there was to be no respite. Sellers's scathing epistle went on until the early hours.

It was 3:30 a.m. when Sellers, without regard for the hour, phoned our English speaking Italian agent Franco Reggiani.

"Franco, I want you to come to the hotel immediately and collect my wife," he said. "She is leaving Rome this instant. Our marriage is finished."

An astonished Franco arrived on his bizarre mission less than thirty minutes later. With him was the green uniformed hotel porter who by now was a nervous wreck.

When they rapped at the door, Sellers hissed at me. "Just get out of here and don't ever come back. I never want to see you again, you bitch."

I was scared. Really scared.

Sellers flung off his platinum wedding ring and flattened it like a stick of gum with the heel of his loose shoe that he picked up from the carpet. It was not the first time. I had taken the ring to Garrards to have it reshaped when he had hammered it into pulp on earlier occasions.

Franco stared disbelievingly at Sellers. Somehow I

managed to put on a pair of jeans and a sweater although I was barely conscious. The valium had made me drowsy and my head was swirling from the barrage of insults I had suffered.

"Here, take her," ordered Sellers as though he was disposing of his garbage to a refuse collector.

I did not have a suitcase to pack the remains of my clothes and the poor, bewildered porter could not help. By now he was as terrified as I was.

Sellers ordered Franco to go and get a suitcase.

"Find an all night store," he barked. Franco returned with one from his own home and packed what few things I had.

In the battle I had hurt my hand and I wrapped a dry flannel from the bathroom round it. As Sellers finally prodded me out of the door I discarded the bandage into a case not wishing to draw attention to myself.

But a weeping girl with a suitcase being led out of the Excelsior by a man who was virtually a stranger to me was an extraordinary enough sight.

Dawn was breaking over Rome. A watering truck was dowsing the Via Veneto: the lights of the night coffee stall flickered out and untied newspaper packages were being bundled out of a van against the shuttered newsstand.

Franco threw out his arms in bewilderment.

"How can he do this to you?" he said, shaking his head in total disbelief. "I have never been called like this before to anyone and I know every big star there is to know . . ."

Then he sighed.

"I don't know where we are going to find you another room at this hour. All the hotels are full."

And so vainly we trudged to the Grand, to the Hassler, and to the de la Ville until we found ourselves back on the Via Veneto at the Flora where thankfully, they had a spare room.

I slept fitfully through to midmorning when the telephone rang. It was Franco's secretary who told me that Sellers had called and ordered the *Bobo*'s captain to throw all my belongings on to the quayside at Brindisi including my three Yorkshire terriers.

"Don't worry Britt," she said. "I am going to fly out there and fetch everything for you."

It was more like a rescue operation. The secretary arrived at the Flora Hotel that night with my dogs and all my luggage, having found them on the jetty as Sellers had threatened.

I was no longer alone. The notorious paparazzi, a hot-rod pack of Rome photographers, had surrounded the hotel.

The story of my exit from the Excelsior had leaked out thanks to the night porter or perhaps an irate guest. I never found out.

I had to get away. I could not stay in Rome a minute longer and I decided to fly home to Sweden to be with my parents.

My escape from the Flora was a conspiratorial affair. My agent's girl took charge of the luggage and the dogs and I left by the kitchen entrance climbing into the back of a car and hiding beneath a blanket for the journey to the airport. All I had with me was my passport and airline ticket which Franco had got for me.

The plane was taxiing out on the Rome apron when through the cabin window I saw the paparazzi in frustrated pursuit. For once they had failed in their assignment.

In time, of course, I was to hear of Sellers's own version of my exit from the Excelsior. It came as always from his lawyers, like any of his earlier communiques.

He complained that I was a woman of utterly selfish disposition who had the notion of being a star and insisted on being treated like one.

If things were not to my liking, as apparently they weren't in the Excelsior that night, then I would break out into hysterical tantrums and temper.

I was accused of attacking Sellers, by punching, biting and kicking him.

Those claims were untrue but perhaps, when cornered, I might have described him as "old and square" and "ignorant."

Sellers always had a complex about our age difference

and he felt conscious of this whenever we went into a
disco or a nightclub together which was a matter he
again complained about through his lawyers.

My marriage was on the rocks. There could be no
more rescue operations. I had to go "underground."

In Sweden my father and uncle jointly owned a house
at Smadalarö on the coast. That was to be my hideaway.

I telephoned England and arranged for Victoria, who
was then only three, to join me. I gave Inger, our nanny,
a holiday so that she would not become entangled in our
affairs.

I was buying time. I wanted the dust to settle before
contacting Sellers again.

We spent four or five days at the house before the
Press finally traced me and once more I made my escape
on the floor of a car—this time an MG belonging to my
brother. We also managed to stow Victoria safely in the
car and in the middle of the night we drove into
Stockholm, but I knew that I could not keep on the run
forever. Besides, I was not a criminal.

The morning newspapers carried pictures of the house
at Smadalarö with the headline, "Britt's Secret
Hideaway." One picture was shot through a pair of Victoria's wooden clogs and an upturned bucket that had
been left in the garden.

I realized I could no longer burden my family with my
problems, but the newspapers were to enlighten me of
Sellers's activities. Far from being the heartbroken
husband, he was squiring Mia Farrow and the gleeful
paparazzi were having a field day.

"Exit Britt, Enter Mia" blazed the headlines and of
course it was said my walkout was over Sellers's new
romance with Mia.

I flew to London to file for a divorce.

Bert barred me from entering our Mayfair flat and I
was handed all my belongings on the doorstep.

"I'm very sorry, Mrs. Sellers," said Bert.

I drove to Elstead and I found my things and all of
Victoria's toys and possessions had been packed in
boxes in the garage.

There was nowhere to go, other than to check into an

hotel. Nanette and Bryan wouldn't hear of it. They offered me their London home, a small but very quaint cottage in Fulham.

I moved in temporarily while seeing Sir Eric Fletcher, the lawyer who had handled Tina Onassis's recent divorce. He advised me to seek a divorce on the grounds of mental cruelty.

When Sellers arrived back in London, after his fling with Mia, the divorce papers were promptly served on him.

He immediately called me and asked me to reconsider my decision.

"Let's have lunch together Britvic and talk it over," he said, using his pet name for me which he always did when he wanted to smooth things over.

Sellers chose a quiet restaurant in Hampstead. It was now mid-summer and we sat outside on a leafy corner of the terrace.

We kissed on the terrace as we took our table: yes, I still loved him. But for once in my life my head didn't give way to my heart.

"You're not really going to divorce me, are you, Britvic?" he said over and over again.

It was all very emotional. His eyes watered and so did mine.

I knew that if I gave in I would be committing my soul as well as my life to Sellers.

"What about Mia?" I rallied. "I thought you were in love with her? It was in all the newspapers."

"It was on the rebound. It didn't mean anything," said Sellers, suddenly uncomfortable in his apparent guilt. "It's all finished now . . ."

"So if I come back with you I have also got to overlook your excursion with Mia?" I said, as he sank his head in shame.

"I thought you had gone, Britvic. That it was all over . . . but now I know I can't live without you," he pleaded with me.

We talked about Victoria and how the divorce would affect her.

"You don't want her to grow up with her parents

living apart, do you? How will you explain it to her when she is old enough to understand?''

I clung to my last vestige of willpower.

I left the restaurant on my own.

I returned to the Fulham cottage where I remained as if a recluse. Swinging London was in full throttle, but I was not tempted from my door.

For some reason, perhaps purely psychological, I felt the pending divorce cast a stigma on my character.

I just wanted to hide away from everyone, although in the circumstances this wasn't too difficult to achieve.

Friends, afraid of taking sides, just disappeared.

One or two telephoned to commiserate. Princess Margaret was one of them. ''I'm very sorry for you both,'' said PM, ''if there is anything we can do . . .''

For the first time in my life I was alone.

It was a very strange experience for me.

— *eight* —

COUNT Ascanio Cicogna, playboy descendent of respected Italian aristocracy, greeted my arrival in Rome like the return of Cleopatra.

Banquets were thrown in my honor, red carpets rolled down for me and the chariots were chauffeur driven.

The Count—"Bino" to his friends—was among a forceful breed of Italian producers ready to build a new film empire to rival Hollywood.

I was to be his star.

"As an actress you symbolize all that we are looking for in Europe. You are not only beautiful but your name means a great deal at the box office," he purred.

My ego was flattered. My first film with Bino's company Euro Atlantica was a Las Vegas style gambling story *Machine Gun McCain* with Peter Falk and John Cassavetes as my leading men.

It was a superb screenplay and I saw the movie enhancing my career.

It was somewhat of a paradox that I should return to Rome to seek fresh happiness in a city where only two months earlier my marriage had perished. But I attached no blame to Rome for that episode.

The new film contract helped to soften the pain of the pending divorce. There was no point in hiding any longer from the pursuing Press. When I arrived in Rome the paparazzi were waiting, but this time I confronted them face to face and delivered immortal statements like, "You cannot live in the past. Only for tomorrow."

Certainly the atmosphere and ambience of Rome got through to me at last. Summer days brought cheer and laughter, generated by the new friends I was making.

I rented a small but comfortable villa on the Via Appia Antica with its own terrace and swimming pool and it was perfect for all my needs.

Bino, who had become wealthy from property and asset stripping, ran the film company with his sister Marina. Their mother, whose family inaugurated the Venice Film Festival, was one of the main investors. Their father was a very prominent industrialist in Milan.

I was strongly attracted to Bino. He spoke impeccable English having been educated at Oxford and it was hard to think of him as Italian except for his tall, dark looks.

A former tennis champion and excellent skier he had so many more qualities than his natural charm. He was 33 and he sparkled with vitality.

However, I did not envisage that we would ever embark upon an affair, particularly when I learned that he was married. His Mexican wife Jaconda and their two boys lived a couple of hours away on the seafront at Porto Ercole and Bino would stay with them at weekends and return to Rome for the rest of the week, retaining his own suite at the Grand Hotel.

I had always been totally faithful to Sellers and the thought of sleeping with anyone else terrified me.

There were times when I was convinced that I would never look at another man again. I could flirt easily enough but anything more scared me senseless.

Bino made me think again. He put me at my ease and I found I was able to relax in his company. There were no pressures and no quarrels!

When we were working we would slip away from the rest of the crew and cast for a quiet snack and drink just to be on our own. And at nights he would take me out.

When I danced with him for the first time I felt little streams of fire flaring up and down my body as we entwined.

I was only unhappy on one count: that I might be regarded as "the famous actress" stealing another woman's husband, but Bino went to great lengths to reassure me.

Extraordinarily he claimed that he had deliberately set up the film and offered me the starring role with the intention of having an affair with me.

"I first saw you in New York two years ago sitting in the lounge of the Algonquin Hotel being interviewed by a journalist and that incredible vision of you never left my mind. One day I just had to get you," Bino said.

It was true I was in the Algonquin at that time. I was being interviewed by a Swedish journalist.

As Bino said, one day he just had to get me. It was time to pass on that reward. His hotel suite at the Grand made the perfect setting: if either of us felt any twinge of guilt we were not aware of it.

I wore a black Ossie Clark mini dress, one of the A-line creations then very much in fashion, and round my waist I clipped a gold chain.

Dinner was wheeled in on a trolley by a waiter but it remained untouched. The bedroom door was ajar and I walked through dimming the lights. Bino's hands clasped my waist and the gold chain slid to the carpet with my dress. I was at Bino's command.

It was a night of ecstasy and fulfillment—there was no turning back. Bino was insatiable as a lover. We would make love in his Mercedes, in my villa or in the hotel but he was never indiscreet.

He always entered and left my villa by the bedroom window to avoid suspicion and he always returned to his hotel at dawn in time for his wife's regular breakfast hour call.

Bino did not want to hurt her but eventually he was troubled by his conscience and living a life of double standards. He asked Jaconda for a legal separation, admitting that he was in love with me.

It was a foolish mistake.

Jaconda, her Latin pride lacerated, flew immediately to Mexico to get a "quickie" divorce but not without stopping over in London to inform Sellers that I was having an affair with her husband.

Until that point Sellers was not going to contest my divorce action, but Jaconda's information put different ideas into his head.

We went to America to complete shooting on *Machine Gun McCain* with location work in Las Vegas, San Francisco and Los Angeles.

Although we were unaware of it, we were trailed the whole way by a private eye. The only incident that raised my suspicions was when I suddenly woke at 5 o'clock one morning to see our bedroom door closing when we were staying at the Beverly Hills Hotel in Los Angeles.

I shook Bino from his sleep and said, "Someone has been in our room."

He threw on a dressing gown and searched the hotel corridor but the intruder had vanished. All our valuables were intact, so what had been the intruder's motive?

We were soon to learn the truth. A showbusiness friend alerted us but by then the private detective had completed his nefarious assignment and we were too late to do anything.

His evidence had already been relayed to Sellers in London who entered a counter petition to my divorce suit. He claimed to have tapes of all my intimate conversations with Bino and he intended to produce them in court.

I felt sick. I felt unclean. How could a man who once professed he loved me resort to this?

He resented the fact that I had found happiness with someone else. Someone who knew how to treat me as a woman. Someone who not only loved me but respected me as an equal. Someone who gave me back my identity.

I lived in agony through the time until the divorce, but one greater weapon came to save me. Sellers, always aware of his public image, withdrew his counter action in what was a gallant gesture by a respectable gentleman.

My solicitor was assured that the tapes produced by

the private detective had been destroyed.

Bino flew back to Rome and I traveled to London for the divorce court hearing. It was 18 December 1968.

The hearing was brief. I was awarded a £30,000 settlement and I did not ask for alimony.

I was given care and control of Victoria, with joint custody. Sellers also agreed to an allowance for Victoria, to be sliced from the interest of a trust fund.

The words of Sellers's counsel Mr. Joseph Jackson QC were significant:

"Mr. Sellers regrets very much that this marriage has broken down and as far as it is appropriate for him to do so he wishes his wife well. He is making provision as befits a man of his status and profession and has taken steps for proper supervision of their daughter Victoria. The child is their common asset."

Maybe to our friends it appeared that we had adopted a very civilized attitude to our divorce. Two nights after the case I joined Sellers for a dinner party at the Mirabelle along with Sam Spiegel, Warren Beatty, Julie Christie, Roman Polanski and Sharon Tate.

I was staying at the Dorchester, but as I was leaving to join my family in Sweden for Christmas, and my room was no longer available, Sellers suggested I could spend the odd night in the spare bedroom of the Clarges Street flat.

Bino wanted to marry me. But his wife's Mexican divorce was never likely to be recognized in Vatican-controlled Italy.

In some ways I was relieved. I was content enough with our relationship as it was.

We were going to buy a fabulous apartment with archways and marble floors on one of Rome's enticing palazzos off the elegant Via Julia. We intended to live there together, but it was not to be.

From England came a threat through Sellers's solicitors that if I lived with Bino, application would be made to the High Court in England to have Victoria made a ward of court.

Again, I was filled with consternation. Victoria was still only a toddler and no one was going to take her away from me. She was my life line.

Under the cloud of that threat, I decided not to live with Bino. I could not risk it.

Bino was stunned and annoyed. But having children of his own he recognized my position. We could still see each other whenever we wished.

I rented my own apartment, a sunny, dual terraced flat overlooking the Via Barbarino and close to the Spanish Steps. I took on a butler and a maid, now I was able to afford the necessary staff to look after the household while I was working at the film studios.

Out riding one day with Bino, I fell from my horse and as I hit the ground the stallion's hind legs lashed out and a hoof tore open my leg. I was rushed to hospital where I had an anti-tetanus injection, but my leg became terribly poisoned and I had to remain in hospital for ten days.

Sellers, who happened to be passing through Rome, came into the hospital to see me. He gave me a copy of the Beatles' new single "Hey Jude": he was in one of his more amicable moods.

The accident apart, my career was going well. Bino announced that I was to play the lead in another of his films, *The Cannibals*, and that three other movies were in the pipeline.

This apparent boost to the Italian film industry caused quite a hive of activity and Bino and I became the focal point of Rome's celebrity echelon.

Flashbulbs popped wherever we went and the paparazzi were always hot on our heels. They were rarely disappointed. Some recognizable faces always appeared at our table in "Numero Uno," the night club where we invariably ended up.

Elsa Martinelli would often join us, so, too, would Bino's sister Marina and her protégée Florinda Bolkan and on the odd occasion we would be invited to parties with King Constantine of Greece, who would throw the

Italian waiters into a spin by ordering vegetarian dishes not mentioned on the menus.

I traveled the world with Bino. It was like a honeymoon and some funny things happened en route.

Like the time we checked into the Dorchester Hotel where I had lived so much of my life with Sellers.

Bino, in his status as an Italian count, was greeted by the bell captain and house manager as "Your Grace . . ." but I could detect their quandary when they turned to address me, having known me for so long as Mrs. Sellers. Now they were not sure if I was the Countess. Finally they settled diplomatically for "Miss Ekland . . . it is so good to see you."

Our next trip to London was equally amusing. Sitting behind us in the first class cabin of our plane, were Princess Margaret and Tony.

I introduced Bino to them, presenting him rather formally as "Count Cicogna."

The Princess smiled and she could not hide the twinkle in her eye. I think she was genuinely pleased that I had found fresh happiness.

Indeed I had.

Bino, on our travels, was the most generous man I had ever met. He bought me a £30,000 ruby and diamond ring in St. Moritz and later in New York, when filming the thriller *Stiletto*, he gave me an emerald and diamond ring that cost him almost as much.

Bino's generosity was genuine; his gestures were spontaneous. That was part of his nature.

Bino lived with grace and style. He drove a Mercedes and he encouraged me to buy a bright yellow Maserati against which I traded my Lotus.

His yacht, the *Rebit*—an anagram of my name— was in final construction at Porto Ercole. Costing £300,000, it was like a floating palace and twice the size of the *Bobo*.

We sailed the *Rebit* into the Adriatic and round Italy's boot heel into the Mediterranean.

I looked back on that summer with lingering memories of love, laughter and sunshine.

They were precious days. Unfortunately I have long
since come to be more cautious of that idyllic dream to
which we always cling so much but which in time dis-
perses like the fragrance of perfume.

Bino's film company had run into a state of collapse
and with it was lost millions of pounds of family money.
Proud Bino didn't tell me.

His last hopes were pinned on the success of *The Cannibals*. It was a very fine film and I got marvelous
reviews in my role as Antigone, the victim of a rebel
massacre. But the movie, alas, was ahead of its time: it
played only to underground buffs and it lost a fortune.
My percentage holding in it was worthless.

The only good the film achieved was to establish the
name of Liliana Cavani as a director whose second
movie *The Night Porter* got the acceptance and success
we so desperately wanted for *The Cannibals*.

I learned of Bino's desperate financial plight only as a
result of his strange manner in New York where I accompanied him on business talks with the British
producer John Heyman.

I did not know the importance of those talks but they
dragged on for three whole weeks and for most of that
time I was alone in the city just window shopping.

At nights Bino was exhausted and he would not sleep
with me, preferring to occupy the other bed.

I was dreadfully hurt and I had to press him to find
out the trouble. Eventually he told me.

"I'm sorry, Britt," he said, "I can't do it. I've lost all
my sexual urge. It's not you or anything to do with you.
It's the business. Things are going wrong. I'm on the
verge of bankruptcy. I didn't want to tell you this, but
maybe it's better that you should know."

I wanted to help Bino in his dilemma. But the funds I
had at my disposal were only a fraction of what Bino
needed.

Soon the crisis was evident. Bino's house, yacht and
belongings vanished and all the jewelry that he had
given to me I returned to him.

Our relationship felt the strain. I was also worried about Bino in other directions. Someone had given him some cocaine for a birthday present. In a way I felt to blame. At a Hollywood party I had shared his first joint to boast to him I was trendy and with-it.

I rarely smoked myself but at a party I would happily go along with a joint if someone produced one. Pot didn't worry me, but I was scared of the heavier drugs and did not sample them until much later in life when I was sure I could cope with them.

Bino would say that as a teetotaller he needed something which would help him unwind.

I don't think Bino ever became addicted, but the weakness for drugs was always evident.

Once more my life was at a crossroads. I had to fly to Sweden where my late grandfather's estate was being wound up and I was given the opportunity of buying the seaside home at Smadalarö.

I had always loved the house so much that I decided to buy it if only to keep it in the family.

I took Victoria to Sweden with me and just a few weeks later Bino arrived to see us.

He was still fighting his financial crash but at least he had remedied the psychological barriers that had prevented him from sleeping with me in New York.

Bino stayed for the weekend. When I saw him off at the airport I felt we had lost the magic that had once existed in our relationship.

Bino sent me a "Happy Birthday" cable. It was only a month later and I was working in Copenhagen on another new film, Hans Abramson's *Tintomara*.

Strange vibrations had overtaken me. I was 27. I had been shielded by wealth. And greatly pampered. What did I really know about life? What did I know about down-to-earth people?

The hippie cult was at its peak and I suddenly had this compulsive urge to become a hippie.

I drove round in a black mini that I bought from Sellers and to complete the new image I wore a sheep-skin jacket and boots.

I got involved with a blond Swedish actor who was in the film with me and in our spare time we would smoke pot curled up on the floor of my hotel room or join up with his hippie friends.

Strangely, I enjoyed their company. Bino departed from my thoughts. They were all pretty broke, but somehow they made ends meet. Among them I was the cheat. I was the only hippie in the group with an American Express card and a thousand bucks stashed away in notes in my hotel bedroom. I felt I had to have something to fall back on if things went wrong. I didn't tell anyone, of course, because to become accepted by the hippie cult I had to underplay my usual famous actress role. I had to be one of them and it worked. I found that I didn't need fast cars, houses, butlers and the rest. I could live happily on next to nothing without all the pressures that come with material wealth.

Disturbing news reached me from Rome. I heard that Bino was homeless. I flew there immediately and gave him the keys of my apartment. It had another three months of its lease to run.

Bino wanted to sleep with me but I acted cruelly and without thinking: I locked my bedroom door on him. He slept in the other room and the next morning it was confession time. We both admitted that we had been unfaithful.

As amicably as possible we declared our relationship over. There was very little sorrow and I went back to my hippie commune in Copenhagen.

I had not seen the last of Bino, however. Six months later he appeared in London. He was desperate for money. His family refused to help him at all.

I loaned him as much as I could and one £1,000 loan he repaid the next morning as he promised.

Bino was a sad, fallen figure. His sparkling wit, his humor, had deserted him.

My heart cried for him. It was so hard to grasp the fact that here was a man through whose fingers had slipped a fortune. Now he was penniless and ostracized, not only by his family, but by his friends too.

I tried to comfort him and he stayed at my house, although we were no longer lovers.

Bino pinned his hopes to one last project: a paddle steamer with a licensed casino running on its decks that would cruise off Rio de Janeiro and entice the playboy jet-set.

A former business associate paid for Bino's air fare to Brazil. Where he was to raise the initial £40,000 for the project was a mystery to me.

Bino struggled in Brazil to get his floating casino launched but the odds were always against him. Some weeks later he tried to call me from Rio. Alas, I was not at home and he did not leave a telephone number with my housekeeper. It was possibly the last phone call he made.

The next morning he was found dead. He had committed suicide.

Italian police had wanted him for questioning on a matter of fraud. Behind him he had left a trail of bouncing checks and promissory notes.

Bino had not mentioned any of this to me when he flew out for Brazil. I was in despair for him: that his life should have ended so tragically.

The irony was that less than six months later Bino's father died and left an estate in the region of four million dollars.

There was yet another bizarre episode. The Italian actress Magali Dorm, into whose affections he had moved after our parting, later maintained that Bino was still alive. She claimed that Bino rigged his suicide in Rio, changed his appearance by plastic surgery in São Paulo and returned to Italy under another identity.

Her belief was never substantiated.

If only it had been. Bino would have found forgiveness in the world somewhere.

— *nine* —

SPIKE Milligan sent me a letter congratulating me on my divorce from Sellers. He was surprised, he said, that I had lasted so long!

Only Spike could have conceived an epitaph like that, risking the displeasure of his fellow Goon, but I suspect he guessed.

Any thoughts I harbored that my divorce from Sellers would put an end to our relationship were premature. Indeed, my relations with my ex-husband after our divorce were almost as bizarre as the marriage itself.

I strove to establish a civilized arrangement but I could never gauge the atmosphere which fluctuated like the extreme climes of an English summer. Thunder and lightning often struck on becalmed days without prior warning.

At first I was at a loss to understand why. We were two divorced people trying to lead separate lives. There was no need to denigrate each other, no need to cause the other any more heartache.

Unfortunately, Sellers, plagued by his own inner conflicts, could never recognize the need for a truce.

I would sob at nights and ask myself, "Why does he want to go on torturing me like this?"

The truth gradually dawned on me. As impossible as it seemed, Sellers still wanted me in his clutches.

He still felt he "owned" me. Thinking back I was able to pinpoint his outbursts and threats to periods when he suspected that I was involved with someone else.

My theory was crystallized by the benevolent airs of Sellers when he knew that I was free from any attachment and he felt that he could stride back in my life at any time.

He would "woo" me with flowers for my birthday and at Christmas. The telephone would ring and it would be Sellers, ready to embark on friendly chats and in magnanimous spirits like this he could not do enough for me.

While Sellers denied me the right to even mention any other man who might figure in my life, I would have to sit and patiently listen to his fresh romantic encounters and his running affair with Lord Mancroft's stepdaughter Miranda Quarry.

I think Sellers mistakenly believed that I might show a flash of jealousy. Instead, I would encourage his burgeoning friendships, saying that it was essential that he shaped a new life for himself.

Miranda appeared as the more likely candidate to win his affections but there were stormy periods when neither would speak to the other.

During those breakdowns Sellers would seek my counsel and I would have to bear all his imagined sufferings with Miranda, but not having met her I could not really pass judgment, which was perhaps as well since I was sure she would have received my sympathies.

They were at loggerheads when the world première of Sellers's new film *The Magic Christian* which he shot with Ringo Starr was staged at London's Kensington Odeon.

Sellers implored me to accompany him to the première.

"I can't go alone. It wouldn't look right," he said. "And Miranda isn't speaking to me right now."

"Can't you find somebody else?" I said.

"There isn't anybody else I can take," he replied.

I was reluctant to go but Sellers kept on and on until

he extracted a promise from me that I would make it if
he could not find a replacement.

Of course I resolved there and then that there was no
way out and, as it was a bow tie and evening dress
affair, I decided to go with some decorum at least.

I had my hair styled by Michael John and I put on an
exquisite Zandra Rhodes gown. Sellers and his son
Michael collected me in his Rolls Royce and Bert his
ever-faithful servant was in his customary position
behind the wheel.

It was almost like old times except that I was a free
agent. Sellers was oozing with flattery.

"Britt," he said, "you look marvelous. I have never
seen you more radiant."

Our arrival at the première together caused inevitable
speculation.

"Will they marry again?" ran the morning newspaper
headlines.

No chance!

All I wanted to achieve with Sellers was a compatible
relationship that would remove any discord likely to un-
settle Victoria's upbringing.

For once, I'm afraid, the gossip columnists missed
out on the real story, because my life did change course
that night, but it had nothing to do with Sellers.

The die was cast at a party at Les Ambassadeurs that
followed the première. Celebrities flocked in: the
Beatles, David Frost, aircraft heir Tommy Sopwith and
a tall handsome Englishman who was introduced to me
as Lord Lichfield.

I had no idea he was the Queen's cousin, nor did I
know that he earned his living as a professional
photographer.

The only photographer I associated with the Royal
family was only a few seats away from me at the dinner
table and causing as many eyebrows to raise as my entrance with Sellers had done.

Lord Snowdon, having arrived at the party ahead of
PM, was engaged in animated conversation with Lady
Jacqueline Rufus Isaacs.

Patrick Lichfield interrupted my thoughts.

"I don't suppose you would care to dance?" he asked. I smiled back and he took my hand. There was an elegance and flair about him that was fetching.

It may have been an old fashioned waltz, I can't recall, but Patrick's conversation was about his work and he asked me if I would care to pose for some fashion photographs for the cover of *Vogue*.

Unfortunately, the session in his Aubrey Walk studios a few days later did not go too well even though Patrick had engaged experts to look after the make-up, the jewelry and accessories as well as the clothes.

Patrick, his aesthetic mind working overtime, could not seem to capture the picture he envisaged. He kept changing lighting, clothes and props.

We worked on late into the night until the fierce studio lights melted me like a piece of wax.

"All right," snapped Patrick finally, his voice ringing with exasperation, "that's it. We'll go with what we've got."

Some welcome bottles of vino were produced and with the studio lights extinguished we were able to relax at last.

Barbara Daly, who had been responsible for my make-up, took her leave and one by one the other assistants disappeared.

We were alone for the first time.

In those few hectic hours in the studio I had come to admire Patrick's endeavors in the cause of duty and his keen eye for detail in creating a picture, rather than expecting it to "happen" which many photographers rely on.

As the Queen's cousin he was proud of his ties with the Monarchy and of his ancestry, and while newspapers tended to paint him as a society "gadabout" I could not possibly describe him as a chinless wonder, even though one or two of his friends fell into this category.

Patrick's family motto is "Despair of Nothing."

Funnily enough Patrick was a bit hung up that we

should have slept together on our first night. He gave
me the impression it was against the principles of the
well-bred.

"I shouldn't have pushed you into it," he said,
gallantly absorbing the blame. But then saying, "What
made you do it?", fishing perhaps for a compliment to
underline his irresistible charms.

I could not help but tease him, "What would you
have felt if I'd said 'no'?"

My friendship with him was to pitch me back into
Royal circles. I argued with Patrick that it might be embarrassing for the Queen and other members of the
Royal family to receive me, now that I was divorced
from Sellers.

But Patrick disagreed.

"They won't be troubled in the least," he said,
although as a divorcee I felt I was being shunned by my
friends and that I was unwelcome in many households.

It was not as though I felt any shame. I was the innocent victim of my marital breakdown with Sellers,
whatever other opinions people held.

Christmas was upon us and Patrick spent the festivities with his mother and stepfather Prince George of
Denmark, but he returned for New Year's Eve which we
were to celebrate at Kensington Palace.

Tony and PM were still trying to maintain a graceful
façade on their failing marriage.

The troubled gaze of PM gave much away when she
greeted me at Patrick's side.

"How are you, Britt?" she said, her words and her
eyes searching to elucidate whether I missed Sellers.

She did not mention his name. In the Royal house,
discretion ruled as always. Tony prudently struck up a
conversation about the progress of my career, and his
warmth and friendliness were unaltered.

I guessed it was a delicate evening for the Royal
couple and I could detect a coolness between them
which could only indicate the temperature of their
marriage.

Tony again seemed to enjoy a rapport with Lady

Jacqueline, who was also a guest at the party, but I was never aware that their friendship had blossomed into the alleged romance that set the pages of the *New York Post* humming.

There were denials from all quarters, but I could not help but think back on a strange conversation I had earlier with Jacqueline in the Yves St. Laurent boutique that she managed in London.

"At least you are lucky in being able to go out with Patrick," she said quietly. "You can conduct your friendship in the open. I can't. What would you do if you were in my place?"

I was at a loss for words, because I could not bring myself to ask her who she was referring to.

Clandestine relationships are always hazardous, to all the parties involved, and the only advice I could offer Jacqueline was to urge on her, "Make sure you are doing the right thing."

Thankfully my relationship with Patrick was conducted without secrecy. Indeed the Press was able to chronicle our day-to-day progress.

We were not too difficult to find.

Most lunch hours were spent in Burke's, then London's most fashionable restaurant, and of which Patrick was one of five partners. Michael Caine was another. We would sit at our reserved table holding hands and gazing fondly into one another's eyes.

Long weekends were spent at Shugborough Hall, his family seat.

Like many tax-plagued historic British stately homes the only reason it survived was because it had been taken over by the National Trust and its rooms were put on daily view to the public. Patrick's allowance from the estate was a meager one. I don't think it was more than £2,000 a year.

Always close in Patrick's mind was his childhood when his parents had the entire run of the mansion, run by a staff of fifteen servants.

Times sadly changed in 1960 on the death of his father, the fourth Earl. The Government's Treasury department took over Shugborough in lieu of death duties and it was then handed to the National Trust leasing the estate through the County Council.

Patrick was banished to one wing of the house, where his accommodation was restricted to a main living room, dining room, a study and a kitchen incongruously stranded on the first floor among three or four bedrooms. His only staff comprised a butler and a maid, who fulfilled the dual roles of gardener and housekeeper.

More demeaning to Patrick was the fact that he could not enter the house by the main door, but had to use the side door that had once been the servants' entrance.

When he saw the queues of visitors to Shugborough he would remark, "It's like living in a zoo." However he was realistic enough to acknowledge that without the involvement of the National Trust the mansion might have been lost to him forever.

Shugborough was truly stately. Bow fronted and pavilion-styled, the house dated from the late 1700s. I could understand why Patrick was boastful of his ancestry. One of his ancestors was an Admiral and the first Earl of Lichfield was the Postmaster-General in the period when Sir Rowland Hill introduced the Penny Post.

Through the months Patrick shot thousands of pictures of me at Shugborough and the beautifully landscaped grounds, with symmetrically planted yews and a Chinese garden house in the background, provided a perfect setting.

Some of the pictures he framed and hung in his London studios, while others found their way to the pages of the glossy magazines.

We spent many summer afternoons on a punt on the River Trent and I deliberately dressed as a crinoline lady, languishing under a parasol as Patrick clicked away for another *Vogue* page.

There was no doubt that he possessed a wonderful flair for photography and his work was always good and tasteful, but I think, not unkindly, that he lacked Lord Snowdon's imagination.

The two were of course rivals within the Royal family, but if any competitiveness existed between them, they disguised it well.

Tony stamped his character on a photo like an artist does on a canvas, and I suspect he regarded Patrick with some disdain as a photographer, though he was careful never to make any comment.

Most photographers are rather coy about having their own picture taken, but Patrick was the exception. He was always very publicity conscious and he never objected to other cameramen snatching woosome-two-some pictures of us.

In fact, Patrick would exploit every situation that derived from being the Queen's cousin. He wanted to project the image of the trendy "Royal."

He wore a specially created Lichfield line of mono-grammed shirts with a coronet as a motif, which were manufactured in America, and I accompanied him on one promotional tour to New York and Dallas.

Our "togetherness" in Burke's and the West End night spots, as well as Shugborough, inspired Patrick to think in terms of hosting a television chat show together, but nothing came of the idea.

For my part I regarded Patrick as my knight in shining armor who had come down on his white charger and plucked me into his arms.

I lived with that fantasy for some time, although life at Shugborough Hall provided me with a less romantic insight into the steady decline of English society.

Guest weekends in the countryside were part of Shugborough's tradition, but the hypocrisy that attended them was almost insufferable.

Unmarried couples who arrived as house guests were shown into separate bedrooms as etiquette dictated, but once the lights went out, the corridors were haunted by shadowy figures pairing with their respective partners.

Dinners would go on interminably; the fare of cucum-

ber soup, venison and Jackson's wine becoming as com-
monplace as fish and chips and a pot of tea after a
while.

The guests were stuffy and snobbish, the conversation
parochial and desultory, and when coffee was served it
was the signal for the ladies to disappear to powder their
faces while the men took cover behind their cigar smoke
and brandies.

My frustrations with all the pretense at Shugborough
Hall came to a rather deafening climax. I could not
resist the huge brass dinner gong mounted at the foot of
the winding staircase. On sudden impulse I picked up
the formidable gavel and struck the gong with three or
four crashing blows. It was, I imagine, like striking the
famous J. Arthur Rank gong, as this was certainly com-
parable in size.

The whole house reverberated to the clanging gong,
and, as everyone came running into the hall and onto
the stairway I fled for dear life.

Patrick admonished me as if I were a mischievous
tomboy and I had to promise that I wouldn't make any
more trouble.

The necessity for me to "play it straight" was of
course paramount in the circles in which Patrick moved.

Several weeks later we were at Windsor to join the
Queen and Prince Philip on a pheasant shoot. I bought
a new Yves St. Laurent blouse, skirt and cape for the occasion.

The Queen and Prince Philip immediately put me at
my ease. Perhaps a cinema star, in the environment she
lived, could be forgiven for divorcing her husband.

By now the newspapers were speculating on whether I
would become Lady Lichfield but I had no designs in
that direction. Titles may fascinate many people but I
had no wish to be addressed as "Your Ladyship."
When we were entertaining at Shugborough Hall I had
never filled that kind of role. It was left to Patrick's
sister, Lady Elizabeth Anson, to act as the hostess.

Marriage was very much on Patrick's mind, I know.
Whenever a man starts using "pet" names a relation-

ship can move into a more serious territory.

Sellers would purr "Britvic" and "Britten" to me.
Now Patrick was calling me "Mousie" and I knew that
he was getting very hung up about me. However, I en-
deavored to divert his thoughts from marriage.

Patrick wanted marriage for many reasons. He was
30 and still a bachelor and there was a need to have
children to continue his ancestral line.

It was essential, too, that he should marry into
money.

The Queen's cousin and a true Earl he might well
have been, but Patrick was basically no more than a
hard working, hard up photographer when the chips
were down.

His income was almost menial against my earnings as
an actress but even then I would not have the financial
resources for which he was really looking and I think on
this count alone I would not qualify as a candidate.

For six months we virtually lived together, using my
flat, his studio and Shugborough.

But it was a style of life which finally became monotonous to me. I knew I could never marry Patrick and I
tried to cool our romance down without injuring his
feelings.

The problem of actually telling Patrick that we should
pronounce an end to it all weighed heavily upon me and
the effect on my system was somewhat psychosomatic
as I developed a rare but violent attack of gastroenteritis
when accompanying Patrick to the South of France to
visit his friend Rupert Dean.

Back in London once more I managed to find the
courage to suggest to Patrick that our relationship was
not working out.

It was hard for him to accept as he was leaving for
America, but I was left in no doubt as to his reaction.

From New Orleans I received a letter from him
pleading with me to reconsider things and promising to
change his way of life for me.

Patrick wrote that fate had brought us together and
that we should give the whole thing another chance.

When he returned Patrick telephoned me constantly and I woke one morning to his knocking at the door of the £55 a week bedsitter I had taken in a mews' house almost opposite Claridge's. He had come to plead with me to marry him.

"It can and will work out," said Patrick. "We can live at Shugborough if you wish or we can buy a new home to move into. Away from everyone. I don't care . . . as long as we marry."

I sat Patrick down with coffee and tried to explain to him that as much as I adored him I did not love him sufficiently to consider marrying him and I pointed out that we lived two entirely different lives. I could not sacrifice my career for the rather facile one I might live as Lady Lichfield.

Patrick could not believe that I was saying "No." Over the weeks he was in constant contact, and he briefed his friends to act as go-betweens.

I got a call from a New York friend who said, "Isn't there any way back? Patrick is really down in the mouth. He's like a shadow of the man you knew."

Some weeks later I caught a fleeting glimpse of Patrick in Mayfair. It was true. He must have lost at least thirty pounds in weight. His suit was sagging on him. His face was tired and sallow.

I got a letter sealed down with his waxed insignia saying that there was no direction in his life anymore. Again he asked me to reconsider our relationship and said that he was half-dying for me. He asked for another chance to prove himself to me and that he would not disappoint me.

It worried me because in the letter he mentioned that he was taking Mandrax because he could not get himself together. He felt that he did not want to go on without me and that if I was with him he could make a fresh start with new visions, ideas and people. On his letter he had stuck a stamp that said, "Love Never Gives Up."

My concern became more acute when another of his friends rang me to warn me that Patrick had become very depressed. A few nights later I got a barely

coherent phone call from Patrick who kept repeating,
"I will die if you don't come back to me."

It was time to be very firm.

"Don't be ridiculous, Patrick," I told him. "There
are millions of other women in the world. Why worry
about me?"

In time Patrick got over his heartache. We were able
to meet as friends from time to time and he was even
able to tell me that on one occasion through our
relationship he had been unfaithful to me with a model
he photographed in the Bahamas.

Two years later, Patrick married Lady Leonara
Grosvenor, the daughter of Britain's richest landowner,
the Duke of Westminster.

I was pleased for them both. It was a perfect match.

Sellers had remained noticeably reticent throughout
my friendship with Patrick. There was not so much as a
single quibble from him and my hunch was that
Patrick's links with the Royal family dissuaded Sellers
from any form of misbehavior.

Sellers never wanted to be seen in a bad light in
public, especially by the Royals.

He would go to great lengths to gain favor with the
Royals, being permanently available as the eternal court
jester whenever their whims were so inclined.

That was not all. He would strengthen his friendship
with PM and Tony with ridiculously generous gifts.

PM and Tony had sent flowers to the clinic when Victoria was born and once they had given her a fluffy
teddy which she adored.

I regarded these kind gestures in keeping with the
level and nature of two good friends, but Sellers would
magnify their significance to absurd proportions.

He reciprocated beyond measure. If Tony just happened to remark that he liked a new camera, or a new
set of lens that Sellers had bought—then my husband
would just give it to him.

Stereo equipment, too, found its way in similar manner to Kensington Palace. In another flash of generosity
Sellers also gave the Royals a *Riva* speedboat.

I would squirm with embarrassment at the demeaning
lengths he would stoop to in order to ingratiate himself
with the Royal family. It was contemptible.

He once sold our custom-built silver blue Aston Martin car to Tony for a fraction of its real market price. I
was surprised that he actually *sold* it: for all the money
that exchanged hands he might just as well have given it
to Tony.

Sellers was an avid car collector; I would not care to
count the number of cars he bought and exchanged
through our marriage, but it would have been enough to
have filled a museum. It was nothing to wake up in the
morning and see a new Ferrari, Lotus, Lincoln, Jaguar
or Rolls Royce standing on our drive. Sellers wasn't
even sentimental about them. The only one he viewed
with affection was an old Austin that he named "Old
Min."

The Aston Martin that went to Tony was one of my
favorites and another was the magnificent blue Rolls
Royce convertible he bought from Somerset Maugham.

After our divorce, no doubt to blow away old cob-
webs, Sellers asked Tony to redesign the white interior
of the Rolls in tan with chrome fittings. It was never the
same and was almost unrecognizable with its new silver
sprayed exterior.

Sellers continued to seek the Royal favor in all sorts
of ways. Having sold our home "Brookfield" to Ringo
Starr for £60,000, he was faced with clearing all the
effects. He did not know what to do with everything and
gazing out of the window one morning his eyes descended on Victoria's beloved, docile Palomino pony
Buttercup, grazing in the field beyond. He immediately
telephoned for a horse box and had the pony delivered
to Kensington Palace as a gift for Princess Margaret and
Tony's children.

Earlier in our marriage I had bred Palomino horses at
Elstead, but Buttercup was very special. She stood only
four feet high and her silky coat was the color of champagne!

Sellers and I both had our own horses and Victoria

"I am not a courtesan or a promiscuous woman but I need to love and be loved."

TRUE BRITT:
PHOTOS

Typical glamour pose, stripes and all, circa 1970.

School days. Front row, extreme left, wearing my special frown for the cameras.

Playing big sister with Kalle on my lap
and Bengt and Bo.

Yves St. Laurent, here I come...
a modelling assignment with hippie overtones.

A day to remember: February 19, 1964.
My marriage to Peter Sellers.

My mother-in-law, Peg,
with the new husband and bride.

My family meets my husband in Stockholm.
Left to right: Bengt, Bo, Britt, Father, Mother, Husband,
Kalle. Note my Father's paintings on the wall. He was
a passionate collector.

Our lives were soon in perspective. A mink for me and denims
for Sellers. Oh no, he didn't always dress like that. He was filming
What's New Pussycat?

Wilfred Hyde White, Princess Margaret, Bryan Forbes and Sellers
all terribly bespectacled in our Elstead home.

With love from
Margaret
1966

Back-to-the-land! Princess Margaret caught us tractor-borne
at Windsor Great Park.
(Photograph: Princess Margaret)

Après water ski with Tony at Windsor Great Park.

Entertaining my Mother and Bengt in Ischia by
reluctant courtesy of Sellers.

Joy and happiness...
the birth of our daughter,
Victoria.

Center: Victoria on her pony "Buttercup" at Elstead.
Bottom: A Christmas party hug for Victoria from Tony.

One of my favorite pictures of Victoria whose umbrella stance says "Always willing to oblige."

Cheek to cheek with Bino on a Roman dance floor.

A mission with James Bond 007. . . or a clinch with Roger Moore in *The Man With The Golden Gun*.

Lou and me.

Lou.

After the birth of
my son, Nicholai.

Nicholai's
first kiss.

The Godfather:
Jack Nicholson
with Nicholai.

Mother love, 1966.

A train journey to Stratford-on-Avon, England, with my friend Roman Polanski.

Rod and me in happier days. Please overlook the worn sneakers.

(Copyright: David Steen/Scope)

Down under on Rod's 1977 Australian tour,
with friendly Koala bear.

would join us on Buttercup whenever we went riding.

She loved Buttercup beyond anything else and she was heartbroken when she discovered what her father had done.

"Why did Daddy give Buttercup away?" she sobbed. "He didn't tell me. I want her back."

I found myself trying to defend Sellers.

"I'm sure he didn't realize what he was doing," I said. "Perhaps he thought you were getting too big for Buttercup now. I am sure he will buy a new horse instead . . ."

But Victoria didn't want a new horse. She wanted Buttercup.

Now, a bachelor once more, Sellers could not have Victoria staying with him, because the routine of meals and schools was too much for him to think about.

Victoria lived with me and spent the summers with my parents in Sweden.

Sometimes, in seasonal fits of friendliness, Sellers would accompany me to Stockholm to see her. The fact that we were together would rekindle the reconciliation whispers, and the Swedish Press had quite a field day photographing us wherever we went.

My mother, who adored Sellers, would have been overjoyed if a reconciliation had come about. Indeed, she devised her own schemes to get us back together; cooking his favorite dishes for dinner and on one occasion, because my brothers were home, ushering Sellers and me into the only spare bedroom.

"You won't mind sharing it, will you?" she said, closing the door on us and knowing that there was only one double bed in the room.

Sellers thought it was a perfect opportunity to let bygones be bygones. He wanted to make love to me but I did not encourage him. I wore a nightgown that came to my ankles and I kept my panties on.

My ex-husband felt frustrated, but I told him that it wasn't right for divorced people to make love. It was much, much wiser that they should stay friends and not complicate things by having another affair.

Sellers listened but obviously did not agree totally with my argument. In the end he gave up and I fell asleep with his arm around me, which was something of a compromise to our discussion.

My mother looked at me expectantly the next morning as if we might announce that we intended to marry again.

"No, mother. There is not the remotest possibility of us marrying again," I said guessing her thoughts.

My mother's expression fell with disappointment, but she did not carry the matter further.

We met again in Paris the following week and he was still very friendly. We had dinner together.

I was back in London on Saturday night and Maggie Abbott my agent, who was also a close friend, telephoned me.

"Have you heard about Sellers?" she said, her voice carrying an air of mystery.

"What about Sellers?" I answered, fearing he had suffered another cardiac arrest.

"He's getting married on Monday to Miranda Quarry," breathed Maggie. "Didn't you see it in the papers?"

My plane had got in late. I had not picked up the evening newspapers.

"That's amazing, Maggie," I said, "because I saw him in the middle of the week in Paris and before that he was in Sweden with me and he didn't mention a word about it. Could you do me a favor and ring him and ask him to call me because he promised to take Victoria on holiday next week on the yacht."

Who could ever predict what Sellers would do next?

He called at 8 o'clock the next morning. His voice trembled for much of the conversation.

"I don't know whether I am doing the right thing, Britt," he kept saying, "but Miranda says it's now or never . . ."

Incredibly, Sellers blamed me for his predicament.

"If you hadn't divorced me, Britvic, I wouldn't be in this dilemma. I wouldn't have to make this choice."

I moved the conversation on to Victoria.

"What about her holiday?" I asked him. "You promised to take her on the *Bobo*. She can't come now if you're going to be on honeymoon with Miranda."

Sellers thought for a moment.

"Can't you take her on the yacht and have a holiday with her at the same time, Britt?"

"Maybe we can arrange something," I answered. "But you know, Peter, all of this is going to upset Victoria. She will not only be disappointed about the holiday but I'm sure she would expect you to invite her to be bridesmaid. You know how much Victoria has always wanted to be a bridesmaid."

Sellers spluttered out his excuses.

"She would have been, Britt. But this is a last minute thing. We haven't had time to organize everything in the same way as . . . well, when I married you, Britt."

I sighed.

As Sellers said it was a very quiet wedding. Where his friends were I don't know. His valet Bert Mortimer was his best man.

— *ten* —

ONE of the greatest shocks of my life occurred at this period. I got a letter from my lawyer Sir Eric Fletcher urgently summoning me to attend a business meeting at his chambers in London's Gray's Inn.

There was nothing too unusual about that and no warning bells sounded. Business talks are a regular feature in any successful actress's life.

Over the previous four years I had earned an average of £30,000 from every movie I appeared in and I had managed to save, by prudent spending, a figure close to £100,000 which I had legally channeled to Switzerland. Some of that money I had invested in gilt edged South African gold mining shares, but the day to day running of my affairs I entrusted to a group of accountants.

Unfortunately, without my knowledge or authority, the accountants had speculated with my capital on the Stock Exchange and they had lost every single penny. What is more, they had borrowed in my name in order to recoup their losses. They had incurred one debt of £20,000 to a Swiss bank and another of £13,000 from bankers in London.

I did not have an inkling about it on the morning I attended the meeting in Gray's Inn but I sensed that something was wrong from the furrowed frown on the face of my lawyer as he greeted me.

"Please sit down, Britt," he beckoned. "I am afraid I have got some very bad news for you. It seems that your finances are in a hell of a state. In fact, Britt, not to put too fine a point on it, I'm afraid you're broke."

"Broke? How can I be?" I said as I felt the agonizing shock reverberate through my body. I looked at my accountants who were grouped in the chamber like shadows from Madame Tussaud's.

"What exactly has happened to my money?" I said, turning accusingly to them, "where has it all gone?"

One of them gesticulated with a despairing hand.

"I'm sorry, Britt. We've slipped up," he whispered. "We were acting in your best interests but the investments we made for you went down the pan . . ."

I was stunned.

"You have lost everything?" I said, recoiling in absolute horror.

"I'm afraid so," the accountant admitted.

Everyone started talking at once and I became a zombie, not hearing a word that they were saying to one another. My head was throbbing with utter disbelief.

The matter had come to light because of a writ served by the Zurich based company Filmtransac who claimed that £20,958 had been drawn out of an account opened in my name and that of one of my advisers.

I was unable to comprehend the intricacies behind the collapse of my financial affairs but my lawyer comforted me at the end of the meeting and promised every assistance that he could.

"I will phone you tomorrow, Britt," he said. "Maybe something will turn up."

It was early afternoon and the sky was cloudy. It began to drizzle and I remember just hopping on a London double-decker bus to get home, believing that I could not afford even to wave down a cab. I don't think I had been on a bus before, except for when I was a child.

On the bus I sat oblivious to all the stares from other passengers who recognized me. My mind was racing like a torrent. I was trying to calculate all my assets but I could not work them out to anywhere near the £33,000 which my lawyer said I owed.

When I got home I gathered my jewels and furs ready

to pawn them and I advertised the sale of my Maserati car which sorrowfully went for a meager £3,500.

I was desperate. I even telephoned Sellers and pleaded with him to borrow £1,000 as I had Victoria's school fees to pay on top of everything else. I had no one to turn to. I hated asking him but he must have realized I was in a crisis because I had never sought money from him before. I promised to repay him within the month. Fortunately I was able to.

My immediate thought was to get work and earn as much as I could. I telephoned Maggie Abbott, my agent in London, and told her to accept any work that I was offered. In the past I had been able to be discriminating, but I told Maggie, "Look, I will do anything. Anything at all. I don't care what it is."

Initially she got me a pretty routine guest appearance on a domestic television show hosted by the British comic Des O'Connor, then I signed for two films that I would not have contemplated under normal circumstances.

For the first time in my life I came to realize the fate of less fortunate actresses who in order to earn sufficient money to survive on are forced to accept roles where they are required to strip off. Usually they have no more choice about such work than "Take it or leave it."

It was this ominous prospect that faced me in *Get Carter*, a gangland thriller in which Michael Caine starred as a racketeer seeking revenge for his brother's murder. I was offered £2,000 for one day's work by the producer Michael Klinger but I had to strip to the waist.

I had never done that before but Klinger to his credit respected all my wishes when I reluctantly accepted the role. The set was closed, the crew respectful and the director Mike Hodges was superb. I was not made to feel in the least conscious about the scene in which I was seen lying partially naked in bed, talking on the telephone to Caine.

Klinger was so delighted with my performance that he sent me champagne and roses.

The scene was harmless, but the critics who reviewed the film later, painted it as rather provocative and some overseas censors actually scissored me out of the footage. I know South African cinemagoers saw no trace of me, which must have confounded them a little as my name figured in large letters on the credits.

If *Get Carter* filled me with consternation, I was positively a nervous wreck over the thought of playing in *Percy* for which I collected the princely sum of £1,500.

Percy was the story of the world's first penis transplant. The young actor Hywel Bennett played the recipient of the new organ which he had to test on the world's females and I was one of his experimental playthings along with Elke Sommer and Julia Foster.

There were no explicit scenes, however, and the critics came to vote the movie as a saucy and funny piece of entertainment.

I felt grateful for the verdict. At least no one had taken me to task for playing in a blatant sexploitation film as indeed it was.

Unfortunately I could not always rely on good providence. I accepted what seemed like a psychotic thriller, *Night Hair Child*, for which a marvelous cast including Hardy Kruger, Lili Palmer, Harry Andrews and Mark Lester were assembled.

Mark, then fifteen, was to play a twelve-year-old schoolboy who seduces his stepmother, in which role I was somewhat dubiously cast.

I should not have accepted the part, but again the money had been the deciding factor.

I was again partly naked for a bedroom scene with Mark and I had a condition in my contract that no still photographs were to be taken during the shooting of that particular sequence.

When the film was premièred the critics were scathing.

"It is a pity that Miss Ekland after canvassing for more U-certificate films for the family and the children, should resort to this type of dirty blatant sexual titillation" wrote one columnist.

I was filled with shame, because my critics were justified in their comments.

During the previous summer I had protested about the number of X-films being shown in London's cinemas and I had joined film censor John Trevelyan in setting up a special children's cinema with matinée screenings of films that would not be offensive to juveniles. I recall we launched the program with *High Wind in Jamaica*. Many leading names in the industry supported the scheme including Lord Harlech, Richard Attenborough, Stanley Baker and Bryan Forbes and I even talked Sellers into joining us too.

By accepting *Night Hair Child* and *Percy* I had betrayed the very principles of our foundation and I understood how my critics felt, but I could hardly tell them that I had accepted such work because I was on the breadline!

It took me all of eighteen months to remedy my financial plight and I vowed I would never enter those straits again.

Through it all my judgment had been constantly in question, such was the mental strain.

I walked out on a film that I was to have made with Tom Bell titled *Quest for Love* only two days before the cameras were due to roll. Joan Collins was the eleventh hour replacement.

My "walk out" was motivated by an opportunity to co-star with the great Marlon Brando in *The Nightcomers*. I should have known I was clutching at straws.

The British director, Michael Winner, promised to give me the female lead if I could assist him in raising the finance for the movie.

"Yes," I said, "of course I will help. I've got plenty of rich friends who will want to back a film with Marlon Brando in."

What I did not convey to Michael was that he had engaged a destitute thespian to find "angels" for him. I ran round in circles for days, ringing every millionaire I knew.

Alas, I would have been hard pushed to have found anyone sufficiently willing to have financed a multi million pound movie, let alone me!

Winner ultimately found his own finance and then announced he had signed Stephanie Beacham as his female lead. I was dreadfully hurt. It was a terrible slap in the face, but there was nothing I could do.

I just had to regard it as one of the hazards of the profession. It was not the first part I had lost. I had been turned down by Joseph Losey and Harold Pinter for *Accident*, I held ambitions to play in *The Seagull* but director Sidney Lumet's mind was set on Vanessa Redgrave and years later I got rebuffed by Dino De Laurentiis when casting *King Kong*.

Those who believe actresses are vain may now know the reason why. When an actress eventually gets a part, it is a very big day!

— *eleven* —

WHEN I give myself to a man, I am at his command. Whatever he desires, I will do.

I have always been discriminating in the choice of lovers, but once in bed, I am like a slave. I willingly accommodate any demands that are made on me, sparing whips, chains and diversions.

Sex is a man's supreme game; his own private and perennial Olympics. He must always be made to feel that he is the dominant force, even if the woman generates the state of play.

My affair with Warren Beatty fell into another kind of category that I had never experienced before, where fantasy became reality.

Warren was the most divine lover of all. His libido was as lethal as high octane gas. I had never known such pleasure and passion in my life.

Warren could handle women as smoothly as operating an elevator. He knew exactly where to locate the top button. One flick and we were on the way.

Nature had sculptured him to perfection and Hollywood might have had good reason to be eternally grateful. For here, without question, was the quintessential sex symbol.

Warren, mature as he was, had never sacrificed his college boy looks. It was almost as though he had just stepped out of Harvard, the dark hair neatly combed into place and his innocently sensual eyes constantly inquiring. He exuded charm, wit and intelligence.

His clothes were elegant and distinctive and hung on

his frame as immaculately as on a tailor's model.

Warren's professional reputation was riding high. So much of the limelight in the past had gone to his more famous sister Shirley Maclaine, but with the triumph of *Bonnie and Clyde* which he not only starred in but also produced, Warren had reached the turning point of his career.

Suddenly he was big box office and could not put a foot wrong.

It was odd. I had first met Warren several years earlier when he was squiring Leslie Caron, the French actress. Sellers and I joined them for dinner one night but then, having been so much under my husband's influence, I must have been immune to Warren's charm.

The situation was remedied in that lingering summer of 1970 when we were to meet again at a dinner party that was thrown for Roman Polanski in London.

Warren's gaze descended on me, and the moment our eyes met I knew we were committed physically.

Warren, the incurable philanderer, was really at a loose end. Julie Christie, his new love, was foolishly absent, and loyalty wasn't his strongest point. I suspected that he kept quite a global roster of bed-mates on tap.

For some reason it didn't seem to bother me. I was anxiously dodging the attentions of Lichfield, who was still pressing me to marry him. I just wanted to gravitate back into the circles I knew best.

I could think of no more satisfactory escape route than in developing a friendship with Warren. What I did not realize was that in the process I would make the fatal mistake of falling madly in love with him.

For a long spell I lied to myself. I was convinced that Warren might abandon all his other women for me, but of course there were always the whispered telephone calls he made to Julie.

We would dine late in the West End and find an intimate corner in Tramp, the in-set disco haunt. Warren had nocturnal instincts.

Then he would drive me back to my bed-sitter, where we would make love until sleep came from sheer exhaustion.

No man had made me happier than Warren, whose affection and kindness flowed as generously as his passion.

I fought hard to keep him, to entice him away from everyone else. When I adore someone, it is like an obsession to the death.

My hopes soared when he followed me to Los Angeles where I flew to appear on the Dean Martin show.

I checked into the Beverly Wilshire Hotel and a day later I got an unsigned cable saying "Arriving tomorrow." I guessed it was Warren, who kept the penthouse in the same hotel reserved exclusively for him.

Sure enough, Warren appeared. "London was dead without you," he said, stroking my face. "I missed you a hell of a lot, Britt."

Our relationship struck a new note. There were no secrets to hide from one another and we were able to live quite naturally. Infinitely so. We would sprawl about the penthouse naked for most of the day and lie out on the terrace and sunbathe.

Warren would drift in and out of the suite making drinks for us and occasionally taking a call from a studio to set up fresh movie deals.

We would go out on the town at nights.

But Warren was always apprehensive about our affair, just in case Julie found out.

"She'd hit the roof if she knew," he said. "But I guess that's one of the gambles we're gonna have to take."

Warren thought it might be fun to see a porno movie as I had never been to one and he took me to a sleazy downtown cinema where we managed to slip into the back row unrecognized.

The movie left me cold and I joked with Warren afterwards. "How can cinema audiences be turned on by simulated sex? I will never make a porno film unless it's for real and only with you!"

Warren laughed.

"In that case we had better get a camera crew to film our activities in the penthouse," he joked.

My stay at the Beverly Wilshire was over far too soon.

I had to return to England for urgent talks about a television play.

Warren, who was then heavily involved in Senator McGovern's presidential campaign, was relieved to see me depart. At least that was the impression he gave me.

I realized that Warren was incapable of lasting love. When he picked a bloom it was only for a season.

As he kissed me goodbye I knew that our affair was over. I should have had the courage to have said, "Thank you, Warren, it was fabulous while it lasted."

Instead on the plane home I brooded about our relationship and once I reached London I pledged myself to a long period of celibacy, feeling that men were not worth the emotional strain.

Years later Warren surfaced in my life once more. Alas his college boy looks were becoming slightly crumpled. The eyelids were heavy, the cheekbones mottled. Much of the charm was still there, but the old magic was missing. It looked like Warren had made himself too available: it seemed to me that practically anyone could have him.

We met at a party in Hollywood where I was invited into an ethnic clique gathered in an upstairs bedroom. Cautiously turning the door handle I walked into a dimly lit room to discover Warren chatting to Bianca Jagger. Jack Nicholson and Alana Hamilton were draped amorously on the other end of the bed.

Had I been invited to snort coke? Or was it for an orgy? Or both? No one would tell me and I left before being accused of becoming a voyeur.

Bianca was quite curt about it later: "If you thought it was going to turn into an orgy, Britt, you were mistaken," she said. "I just hope I never get like you."

Alana was equally abrupt. "Was it something I said, Britt?" she pouted.

"Nothing," I replied. "But I don't play games."

It was very strange. Alana, tall and blonde and a decorative participant in so many Hollywood parties, twice appeared on the tail end of my relationships.

I once had a ten day affair in the South of France with

actor George Hamilton, who returned home to California to marry Alana and have a son they named Ashley. The marriage was brief and they were quickly divorced.

Alana next surfaced on the scene as the companion of another of my former escorts Rod Stewart. She married him too, not waiting to see what I had in reserve for the following season!

In fact I might well have married Rod, but that saga I am going to touch on in later chapters. And for that matter, I could also have married George.

George proposed to me on several occasions during our whirlwind fling and sent me roses with the message, "I did. I do. I will."

Colliding on holiday was a tonic for us both. George had gone to the South of France to think things out when he was feeling down and depressed, while I was still feeling hung over from the eclipse in my life of Warren Beatty.

But instead of crying on one another's shoulders, we began to laugh our troubles away. It was so funny because George did a marvelous impression of Warren, which rather mocked all the feelings I harbored for him.

George was as handsome as Warren but his real plus was his tremendous sense of humor. He could mimic so many other Hollywood stars and he could conjure up the most amazing and amusing anecdotes.

I met George on my first night in the South of France at a champagne soaked dinner party thrown by our mutual friend, songwriter Leslie Bricusse, at his St. Paul de Vence home.

My avowed celibacy was no more. George took care of that and finally I had to push him back on the plane to Los Angeles where he was committed to finish a movie.

"I want to marry you," said George.

"Think of me as the girl you saw in the holiday brochure," I laughed, refusing to take him seriously.

My sojourn in the South of France provided me with an enviable suntan when I started work on the film version

of the Agatha Christie thriller *Endless Night* with
George Sanders, Hayley Mills, Hywel Bennett and Per
Oscarsson. It was shot on location in England on the
Isle of Wight and it rained incessantly.

I had to dye my hair red so that I would be distinguishable from the blonde Hayley Mills, who played
an American girl who, in the film, was to become the
sixth richest woman in the world. They dressed Hayley
in pretty white clothes and wrapped me in khaki to take
the role of her German secretary.

Missing the sunshine of the South of France and
hearing that Hayley kept a home in Menton, I suggested
to her that we might take a break from the inclement
weather of the Isle of Wight.

Hayley would have loved to have gone that instant,
but her newly-acquired husband, Roy Boulting, vetoed
the idea. Frankly, he thought I would exert a bad influence on his almost child-like bride.

I didn't press the matter. I thought back on my own
restrictions when I was married to Sellers and the age
gap that existed between Hayley and her husband was
even more acute. Hayley was then only 26 and Roy
Boulting was in his late fifties.

Endless Night was appropriately titled. It trudged
relentlessly on for nearly three painstaking months by
which time we were all totally exhausted. Although
critics hailed it as an "entertaining pastiche" it turned
out to be a box office failure.

As an actress the prospect of a flop must be considered another occupational risk. One can only hope to
benefit from the experience.

It is never wise to look back and like most of my con-
temporaries I treat every new project in the same way as
a mountaineer regards Everest; as the ultimate challenge.

In fact at this period of my career I was fortunate in
finding myself very much in demand. I shot *Baxter* with
Patricia Neal, a tender story of an American boy suffering from a speech impediment. During filming my
career might have been prematurely halted by a crashing
beam that fell from the set. It sliced close to my head

and tore off a wig that I was wearing, in the narrowest of escapes.

In Paris I filmed *Time for Loving* with Mel Ferrer in which I played a French schoolmistress occupying an apartment in Montmartre into which was set four different love stories. Susan Hampshire and Joanna Shimkus were the other two female leads, while in London I was cast as Charlotte Rampling's alter-ego in the psychological thriller *Asylum* in which Peter Cushing, Robert Powell and Herbert Lom all starred.

In a more poignant play for television I appeared in the British adaptation of August Strindberg's *The Stranger* with Marianne Faithfull.

It was a very demanding play for us both, cast as two women whose friendship is put to the test when they discover they are wife and mistress to the same man.

For Marianne, her affair with Mick Jagger at an end, and bravely fighting off her addiction to heroin, it was a marvelous come-back performance.

I don't think many people knew of the courage she showed in undertaking the role, while still enduring the after-effects of "cold turkey."

She was desperately sick at my home, but I made her as comfortable as I could and I did not tell anyone of her predicament.

I was joyful for Marianne. She was a warm, kind human being who had lost her way and was determined to get back onto the right path.

She needed friends and I was happy she came to regard me as one.

Marianne's casting was the inspiration of Patrick Garland, the brilliant young director of the National Theatre and the only man with whom I can safely say that I enjoyed having a long and culturally rewarding friendship that stayed on a strictly platonic level.

— *twelve* —

FROM my student days at drama school a certain passage from Hamlet stayed engraved on my mind.

Shakespeare wrote: "There is a divinity that shapes our ends, rough-hew them as we will."

It has been so true of my life.

That guiding divinity of which the bard spoke brought me before the somewhat sinister figure of Lou Adler and, having deposited me in his court, left me to mix the chemistry.

Some of my past lovers were molded in the fashionable "film star" image but Lou was the complete antithesis to any of them.

He presented a monolith of mystery beneath a wide-brimmed Mexican hat that he wore like a status symbol.

He struck me, on first glance, as a Cuban revolutionary, but he might easily have been mistaken for a Rabbi or just a simple hermit, while Maggie who introduced us, regarded him as "that dark, enigmatic Jew."

I could hardly have guessed that Lou was in any way linked with the pop music industry, but then I had never met a Svengali before.

Here was the man who discovered the Mamas and the Papas, and Carole King, who owned Ode Productions, his own multi-million pound record company and was heavily into film production.

A behind-the-scenes manipulator maybe, but one who possessed the creative talents that had rewarded

him with scores of gold discs for the hit records he had
produced for his artists.

It was in Burke's on a rare day when Patrick Lichfield
was absent from his fold that I first met Lou, at a table
crowded with American film people.

Maggie was among them and she summoned me over.
Of all the people at the table I was intrigued by Lou
whose bearded face was hidden by the furry collar of his
jacket. He said very little but I felt his dark eyes
penetrating me as others talked.

He had come to Europe with Robert Altman, one of
Hollywood's new crop of *avant garde* directors. They
were on their way through London to the San Sebastian
film festival for their movie *Brewster McCloud*.

But Lou was there primarily to organize the concert
appearance in England of his singer Carole King who
was touring with another folk idol James Taylor.

I told Lou over the dinner table that I hoped to go to
the London concert at the Royal Festival Hall.

"Phone me if you have any trouble with tickets," he
said sardonically.

I might have guessed from that remark that the concert was a sell out and the next day I called Lou rather
than hassle with black market touts.

Lou was staying at the Newton House hotel.

"Can you let me have four tickets?" I asked him
selfishly, thinking I would take some friends along as
well. There was a heavy pause.

"I'd like to get my hands on four tickets myself."

Another pause.

"But I just might be able to get two tickets for you."

As it transpired, the boy I intended going to the concert with, an Argentinian student, was delayed at night
school and I ended up going with Lou!

After the concert Peter Asher threw a party at his
Hampstead house and Lou didn't mind when my young
Argentinian friend joined us there.

It was a perfect evening and Lou, in a gentlemanly
gesture, later drove the pair of us back to my Mayfair
flat in his Rolls Royce.

Of course I had not heard the last of Lou. My telephone rang early the next morning.

"How would you like to come to the San Sebastian film festival?" drawled the American voice.

I recognized it instantly.

"Not if there are any strings attached," I said.

"That's a promise," he replied.

I had never gone away with a stranger before, but the idea was intoxicatingly romantic. I wanted to explore the shy, intriguing man behind that engrossing beard.

It was July and San Sebastian basked in the rays of the summer sunshine.

The atmosphere was infectious. Blissful days were spent sunbathing on the beach and every night there was a floodlit gala film première where tumultuous crowds would greet the procession of movie stars.

Afterwards the laughter would echo over the narrow streets from the little intimate restaurants that would stay open practically all night long. I must have lived on white wine and seafood.

Lou had booked a two-bedroom suite in a traditional Spanish hotel furnished with beautiful antique pieces. I was quietly impressed because Lou had not been presumptuous to book us into one room.

It was inevitable, of course, that we would eventually sleep together.

Lou had already shown himself to be so different from any other man I had met. He was indeed a very private man. There was no fast talk or bullshit. He was sincere.

Now he was at my bedroom door wearing a blue bath robe.

It was remarkable. Lou, the grizzly bear, was smooth chested! At least he was in trend.

My thoughts ran back to Sellers, whose hairy cladded chest did much to perpetuate the arguments of mankind's evolution from the gorilla.

I could not resist Lou. Or turn him away. Not when he removed his Mexican hat. I knew he was serious.

The San Sebastian film committee, delighted by my

unexpected presence, invited me to present some of the awards at the final ceremony and I had a special gown and my jewelry flown out from London for the occasion. One of the presentations I made was to Anthony Friedmann who won a special award for his direction of *Bartleby* which starred Paul Schofield and John McEnery.

It was a glittering, star studded night, but unfortunately Lou missed the whole show, having had to rejoin the Carole King concert tour in England.

I caught up with him a day or two later but there was little time left to spend together before his departure back to Los Angeles. But my instincts told me it wasn't a flash-in-the-pan affair. There were ten years between us. Lou was 37. He had been twice married. His first marriage had lasted only a few months as far as I could gather. He had then married singer-actress Shelley Faberes, best remembered for her hit song "Johnny Angel" but for years they had lived apart.

In that time he had been with actress Candice Bergen and more steadily with Peggy Lipton, star of the long running American television show *Mod Squad* but even that romance was now over.

Somehow I regarded Lou as a typical Sagittarian. He obviously enjoyed his freedom and he didn't like to be tied down. Even his life style indicated that. It was organized like a true bachelor's.

His home was in Bel Air, but he loved the open air life. He was a sun freak, and in his youth he had set up office on the beach at Santa Monica with a phone booth at the rear so that he could take calls without abandoning his li-lo for longer than necessary.

Lou was never ostentatious although on my arrival in Los Angeles in September, after a rapid exchange of telephone calls and letters, you might be forgiven for thinking so.

He arrived in a blue Maserati to collect me at the airport and stacked my luggage into his "second" car, a chauffeur-driven white Rolls Royce with tinted windows, television and cocktail bar. My bags had never been treated so well!

We drove to Lou's house on Stone Canyon: a modern split level home with a glass paneled lounge overlooking a kidney shaped swimming pool.

It was all very pretty on the ground floor but upstairs Lou's bachelor traits were exposed.

There were no curtains in the bedroom, and the beds were simple mattresses laid on the bare floors.

In Lou's room the emphasis seemed to be on his recording equipment which from a floor level bed towered like skyscraper blocks.

In the bedroom we were to share, he had a wardrobe, where I could hang my own clothes, and a television set too, even though it occupied an area more suited to a dressing table.

I laughed. "How long did you say you had lived on your own?" I asked him.

Live-in relationships have to start somewhere and this was the moment when we could put our feelings to the test. After a fortnight we were optimistic enough to think it could work out.

Lou had his eccentric little ways, and his privacy, but I did too, even if I didn't recognize it. Lou, a little ashamed at the way the house had been let go, asked me to refurnish it. He gave me *carte blanche* to do whatever I wished.

The first thing I did was to sack his maid who spent more time vacantly watching the television than she did in carrying out her household duties.

Next I ordered curtains, a huge brass bed and carpeting. I got the decorators to splash on some fresh paint.

Later I introduced some fine pieces of art nouveau, and as a result Lou became a collector.

Even his Norwegian elk hound dog Joe Buck, fat and lethargic from being quarantined in the house, began to look sleek and slim from daily exercise.

He lived well but quietly. He would rather eat at

home than go out to a restaurant. I would cook him the
English and Mexican dishes he loved. Once, he took
over the kitchen and cooked a special fish recipe he
served in pastry. I don't think a man had ever cooked a
meal for me before. Or we would have room-service
from the Bel Air Hotel which was across the street. It
was quite funny, and strange for neighbors to see
waiters rushing the cart down the stone yard.

Our fridge was stocked with Dom Perignon champagne and fine bottles of French wine, but we did not
drink a great deal except when friends came to the
house.

We spent a holiday together in Puerto Vallarta. It
might have been the honeymoon, such was the joyous
setting of our rented villa. Mariache music echoed to us
from the old square of the Mexican resort, dominated
by a centuries-old bell tower.

Only one thing spoiled the holiday and that was on
our return to Los Angeles when we ran into trouble with
the Customs. The Customs officers were looking for
drugs and I was stripped and searched, while Lou, much
more suspicious in his hippie garb, was allowed through
without question.

"They don't go for the obvious person," grinned
Lou. "They thought if we were carrying drugs then you
would be the one most likely to conceal them."

Neither of us was carrying drugs. Lou occasionally
smoked grass, so did I.

But I didn't like the idea of anyone regarding us as a
couple of dope peddlers.

I thought I should do something about my image,
feeling that my classical gowns and expensive jewelry
and furs didn't fit into the casual Californian life style.

Lou, the quiet millionaire, took me to a secondhand
clothes mart called Crystal Palace.

I searched through the racks and found a range of antique clothes that were really in vogue. I bought several
'twenties and 'thirties style dresses that suited me perfectly.

No one thought less of a star buying secondhand

clothes, because it was the "in" thing to do. Besides, if a millionaire could go around second-hand, so could I. After all I was still economizing.

In the winter we each bought a chinchilla coat, only I had mine made up out of scraps of sable and other odd furs I already owned and only its sleeves were genuine chinchilla.

I would always buy my own clothes, but sometimes Lou would come home with an unexpected present like the pair of gold rings inscribed with the theatrical masks of comedy and tragedy. I wore them all of the time.

What I wore did not always please Lou. Once, when he was campaigning for Senator McGovern—he and Warren Beatty shared the same political beliefs—he organized an all star concert at the Los Angeles Forum at which Barbra Streisand, James Taylor, Quincy Jones and Carole King were among many others to appear.

I thought I would surprise Lou with an entirely "new look." I put on a blue denim suit with one of his McGovern T-shirts and I flounced into the auditorium with a new Afro hair-style. Only I was the one who was surprised. He didn't recognize me!

Because I was unsure of Lou's reaction I had brought a second outfit to the theater with me—a lacy cream dress, shawl and beaded skull cap.

My hair was the only problem but sure enough there was shampoo in the Lakers basketball team dressing rooms as well as a hair dryer and twenty minutes later I was the Britt he knew.

It was my own fault. As a woman I had always dressed to please myself and I vowed I would do so in future, but on that occasion I had actually gone out of my way to please Lou.

Lou and I were commuting between Los Angeles and London, where I still had my home to look after and Victoria's schooling to attend to.

We normally flew TWA and on one of our flights back to California we were diverted to a remote airfield in Iceland when the pilot was radioed that we might be carrying a bomb aboard.

Everyone remained reasonably calm after the intercom announcement that we were descending for an emergency landing, but one could sense the undercurrent of panic.

The plane landed safely and all the baggage was fastidiously searched, but no trace of a bomb was found. The operation added hours to our journey, especially after further delays caused by the investigation of a sealed art collection that was aboard.

Eventually, in freezing weather, the passengers trooped back aboard but by now the crew had worked their maximum hours and we had to go into New York for them to be relieved. This put us almost a day behind on our arrival in Los Angeles and we all were zapped out like the rest of the passengers aboard.

What I did not realize was that I might have been the unwitting cause of the bomb scare. A TWA executive aired his suspicions about the episode later. He blamed the hoax call on a disgruntled fan at London Airport whose autograph book I had unconsciously thrust aside when running to catch the plane.

I was stunned to imagine that such a thing could happen. In normal circumstances I always gave my autograph and I could not believe that one fan I happened to ignore could make a malicious call like this. The TWA man shook his head. "Miss Ekland, it can happen, believe me," he said.

My relationship with Lou was growing closer every day and he invited me to spend a holiday in California.

Then Sellers came on to me.

He urgently needed the use of my flat. By then I had moved back to our old matrimonial home which I was renting at £5,000 a year.

Sellers had to be in London because Miranda had been taken ill with meningitis. The Inland Revenue had given my ex-husband a special dispensation to remain in England because of her illness.

Sellers said that if I granted him that favor he would consent to Victoria flying out to Los Angeles with me without raising any objections.

I agreed and I handed him the keys of the Clarges Street flat that he knew so well and which must have provoked many memories for him.

Lou and Victoria got along famously together. His natural love for children shone through and he had even redesigned one of the empty bedrooms at Stone Canyon for her.

It was sad that Lou had not had children of his own. Through his second marriage he had thought of adopting one when considering the plight of refugee and underprivileged children across the world.

He supported many children's causes and in Los Angeles he had formed a basketball club for young boys. Basketball was his keenest recreation and he loved to encourage youngsters into the sport.

By the spring of 1972 I actually summoned courage to ask Lou why he remained married to his wife. Until then our relationship had been founded on the understanding that whenever we could be together then that would be the way but if we were separated by work or any other activities then neither would make any demands on the other.

However our involvement gathered a degree of permanence when we moved into a very pretty beach house Lou bought at Malibu, where the Pacific waves smacked the shore almost directly beneath us.

I saw the house as our first real home together; a home we had found and furnished as any man and wife would have done. I was proud of it.

When the final strip of fresh wallpaper had been hung and we sat down to bask in our achievement I broached the subject carefully.

"Lou," I said. "Why don't you get a divorce if you don't live with your wife? Why stay married to her? You never see her . . ."

He didn't say anything for a full minute and then went to the kitchen to get some ice cubes for our drinks.

"The day I want a divorce I can get one," he said sullenly. "All the papers are settled . . ."

"Then why don't you go ahead with it?" I asked.

"Don't you want to marry again?"

Lou sprawled into a chair and swallowed hard and didn't answer.

I knew how Lou felt. With two failed marriages behind him, he was diffident about contemplating a third.

The long, hot summer days gently lulled us into the transient happiness of which Lou spoke. Our friend Robert Altman was filming further along the beach and he and the cast would drop by for evening drinks and we would entertain other chums like Jack Nicholson and Michelle Phillips.

Mick and Bianca Jagger came to one of our parties and Bianca sunbathed by the pool—which left the men stirring their drinks for longer than usual.

Ryan O'Neal lived only three or four houses along and the beach scene really hummed when Ursula Andress flew in from Rome as his house guest.

One day, almost as though she was repeating her role in the first James Bond movie *Dr. No*, she came wading out of the sea wearing just a tee-shirt and a pair of bikini pants.

Our guests on the terrace almost freaked out at the sight of her. She was just sensational.

"I just thought I would drop by for a drink," said Ursula casually, as though she always made her arrival that way.

The house took on a more domesticated air with the presence of Victoria from London and my mother and brother Bengt from Sweden.

Lou's sister and mother also visited us and we were really a family unit although we had to arrange for some of them to stay at a nearby guest house.

It was while the family were staying with us that we lost Joe Buck. I think that Lou loved that dog more than any human being alive. I had seen Lou in quiet, pensive moods before but I had never seen him the victim of such gloom. He wouldn't speak, he wouldn't eat and he locked himself away on his own.

We craved the assistance of the police and the animal organizations; we telephoned friends. I tramped miles up and down the beach searching for Joe but there was not a sign of him anywhere.

I inserted advertisements in the local papers and I even nailed homemade posters on a lot of telegraph poles in Malibu offering a reward for Joe's return.

There was nothing more any of us could do. I felt I was to blame. Joe had been my responsibility.

I kept apologizing to Lou but it was as if he wasn't listening. It was almost as though I had not only destroyed his relationship with his dog, but with me too.

We suffered for three whole days. And then, without any announcement, Joe Buck just sauntered back into the house and sprawled out beneath my feet. I could not believe my eyes.

He had clearly been in a fight. His mouth was torn and so was his ear. Stitches were needed to treat his wounds and I drove him to the vet.

Lou was overjoyed when I phoned him at his office.

"I'm coming home straight away," he said cancelling the rest of his business meetings for the day.

The reunion between one man and his dog brought tears to my eyes and Lou could not find enough ways to express his gratitude.

He knew that I wanted to see Elvis Presley in concert in Las Vegas but I had not pressed him to go. Suddenly, he booked not only for me, but for the entire family —his mother Josie, his sister Paula, and her husband along with my mother and brother Bengt. Only Lou insisted we should do it in some style and the two families were left boggle-eyed.

He booked our plane tickets; two limousines awaited on our arrival, we were also given individual suites on the top floor of the Las Vegas Hilton stocked with fruit, flowers and champagne and reserved for us were the best tickets in the house for Elvis!

Lou's mother, a frail but friendly Jewish woman in her sixties had been to Las Vegas before, but a £1,000 a week suite with king size beds and color television in every room was a luxury beyond her wildest dreams. Lou's brother-in-law who was a humble refrigerator

repair man and my own mother and Bengt were
similarly lost for words.

The joke was that I got smashed on champagne
before the show even started and I was out for the count
in my room when it was time to see the show. I missed
Elvis entirely!

I was too embarrassed to tell Lou what had happened
when we got back to Los Angeles and I swore the others
to secrecy!

"Just how was Elvis?" Lou enquired. And evasively I
replied, "Thank you darling. It was a marvelous trip.
Elvis was just wonderful."

I suppose I had always been a music freak. I once
spent £20 a week on records and at this time many
British bands were coming into America attempting to
emulate the success that the Beatles had enjoyed in the
early 'sixties.

Because of Lou's association with the record industry, we would often get sent pop concert tickets and I
remember passing on a couple of tickets to Bengt to see
the touring Rod Stewart and the Faces at the Hollywood
Bowl.

I told him, "You might like them, but I'm sure I
wouldn't be a scrap interested in them."

You can't snub providence that way. Two years later
Fate dictated my path should cross with Rod's.

At that time, however, I thought my entire future
would be with Lou. Not only was I deeply in love with
him, but I discovered that I was bearing his child.

It was a moment of shock as well as joy. For nearly
eighteen months I had been consulting a gynecologist
because of a menstrual problem caused by anemia. I
was told that I could not possibly conceive as I was not
ovulating, but this could be remedied by injections.

I took the course of injections, if only to recycle my
menstrual period, but still I had problems. Lou and I
didn't think there was any point in bothering with con-
traception. To all intents and purposes I was infertile.

I went to Scotland to film *The Wicker Man*, a story
with paganistic overtones, and for some weeks I refused

to acknowledge the usual symptoms that are associated with pregnancy. My breasts had swollen and I was suffering from morning sickness.

"It's impossible," I told myself. "It must be something else."

Finally, I went to London to take a pregnancy test in Harley Street, just to dispel my fears.

My disbelief when the test was pronounced "positive" must have been all too clear.

"Don't take it too badly, I'm sure you can cope," said the doctor sympathetically.

"Oh, it's not that," I replied. "I didn't think I'd ever have another child."

"Then let me be the first to congratulate you," he said.

I could not wait to telephone Lou but the eight-hour time gap between London and Los Angeles made it difficult. As I drove back to Scotland my nerves must have been transmitted to the engine.

The car broke down twice on the way and I had to put up for the night in a wayside inn, where they gave me the best room in the house.

The only telephone was in the main hall and, at the risk of being overheard by everyone, I called Los Angeles and got hold of Lou.

"You're what?" he said, his voice pitched high with surprise. "You can't be . . . you are? . . . well, when is it due? . . . congratulations."

I continued my journey to Scotland early the next morning, slightly confused by Lou's reaction. Had he been genuinely pleased or had I detected a note of frustration in his voice?

The thought niggled me as I crossed the border into Scotland.

Lou had always said that he wanted children; was he now changing his mind? I had to be sure and I decided that we must, at the earliest opportunity, discuss all the implications involved.

Back in the Highlands once more I safely guarded the nature of my true mission to London from the other members of the cast but an extraordinary incident occurred.

Diane Cilento, who was starring in the film with me, had spent many years in the study of the occult and to while away the time she would read Tarot cards. At the end of a day's shooting, I succumbed to the temptation for Diane to spread her cards out before me.

I was amused as she began to relate my fortune to me, but then suddenly struck dumb.

Diane looked deeply into the upturned cards laid out in rows at her fingertips and she said, "You are going to have another child, Britt, but it is unlikely that you will marry the baby's father."

It was not possible for Diane to have known about my pregnancy and I could only stare in wonderment at her.

I was glad when the movie was wrapped and I could return to London to meet Lou who was on his way through to the South of France on a business jaunt.

I went with Lou as far as Paris and we booked into the Plaza Athenee. Dinner in our suite gave us the first opportunity of talking about our unborn baby.

Our conversation was strained. Lou was totally impassive to everything I said. Perhaps I anticipated too much, for I allowed myself to be carried away by the excitement I thought he would share.

It seemed as though Lou had already determined his own answers.

Finally, he had to open up.

"Britt, I've got to be honest with you. I'm not going to marry you and I don't think we can ever live together on a permanent basis . . ." he said.

I felt suddenly awkward, I didn't want Lou to feel that I was blackmailing him in any way.

"Of course you can't marry me because you're still married to Shelley," I said. "But isn't this good enough reason to divorce now?"

Lou pensively forked over his meal. His eyes didn't move from the direction of his plate.

"Britt, as far as I am concerned things won't change

between us. We will still see each other when we can. Okay, if you want to keep the baby, then fine—I'll support you 100 per cent of the way. But the decision must be yours.''

I sat thinking about Lou's words for several minutes. There was a heavy silence in the room.

"Are you suggesting, Lou, that I should have an abortion? Is that what you are saying?" I asked.

He shook his head and looked up from his dinner plate.

"I didn't say that at all. I said the decision is yours. If you want to have the baby, knowing that we won't marry, then okay, go ahead. I'm not going to run out on you either way . . .''

I flew back to London alone. I had to think very deeply about it. My upbringing dictated that if I was to have a child I should be married. I was afraid, not so much for my own sake, but for the stigma that our child might have to face.

Then I thought of two fellow thespians, Vanessa Redgrave and Catherine Deneuye, both of whom had children out of wedlock. No one had thought badly of them and both were enjoying prominent professional and social lives.

Besides, we were now into the 'seventies and old taboos had been broken down.

At the same time I still had Victoria to consider. How would she think of her mother? How would she react to having a half-brother or sister. I had always thought Victoria needed other company. There was the imminent danger that she would become too selfish in being brought up entirely on her own and I honestly believed that she needed to start caring about someone else other than herself.

So the argument was tossed over like a nightmare in my mind but I had not lost sight of the spiritual aspects.

I could not bring myself to contemplate an abortion, not when I had prayed to God that I might conceive if merely to demonstrate that I was not infertile.

I had always been a religious person, and now that God had answered my prayers, I knew that I would have my child.

I told Lou and he was true to his word. "I'm glad," he said simply, but in a voice that left no doubt as to his sincerity.

For as long as possible I kept my condition secret. I went on an intensive slimming diet, losing twenty pounds in weight. I wore lacy dresses, kaftans and outfits that disguised my figure and when at a party in a crêpe overlay dress Joan Collins asked me suspiciously, "Is this the new fashion?"

Victoria's nanny, Britt Inger, who was a trained nurse was the first to guess I was pregnant and so I realized that I would have to confide in members of the family at least.

Victoria was excited. She was then nine years old and the idea of a new baby was like having a real live doll for her pram.

It was in Los Angeles when I was seven months pregnant that my "bulge," now impossible to hide beneath a black dress, caught everyone's eye at the Bette Midler concert I attended with Lou. A gossip columnist wrote, "Lou Adler and Britt Ekland are expecting a visit from the stork any day."

I decided to have the baby in London. I wanted our child to have British nationality, as I had come to regard England as my home and believed that England was so civilized and realistic compared to other parts of the world, but Lou did not necessarily agree.

Naturally he loved America and he would have been happier if I had stayed on in California and had the baby there.

But I had to return to England to be with Victoria during her schooling and I said to Lou, "It would be a great advantage to have the baby in London."

Lou fortunately saw it my way and I was given an injection to safeguard my unborn child on my flight to London and my American doctors advised me to take things "very quietly" till the final countdown.

Yet my arrival in London coincided with Sellers's romance with Liza Minnelli. It was all red roses and wedding bells and the Press was knocking on my door asking me to pass judgment as one of his ex-wives.

Of course I knew about Liza. Victoria came home with a photograph of Liza and Sellers together and said, "Look Mummy, Daddy has had his photograph taken with Liza." Later Sellers came on the line.

"This is it," cried Sellers in a delirious mood. "I am going to marry Liza Minnelli. We're madly in love . . ."

Once more I offered my congratulations, but I had reservations about the planned wedding. I just couldn't see Sellers handling a superstar like Liza who was much more mature than any of his three earlier brides had been. Sure enough, a couple of weeks later, the friendship fizzled out and I felt sorry for Sellers.

Sellers constantly complained about the environment in which I brought up Victoria, but before the Liza Minnelli episode, Sellers had been escorting fashion model Titi Wachtmeister and for Victoria, then only nine this was a trifle bewildering as she had known Titi, a Swedish ambassador's daughter, from an early age as my brother Bengt's girl friend.

In her innocence she would say, "Daddy had tea today with Titi but Ben wasn't there."

Titi and Bengt for whom I reserved the water bed in my Clarges Street flat had parted several months before Sellers entered the scene, but I could not explain that to Victoria.

It was Victoria's excitement at the prospect of having a baby brother or sister to look after that brought me back to making the final plans of my confinement.

Lou flew in a few days before the date set for our baby's arrival and only a couple of nights before entering London's Avenue Clinic we went to the opera with Sam Spiegel.

If the Covent Garden production was spectacular, I am afraid it was upstaged by Nicholai who came into the world on 10 June with all the computer control of a

NASA space landing. Indeed he was a perfect Gemini.

His arrival was greeted by a salute of champagne corks as Lou, wearing a green hospital smock, led in a celebrating clan of his friends including Jack Nicholson, who was to be our baby's godfather, and his more recent girl friend Anjelica Huston.

Nicholai was just under seven pounds in weight and he was a beautiful baby with a mop of jet black hair.

I had been convinced that I would have a boy. I had knitted booties and sweaters and outfits all in blue and even bought a cot with a blue hood, blankets and accessories.

When I had Victoria, I made such a fuss about having a nursery especially for her. But with Nicholai I thought I would try a fresh approach. I asked myself why a baby should be isolated in a nursery.

We tend to rear infants like prisoners, cut off from everybody else in the house. So I decided against a nursery. Instead, we kept Nicholai in his cot in the living room where he would sleep as contentedly with the record player booming out, cigarette smoke wafting round the room all day, the vacuum cleaner going and odd people wandering in and out. Nicholai didn't bleep. Not once was he disturbed by the noise around him.

Lou left for America after five days; he could not abandon his work any longer than that.

I did not see him again until a month later when only twenty-four hours remained in which to meet the legal requirements for Nicholai's official registration.

Lou didn't see the necessity of it all but I had to remind him that we faced prosecution if Nicholai wasn't properly registered.

I managed to persuade him to drive with me to the Hampstead Register Office but once we were there an argument developed between us.

Lou adored our son's christian name of Nicholai which I thought combined our Swedish and Russian ancestries and projected the romantic ring of Tolstoy; but the argument was over my insistence that Ekland should figure somewhere in his surname.

"All right we will have Nicolai Ekland Adler but without the hyphen," he said.

Nicholai now has a bone-inlaid rosewood music box with his initials N.E.A. engraved on it. Lou commissioned experts in Switzerland and Los Angeles to make it.

When the lid is opened it plays a song that Carole King specially composed for me during my pregnancy and which she later recorded on one of her albums.

The title was very appropriate for any mother-to-be . . . "That's The Way Things Go Down."

— *thirteen* —

IN late summer we were heading back to Malibu: Victoria, nanny and our radiant robust fledgling Nicholai, now nearly two months old. I knew they would love the sand, the sea and the Californian sunshine.

Lou, having been on a lightning visit to Spain to see Jack Nicholson filming *The Passenger* with Maria Schneider, was on his way back to join us.

Almost three months had elapsed since leaving Malibu and I was excited about the prospect of being home once more. But when I unlocked the beach house front door I was filled with a strange sensation. Something was wrong.

Maybe it was a woman's intuition, maybe it wasn't, but I found myself checking round the rooms. Everything seemed to be in place. Our silver-framed photographs still occupied the sideboards and tables and our little pieces of art nouveau that we had collected in Paris were not missing.

However, I could not erase the uneasy feeling that something was amiss. My feelings could have been dismissed as being due purely to the emptiness of the house, but a sudden notion struck me. Someone other than Lou had been living there during my absence.

I went into our bedroom, leaving the nanny with the children in their room. It was all very neat and tidy, but then my eyes settled on something that sparkled on the dresser. It was a pair of earrings. I picked them up and examined them. They were certainly not mine.

My whole body trembled. I had trusted Lou implicitly. I had never envisaged that he could possibly be unfaithful to me. We had given ourselves license to do whatever we wished when we were not in each other's company but I had not interpreted that as meaning we could indulge in other affairs.

My suspicions of Lou's disloyalty heightened when I found a hairpin buried in the beige pile of the bedroom carpet. As far as I was concerned, that was the conclusive evidence.

I fell in a crumpled heap on to the bed. I was sick with anguish. It was as though my whole world had collapsed once more.

Some silly but curious little things flooded back into my mind. I remembered flying with Lou to the Montreux jazz festival and he had been wearing a gold whistle on a chain round his neck.

At the time I thought it was unusual because he was not the kind of man prone to wear medallions and jewelry. The only item he wore of mine was an original Cartier watch I bought on one of my many expeditions down the Portobello Road in London.

It should have occurred to me at the time. Lou would not have bought the gold whistle himself and it must have been a present. But who from?

My tortured mind ran off in all sorts of crazy directions and I drove myself insane just trying to pin down Lou's secret.

Suddenly it became all too transparent. Why hadn't I guessed it before? Was I so blind?

Twice in my early days of pregnancy I had been approached by Michelle Phillips as to whether I was expecting a baby. Once I had replied, "I should be so lucky" when trying to keep it all a secret. On the other occasion I could not really understand her mounting curiosity.

Michelle, who had sung with The Mamas and the Papas, had been married to John Phillips in the group, but after their divorce she became involved with Jack Nicholson.

We used to spend lovely weekends at the racquet club
in Palm Springs with Jack and Michelle, but eventually
they drifted apart. Jack found solace with John
Huston's daughter Anjelica, but while I had been in
London I had lost track of Michelle.

Michelle was tall, blonde and vivacious but I knew
that Lou had never thought of her as being sensual.
Now the truth dawned.

We engaged a Swiss housekeeper at Malibu who had
been looking after Lou and the house while I had been
having Nicholai.

It may have been unfair and unreasonable of me but I
interrogated her in the kitchen.

She was reluctant to betray Lou but I threatened her
with dismissal if she did not tell me the truth. After all, I
had hired her.

Finally she broke down. "Yes, Britt," she said, "they
have been here."

From the sorrowing housekeeper I discovered that
Michelle had spent most weekends with Lou at the
house. She had also brought along her daughter Chynna
from her marriage to John Phillips.

I promised the housekeeper that I would not tell Lou
about our conversation.

Lou got in from Spain. He was at the Airport but he
had lost his luggage. Could I help? I got on to the airline
and organized the search.

When he came home he looked distinctly weary and he
appeared sensitive, as if assessing my reactions to
everything he said.

I acted perfectly normally and deliberately lulled him
into a sense of false security.

Exhausted from jet lag, he slept undisturbed for the
night.

In the morning we made love and I offered no ob-
jection. It was cruel, it was calculated and it was
probably unforgivable. But I knew that by allowing Lou
to make love to me he would suffer so much more pain
by the accusations I was now ready to unleash.

After all, I loved this man. I'd had his child and I'd

gone through with it on his terms.

I might have been able to accept it if it had been a one night stand with a floosie. But he had been unfaithful with Michelle, supposedly as good a friend to me as to Lou.

I should have known better. It's always the close friend you least suspect . . .

I watched Lou getting dressed that morning, believing that he had successfully managed to deceive me.

"Lou," I began quietly, "there is just one thing you have forgotten to tell me about . . ."

"What's that, Britt?" he asked.

"You haven't mentioned your affair with Michelle Phillips."

The words struck like a thrust of a blade.

At first Lou tried to dismiss it but I told him the deception was over.

Over the next few days he complained of feeling sick. I was used to Lou suffering from migraine attacks whenever something unpleasant was on his mind, but this was something new.

I called his doctor who advised his admittance to hospital for tests suspecting that Lou's trouble was dehydration.

When Lou was discharged and returned home I decided that the only way our relationship was going to survive was for me to make some kind of mental adjustment in my attitude to his infidelity.

It was totally against all my principles. Unfaithfulness was something I never thought I could bring myself to tolerate. When linen is soiled, it must be discarded.

But I could not find it in my heart to discard Lou. I was still desperately in love with him and even at the cost of my pride I decided that I must make an effort to reestablish our relationship, particularly for the sake of Nicholai.

Lou was penitent. For my birthday he gave me an expensive fur jacket, a gift that made me reflect on his past generosity when he had bought me a custom-built Volkswagen and a set of Gucci luggage.

But the real token of Lou's love was his caring for us
as a family and I came to believe that every man must be
allowed his one foolish indiscretion.

Our friends may have pondered on our future
together as I suspected that most of them would have
known of Lou's fling with Michelle. It's difficult to hide
these things in Hollywood even for someone as private
as Lou.

That we were trying to iron out our difficulties must
have been clearly shown at the surprise birthday party I
threw for Lou.

I organized a champagne breakfast for Maggie, Herb
Alpert, Robert Altman, Jack and a dozen more of his
friends, directing them all into the house while Lou was
taking his morning shower. When he appeared, ready to
drive to the office, he was confronted by a chorus of
"Happy birthday, Lou . . ."

The only notable absentee from the clan was
Michelle, but, as Lou might have guessed, I did not invite her.

Just when our troubles seemed to be dissolving, Lou
tossed out the idea of going on a skiing holiday with
Jack to Aspen in Colorado. It was the Christmas season
and I thought it was strange that he should not even
think of inviting me.

"Why can't I come with you?" I was finally forced to
ask him.

Lou made all sorts of feeble excuses, saying he would
only be away for three or four days.

Aware now of my suspicions he suddenly thought
about the trip in a new light.

"Of course we could all go," he said, with a fresh
burst of enthusiasm.

Christmas on the snow covered peaks of Aspen was
the tonic we both perhaps needed to resurrect our
relationship.

Alas, it did not turn out that way.

Our party became unwieldy.

Lou and I shared an apartment with our friends
American singer Cher and record mogul David Geffin,

while Jack and Anjelica moved into a nearby house with Roman Polanski and three New York models, Susan Blakely, Ingrid Boulting and the Dutch born Appolonia von Ravenstein known to her friends as "Apples."

No one ever mentioned Sharon Tate's terrible death at the hands of the Charles Manson cult, but we all knew that Roman hid great pain. Only in parties like these could Roman relax.

There was one constant round of parties and as the festivities progressed I grew more and more anxious about Lou who became increasingly affectionate towards "Apples."

I could not help but feel jealous.

Lou would disappear without any excuse. One afternoon I made the mistake of going to search for him, only to find him sprawled out in the jacuzzi across at the house with "Apples" and two or three others as if giving patronage to a Roman bath.

I grew desperately unhappy. I suspected that Lou might be having an affair with the beautiful red-haired Dutch model but I could not bring myself to accuse him of it. I had no evidence.

Back in Los Angeles once more I just had to ask him outright. I could not contain my lurking suspicions any longer.

Lou dismissed my anxieties lightly.

If it had not been for his friendship with Michelle I might well have accepted his word. I remained unconvinced.

Our relationship descended into a hopeless phase of deceit and it hit rock bottom when I decided that double standards weren't strictly a man's game—although Lou might have thought so when he spent New Year's Eve at Malibu without me. He reasoned it was time we got out of one another's hair for a while.

I marched resentfully out of the house and drove over to Stone Canyon, determined not to question Lou any further but to leave him to his own devices.

Early in the New Year, I had to return to Colorado to film *The Ultimate Thrill*, a skiing story set in the moun-

tains and now that Lou had gone on his own tack I em-
barked on an affair with a young film man which was a
cheap and ghastly mistake that jarred my emotions.

In fact, nothing went right in Colorado. My hotel
room was raided and £40,000 worth of my jewelry and
furs were stolen.

I had been asked to wear them as costume pieces for
the movie and I had mistakenly believed my belongings
were insured.

No trace was found of them, despite intensive police
inquiries.

I telephoned Lou then in New York, but of course
there was nothing he could do to assist.

Maybe both Lou and I had a lot to answer for when
we got back to Los Angeles, but he didn't question me
about Colorado and I didn't cross-examine him.

That was to be the pattern of our future liaison. No
one would intrude on the other's privacy. But I remember lying awake one night stricken by recrimination and
asking myself, "Whatever happened to our love?"

In the spring I was in London looking after Victoria's
schooling and administering my own affairs. I wrote
long and endless letters to Lou, enclosing snapshots of
our thriving son.

It was not as though I missed a man about the house.
I had become pretty independent. I could mend a fuse,
hammer a picture to the wall, plaster up wallpaper and
even strip down a car.

Yet I felt lonely and abandoned.

It was a bleak period but things were to change much
more rapidly than I envisaged.

Ryan O'Neal was in town, making me feel alive and
wanted once more.

We were old friends dating back to the time when
Sellers had been filming in Hollywood and only the year
before Ryan had taken me out to the Wings concert
in London when I had been heavily pregnant with
Nicholai.

Now we were meeting under different circumstances

and Ryan, who had a keen ear to the grapevine, knew that my relationship with Lou was floundering.

We shared a mutual understanding of one another's problems. Ryan, who was bringing up his daughter Tatum practically single handed, could relate to my own task in rearing Victoria and Nicholai.

The thought of having an affair with Ryan had never crossed my mind. I had never seen him in the light of his screen reputation as a heart throb, an identity he had gained after his very moving role in *Love Story*.

To me he was just a nice, friendly guy and I am sure that he did not see me as a sex siren.

Ryan took me out to dinner parties and night spots and unconsciously we drifted together. The question of going to bed with him was academic; it wasn't a mad, passionate love affair as I had experienced with Warren Beatty or, for that matter, with George Hamilton.

I think my interlude with Ryan fell under the category of comfort and consolation. It was all over soon, as our careers took us in opposite directions.

The memory was always a pleasant one and although I was to see Ryan on many occasions in the future we abstained rather than spoil anything we had valued before.

During the spell that I was in London producer Albert (Cubby) Broccoli was casting for the new James Bond film *The Man With The Golden Gun*. I went out and bought a copy of Ian Fleming's book, read it and was convinced that I could play the role of the spy girl.

Broccoli admired my grit when I phoned him through and bowled over to his office. He was right in the middle of casting and I could not have timed it better.

As the weeks slipped past I thought I had lost the opportunity. I heard that another Swedish actress, Maud Adams, had been signed.

I was bitterly disappointed but it was no more than any actress must face. I dismissed the whole thing from my mind.

Then I got a call from Broccoli asking me to see him. Behind his huge desk in Mayfair he was smiling.

"Of course," he said, "you may have read the book but our script is very different. I would like you to take it home and read it. Look especially at the part of Mary Goodnight. I think you might be right for it."

Mary Goodnight was Bond's assistant and it was a superb role. I leapt at it.

Jumping on the Bond bandwagon was the perfect antidote for my depression.

My 40,000 dollar fee may not have been spectacular but the expenses were generous and I was given VIP treatment to the most exotic locations in the Far East. For once I could also shamelessly bask in the Bond publicity machine.

Some months earlier I had two unsightly moles removed from my skin and on the day I was due to fly out to Thailand I went to Harley Street to have the third one nicked from the pit of my back. This one had to be scooped out because it contained live cells and I had to have eight stitches in the wound. I flew out on the late plane, feeling comfortable but with my back bandaged. The stitches were removed by a nurse during filming on the isle of Phuket.

Shooting the Bond movie was something of a dream. I had never worked for a more generous and affable producer than Cubby Broccoli and Maud Adams, who was to become a close friend, shared my view. He treated us both like superstars.

There were moments when that was a heavy mantle to wear and I remember throwing my first tantrum as an actress when I tore up several sheets of inferior film stills that had been shot of me.

Fresh photographs had to be taken but this time the work was in the safe hands of David Steen whose photography I was already familiar with.

I got along with Roger Moore very well. He was intelligent, witty and brimming with dry humor. No doubt as Bond he was girl-bait but I did not fancy him.

Yet Roger's wife Luisa, was extremely possessive of him and she could not hide her feelings on occasions. She was upset whenever he talked to another woman. I guessed it was hard on any wife to see her husband thrown into a harem, even though it's all make believe on a film set.

The Bond film schedule spanned four months but I did not mind. My children Victoria and Nicholai were with me, together with a nanny and governess and I think the period was one of the happier ones in my life.

That autumn I was in London with Lou who was co-producing the film version of the *Rocky Horror Show*. Everything seemed to be happening at once. We had barely got organized in my Clarges Street flat again before I was off to Bavaria to shoot *Royal Flash* with Malcolm McDowell and Alan Bates.

It meant that I would be away for several weeks and for the first time Lou showed a grain of jealousy. Close to the end of my film's schedule he was going to lay on a Lear jet so that I could fly back to spend a weekend with him, but I cancelled the arrangement because of more pictures that I had arranged with David Steen. Lou beefed on the telephone, "If you would rather have your photograph taken than see me then go ahead . . ." I was secretly delighted. Maybe Lou was in love with me after all.

In Malibu, Lou was in the process of rebuilding the beach house and he bought a property on rising ground at the rear as an operations center. I helped him with the designs and layout.

Then it was off to New York for a party hosted by John Phillips and his new wife Genevieve. It coincided with my birthday.

Mick and Bianca Jagger were there and Lou enticed the Rolling Stone into parting with an art deco diamante pin that I later learned his wife had given him as a present. Lou clipped it to my lapel, and said, "That looks very good on you, Britt."

"Yeah," agreed Mick reluctantly, "she can have it."

In London we attended the Royal première of *The Man With The Golden Gun* and Lou joined me on various dates for the massive tub thumping promotional tour for the movie.

But the days of our relationship were numbered. We flew to Switzerland for what was to be our last Christmas together, although I could not possibly have foreseen that eventuality at the time.

It was very much a family affair and many of our friends came across to join us. Among them Jack Nicholson, marvelous always as Nicholai's godfather and who volunteered to play Santa Claus for the festive parties.

Unfortunately, I wasn't able to appreciate it all. I spent most of the time in bed suffering from tonsilitis.

After only a few days with us Lou returned mysteriously to the States, but as three weeks' rent had been paid for the Gstaad villa, I stayed on with the children.

It was in New York, just a few weeks later, that Lou's bombshell exploded. We had been happy enough, taking in the usual round of Broadway plays and films, but near to the end of our trip he said, "Britt, I don't want to make it hard on either of us. But I must tell you that it's over."

I was stunned. Lou didn't make those kind of statements without good reason, but this time his feelings, his inner thoughts, were locked within him and he was not going to reveal them.

Only when I was back in Malibu was I able to learn the bitter truth of Lou's deception over the previous months. I pieced it together with the reluctant help of our nanny, Britt Inger.

Living only two doors from us in one of the beach houses was Phyllis Somers whose marriage to Lou's lawyer and friend Abe Somers had gone bust the summer before.

Lou encouraged me to befriend and console Phyllis.

Of course I had done so without hesitating. I was always ready to support any woman.

Besides, I already regarded Phyllis as a friend. Her little daughter Eve had taken swimming lessons with Nicholai.

So most days I rang and tried to cheer Phyllis out of

her depression. I remembered how I'd felt through my divorce period.

Phyllis, a glamorous young blond model with the all-American looks of a Cheryl Tiegs, moved into the beach house after the split. She was glad of my company.

When Lou opened the *Rocky Horror Show* at his new club, the "Roxy," we were all there.

When I look back on that night now, I shiver. There I had been in front of all our friends, playing helpmate to Phyllis totally unaware that she and Lou were having an affair.

I could only blame myself for not having recognized the telltale signs.

Our sex life at one stage had ceased to exist. I was very frustrated by it but excused Lou on the grounds of tiredness and business pressures: he was then handling the affairs of so many artists including the American comedy duo Cheech and Chong whose album he had promoted to the No. 1 spot in the national pop charts.

Lou was also a man of conscience. I don't think he could have conducted two affairs simultaneously, and by this time his thoughts were probably channeled to Phyllis, but I still didn't see through their involvement.

I was blind to all the evidence. I went to Phyllis's house one day and noticed some roses in her flower vase identical to the icy mauve colored ones that Lou always sent me. I also noticed she was wearing a Tiffany wristwatch similar to the one that Lou had given me.

Phyllis would complain about the money and the way her ex-husband was treating her. But having sold her Jaguar car she bought a 17,000 dollar pale blue two-seater Mercedes and I wondered how she could afford it but I didn't ask.

We became such close friends that I actually worried about her, particularly when she disappeared.

I looked by on the house when I got no answer from my telephone calls. Her other friends were also left in the dark as to her whereabouts. I was on the verge of telephoning the police as I feared that something terrible might have happened to her when she finally turned up and explained that she had been to Palm Springs to do a commercial. There was no reason to doubt her.

Only later did I discover that she had been away with Lou and joined him in New York and on a subsequent occasion they went to Hawaii.

Through it all there was only one time when I suspected Lou. It was when I found a Polaroid picture in our house of Phyllis holding Nicholai up in her arms. I asked Lou, ''You're not having an affair with Phyllis, are you?''

Lou shrugged away my doubts.

But when the crushing truth came out I was broken hearted. I felt betrayed by Phyllis. I had shared her sorrows and sympathized with her.

In the past Lou had always referred to her as my look-alike because of the way she imitated my clothes, my hair and my make-up.

I was ready to remind him of that in the final hour of our parting.

''You're a fool,'' I snapped at him, ''how can you trade a Rolls Royce for a second-hand Ford?''

I packed my things and left for Stone Canyon.

Lou was not without feeling, however much I held him in contempt at that moment.

He told me that I could stay at Stone Canyon for as long as I wished or that he would buy me any other house I wanted.

''I think you know that I will always ensure that both you and Nicholai are secure,'' he said.

Lou has kept to his word.

Ironically his relationship with Phyllis developed almost identically to the one he had shared with me. He stayed married to his estranged wife Shelley while living with Phyllis at Malibu.

In September, 1978 Phyllis gave birth to Lou's second son, Cisco.

I could not easily come to forgive Phyllis for her part in the conspiracy, but to show her that I bore no ill-feeling I sent a basket of flowers as a gift to mark Cisco's arrival.

I think Lou proudly regards his sons Nicholai and Cisco as the twin pillars of his Slovac ancestry.

When Nicholai goes to stay with his father, he is already playing Cisco's big brother, and that is the beauty and innocence of children who must never be tainted by the foolishness of adults.

As strange as it may seem to others I have now built a very special relationship with Lou. We rely on each other's advice in times of crises.

Maybe we have got more going for us now than at any time through our relationship.

— *fourteen* —

THE second word my innocent, gurgling son Nicholai could say after "Dad" was "Rod". Only Nicholai pronounced it as "Wod."

It was sufficient revelation for the world to guess that I was head over heels in love with Rod Stewart, the tartan scarved rock star with the pebblestone flecked voice that shattered the pop charts.

Rod came into my life six weeks after I parted from Lou and I rose back into the sky like a gull whose oil-soaked wings had been cleansed by a detergent.

I had first seen Rod on the stage of the Rainbow Theater in London at the *Tommy* charity première produced by Lou Adler.

With his mousey-colored cactus-spiked hair, an elongated, mobile face and his limp figure swathed in yards of tartan, he resembled a rag doll.

When I next ran into him, at Mick Jagger's birthday party, I could not resist the temptation of crushing down the spiky hair and goading him, "Is this for real?"

Needless to say, he was not amused.

Many of my girl friends thought he was the sexiest beanstalk on two legs, but others felt that way about Mick Jagger. Neither Jagger nor Rod Stewart had appealed to me in the slightest.

I regarded pop stars a little contemptuously, having seen from the inside how the music industry manipulated them like pawns on a chess board.

Rod Stewart was playing Los Angeles in March 1975 and Joan Collins and husband Ron Kass, two close friends of mine, persuaded me to join them for his concert at the Forum.

In a melancholy state over my break with Lou, I was reluctant to move out of the house. I did not want to see anyone, or talk with anyone. Joan wouldn't give in.

"Come on, Britt. You've got to pull yourself together," she said, "an evening out will cheer you up."

The Forum was packed as we took our seats and when Rod Stewart came out on stage, in the most poisonous of green suits, the auditorium erupted into scenes of hysteria.

Stewart was much taller than I had first thought. When straightening his back I imagined he was somewhere near six feet tall and I later learned that he suffered from a curvature of the spine which should have been corrected as a child. He had been left humpbacked.

Because of the S-shaped spine one could hardly distinguish his neck but the one advantage of the curvature was that his rear end protruded and no one wiggled quite like Rod on stage.

When the concert was over Joan and Ron led a foray of celebrities backstage to congratulate Rod on his performance and against popping champagne corks we were properly introduced.

Ron and Joan immediately invited Rod to join us for dinner at Luau's.

Rod, an extrovert on stage, was terribly shy in private life and all through dinner he sat coyly at the table like "Little Boy Lost," saying hardly a word.

We went on to singer Cher's house party and it was only then that he began to thaw out.

I got the impression that Rod was intimidated by my image, but slowly he came out of his shell and at Cher's we found a quiet corner and immersed ourselves in conversation. Out of the corner of my eye I caught a glimpse of Ron and Joan smiling towards us, obviously feeling that their matchmaking efforts had succeeded.

By the end of the night I knew that I would have Rod but I wasn't going to be a one-night groupie. My strategy would be entirely different with Rod than with any other of my lovers. There would be no harm in keeping him waiting, because I figured that Rod needed to respect a woman.

That week I saw a lot of Rod and a night or two later we were on Santa Monica Bl. in the vestibule of the Troubador Club.

Rod was heading for trouble. His long-standing English girl friend Dee Harrington had suddenly arrived from London and she had caught up with us.

At first I thought it was just another groupie who had rushed in to the restaurant for Rod's autograph, but then I realized that something was amiss.

"I am going to take the next plane back to London if you don't want me to stay here with you," I heard the English girl tell Rod, her voice desperate.

I turned away. I did not want to get entangled in their exchange. At the same time I was making no claim on Rod, or trying to impair his loyalties. I could not possibly know the state of their relationship and I was not going to intrude. I saw Rod trying to calm the situation, but then Dee was gone and Rod came to join me at the table where I had taken discreet cover. He did not mention the incident.

His composure, in such a moment, was remarkably cool. There was not the slightest trace of anxiety, although I felt strangely to blame when I heard that Dee's melodramatic departure had been the final act in the parting of their ways.

I should not have felt vexed.

Rod would have to establish a set of new principles if ever we were to become involved.

I trusted my men and I could never torture myself with jealousy again. But with Rod it would have been foolish to have turned a blind eye to the trappings around him.

It was at a party at singer Joni Mitchell's that I knew I was weakening.

Bob Dylan and Paul McCartney took over one of Joni's magnificent rooms and began a jam session. They wanted Rod to join them but he could not detach himself from my side.

Later, Rod told friends of that moment.

"I don't think anyone has ever turned down the chance to jam with Bob Dylan before, but I was so much in love with Britt," he said.

It was true. Rod admitted that he was in love with me that night; and I could not easily say I felt less about him. As always, I had fallen in love before anyone could even get out their stop-watch.

From that moment on we were inseparable, kissing and cuddling in our new found passion. We were oblivious to the stares and embarrassment we caused.

It mattered little that our first time in bed together yielded no greater reward than that of any other of my experiences. Perfection, however, was ultimately achieved.

Very soon we were making love three or four times a day. We were like two pieces of interlocking jigsaw and we matched physically. We were both slender, small boned and long legged.

Members of Rod's band said he usually fancied big boobed amazons. I was hardly that, and I asked Rod, "Do you want me to have a boob job?", thinking he must be dissatisfied with my miniature equipment.

Rod was uncomplaining. He thought I was perfect as I stood. He liked my teenage-preserved figure and my long blond hair. I think the little-girl image was different for him and he liked it.

He liked me always to dress in virginal white stockings, panties, petticoat, negligee and peel it all off like the leaves of an artichoke.

And in bed, I wore only "Joy"—his favorite perfume by Patou.

We would make love in all sorts of crazy places. Once, just for the kick of it, we made love on the back seat of my Mercedes which we chose to park in the long, unlit drive of the house belonging to my neighbor

Goldie Hawn—whom I'm sure would have been very understanding if she had found out!

Rod was eighteen months younger than me. At last I was with a man virtually of my own generation. For so much of my life I had been influenced by the father figure. I had missed out so much on my youth.

My early twenties had been stifled by Sellers and his indoctrinations on the immaturity and rashness of youth. With Rod I could go to parties and discos and let my hair down.

Rod had not always been a pop star. The Press relished the fact that he had once worked as a grave-digger, but as far as I gathered Rod only lasted in the job for a week before laying down his spade in preference to his soul.

At least the experience had a therapeutic effect on him. Rod said he was cured from all the complexes he once held about death.

Rod was born in London's Highgate and he was more of a Cockney than anything else; but from his early teens he had developed a genuine patriotism for Scotland which was fired by his father's origins.

His father, Bob Stewart, was born in Scotland but had run away to sea as a boy and later settled across the border. He married a London East End girl named Elsie. Rod was the youngest of their fold of five and he was continually spoilt.

They were a working class family. Bob ran a news-agent's shop until his retirement when he found himself collecting the rents of the houses his pop superstar son had bought as investments. His only pleasure from life, as far as I could see, was his interest in dog racing and his excursions to the betting shop.

Bob was a dour introvert who spoke in clipped sentences. My impression was that he disliked women intensely, although not once did he shrink from his burden in caring for Elsie who was confined to a wheelchair with a weak back although her troubles were unrelated to Rod's. She could walk a few steps, but that was all.

They lived in Highgate, but looked after Rod's mansion at Windsor whenever he was away on tour.

It was a huge manor house only a stone's throw from Windsor Great Park which brought back a flood of memories to me. Its atmosphere was distinctly Victorian and the enormous rooms were a maze of paraphernalia. By far the most bizarre feature of the house was the paneled hall where rich Chinese carvings fought the eye for recognition among a collection of hanging antelope horns and wild animal heads.

I had the feeling that the house had once belonged to a big game hunter or taxidermist. Something like a hundred bird cages housing a variety of exotic tropical stuffed birds occupied the breakfast room, which did little for my appetite.

The red-based Stewart tartan glared from the carpet as well as the wall fabric in the dining room where the immense oak table could comfortably seat twenty-five guests or more.

Obviously some work had been done on the kitchen which was ultra modern, but I could not take easily to its circular layout.

Rod's den was a pool room complete with tartan scarves, soccer pennants and shirts draped from the wall: my young hero was a football fanatic and in the months ahead I would be sitting on many a cold windswept grandstand with him screaming for Scotland. There was a heated indoor swimming pool, walled with giant black and white prints of Rod and above were ten bedrooms, simply furnished and decorated.

We occupied a small and pretty Victorian bedroom, while the adjoining master suite was having a face lift. I thought immediately of Sellers when I first glimpsed one of the many bathrooms. It was all purple! Obviously Rod didn't hold the same superstitions as my ex-husband.

Rod had never lost his schoolboyish love of soccer. Essentially he was a frustrated footballer and he would often play for the Showbiz XI with other soccer-mad celebrities.

Another schoolday passion was evident in the house: his mania for model railways. He had an incredible

track, worthy of Olympia exhibitions, laid out between
two bedrooms, the walling conveniently sawn through
to allow a free run of the lines which passed through
tunnels, stations and plastercast countryside.

It was a magnificent house with paddocks and a tennis court in the manicured grounds. No doubt in earlier
times baronial houses of this dimension belonged to the
aristocracy, but in England the demise of traditional
society meant such properties fell into the hands of the
new rich: the unwelcome pop fraternity.

I was aware that Dee Harrington had once lived there,
but her possessions had magically disappeared from the
scene by the time I arrived. I stayed there when not
using my London flat.

Sometimes Rod's folks would make a slip of the
tongue and call me Dee but I didn't mind. While his
wheelchair bound mother was a stern woman, I got
along with her very well and his father I think I came to
understand once I realized his distrust of women. Rod's
dad even came to bring me tea in bed!

Rod never really mentioned Dee and when he did he
cruelly painted her as having been no more than his
housekeeper who slept with him whenever the whim
took him.

"Dee knew I had other women," Rod told me early
on, "but she didn't mind."

I looked at him straight between the eyes.

"Then that's where I am very different," I said. "I
would mind a great deal. In fact, if you screw another
woman while you're with me, I'll chop off your balls."

Rod's face puckered with fear. He knew that I meant
every word.

There had been many past affairs in Rod's life. He
admitted that he had an illegitimate child by a Bristol
beatnik which was later adopted.

"She was a pretty little thing, but just like any other
baby," said Rod, who made the token gesture of seeing
the child.

When launched into the pop world, Rod found that
girls and groupies came easily. Even those in more
distant and sophisticated areas came within his grasp.

One of them was a well known English actress. But many of Rod's so called "romances" were embroidered just to stimulate publicity.

His friendships were heavily fabricated and the situations exploited by Rod's personal publicist, a lackey with the tongue twisting name of Tony Toon.

Toon would indulge in the slickest and cheapest of gimmicks in order to gain his client as much space as possible in the British Press.

Rod would only have to burp and we would cry out, "Why isn't that on the front page, Tony?"

He would hover around us like a hawk and occasionally Rod would throw down a few crumbs as though feeding a pigeon and Tony Toon would peck them up. He was totally subservient and hero-worshipped Rod.

Sometimes he would exceed his authority and Rod would bawl him out, but these occasions were rare. Rod happily went along with all the gimmicks although I thought he was ill-advised in backing Toon's story that he had once stood up President Ford's daughter on a date.

"It wasn't true. I didn't stand her up. I just couldn't get back to Washington from my tour in time to take her out," explained Rod, shrugging his shoulders. "I want the publicity and Tony's only doing his job."

His face brightened, "But it made the front page everywhere and that's why I employ him."

Tony's duties didn't end there, as far as I could gather. In so many respects I felt pity for him. Tony was nothing more than Rod's handyman.

Whenever Rod couldn't face the truth, or had something unpleasant to say to someone, then he would delegate the task to the wretched, luckless Tony Toon.

Rod's personal manager Billy Gaff stayed at a convenient arm's length and only came into view when touring concert program or business matters were concerned.

So it was left to Tony Toon to act as the go-between and the bricks often flew.

Before I was on the scene Toon would have to

organize the groupies outside the door. Rod told me once Tony was rash enough to pay a hooker a hundred dollars in New York to go to Rod's bedroom.

Rod's sense of pride was damaged and he remained sore about it.

"That's the closest I got to sacking him," Rod said. "Me *paying* for it . . . ?"

Tony, willowy thin and in his early thirties, didn't seem to have a private life of his own and if he did he kept it away from us.

My alliance with Rod was Heaven-sent as far as Tony was concerned. We were the "hottest" couple in the world, in terms of news-media exposure, and Tony glorified in us, describing us as the "Burton and Taylor" of the 'seventies.

I found myself almost echoing Tony's publicity blurbs and playing on the Burton and Taylor theme. What I lacked in diamonds—and it became transparently obvious that Rod wasn't going to give me any—I compensated for by wearing the gaudiest of costumes to match those of my new pop hero.

In our relationship it was Rod who wore the jewelry. I bought him an eye-catching piece of carved jade mounted on a delicate gold chain and another chain with the replica of a mouth fashioned in diamonds, a symbol of Rod's own pouting lips. I also gave him a Cartier watch and he would borrow my gold chains, tethering them from one pocket of his waistcoat to another with safety pins. Unfortunately, he lost most of the jewelry including two of my chains, but personal losses count for little when life is conducted out on the road.

Rod wanted to set up home together, but for the first six months I refused to live with him. I wanted him to be sure to know the extent of his commitment. A woman with two children to support would present a burden to any man: I was well aware of this situation. I didn't doubt that Rod loved me, but could he really accept my children too?

Rod got along well with the children and he didn't

regard them as being a lead-weight to our relationship at all.

"It's like starting out with a ready made family," he would insist, "and it will be good to have kids around the house. A home isn't a home without kids . . ."

I had to think carefully. It wasn't just the question of two children but I had to allow for their friends too.

Tatum O'Neal was already a Rod Stewart fan and she looked so much more grown up than my daughter, wearing high heeled shoes, see through dresses and the latest teenage trends. In Ryan's daughter I could see the teeny bopper emerging and very soon I would have to come to terms with it in Victoria.

I told Rod that we should really think more seriously about setting up home on a permanent basis and as the weeks sped past he became more and more agitated that we were not living together.

I was still maintaining my independence at Stone Canyon and I think this irritated Rod considerably because he knew the house belonged to my last lover Lou through whose benevolence I was living there.

While Rod insisted that he accepted my past, he could not resist making the odd jibe about it.

He would refer to Lou as "the Rabbi" and if Sellers ever got mentioned he would be prompted to remark, "That *old* man of yours . . ." Then he would preen, "Aren't you lucky to have someone at last who is so young and gorgeous?"

Rod didn't like old ties, although it took him a considerable time to shake free from Dee Harrington who pestered him with calls and then laid claim to a horse kept in Rod's paddocks at his house in Windsor.

"Why don't you give it to Dee?" I said to him one day. "She deserves it. What else has she got from you?"

Rod parted reluctantly with the horse and Dee's phone calls petered out.

It was not until August that I finally agreed to live with Rod. He had convinced me that we would spend our entire future together. We were to be man and wife in every respect and we regarded the documentation as extraneous to the consuming force of our love. We made a pledge to be loyal to one another, echoed by Rod in America's *Time* magazine, "We've got a pact to be faithful to each other." We started househunting in earnest. We found one property overlooking Sunset Boulevard but the negotiations fell through at a late hour.

It was judicious. An empty mansion in Carolwood Drive, whose owners never realized its potential, came into our grasp. We knew that we had found the house of our dreams.

Rod paid 750,000 dollars for the twenty roomed, cloistered mansion and when asking me to redesign its interior from beginning to end he opened a special account for me, the "Carolwood Account" with the City National Bank into which he paid 100,000 dollars from his record royalties.

It was a huge task and I set about making sketches of every room, planning its decor and color schemes so that a distinguishable influence could be detected in the house from the moment one entered the front door.

Rod, to my utter delight, had fallen in love with art nouveau and I was able to ship in lamps, candelabra, mirrors and many other furnishings from Paris. From Sotheby's in Los Angeles we bought £6,000 worth of Old Masters. Crockery, linen and cutlery came from London, New York and Hong Kong.

Before we began we had to evict some wild cats who had made their home on the terrace outside one of the first floor bathrooms and the house, infested with bugs of all descriptions, had to be fumigated.

Builders, decorators and designers descended on us. So did the furnishings. From Anthony Redmile in London came a collection of silver artichoke tables, a pair of pelicans made of ostrich eggs, a couple of sofas backed with elephant tusks and upholstered in cowhide, and other *objets d'art*.

Gradually the house was transformed. The major undertaking, at a cost of 30,000 dollars alone, was the entire wood paneling of our living room which was the size of a basketball hall!

Above were six bedrooms and as many bathrooms

and there was an intercommunicating lift between the two floors, but an unremedied fault kept it out of service. It was as well because the lift would have run straight into my upstairs loo and Rod didn't like the idea of any of our guests finding me with my knickers down!

It took several months to complete the house but in the end it resembled our dream—like a shrine of our love, set amid the aromatic scent of gardenias and flowering shrubs beautifying the two and a half acres of grounds providing us with a swimming pool and paddle tennis court.

I had never been happier. And with Rod I found total unison.

Rod loved playing the host at Carolwood. We had a housekeeper but Rod enjoyed helping me to arrange the meals. He would lay out the tablecloth, the cutlery and the wine glasses. He would open the wine in time for it to acquire room temperature or if it was to be champagne then he would prepare the ice bucket which was an exotic affair with sculptured nudes and candleholders protruding from its rim.

I would cook the meal and prepare a menu. Rod's passion was escargot but he was not tempted by anything more exotic and he was always happier with liver or steak and kidney pie.

My own tastes were equally simple, preferring fish or chicken as I had become a semi-vegetarian after facing too many Texan sized steaks!

Whether we expected guests or not we would always make a point of dressing for dinner.

Rod would put on a tuxedo and I would climb into an evening gown and in our own candlelit dining room we created a more romantic ambience than we could have found in any restaurant.

There was a staff cottage in the grounds and I made this very comfortable for Tony Toon to move into. Tony, who acted as Rod's secretary as well as his publicist, only came into the main house when he was invited but every morning he would shuffle into the kitchen with a cigarette dangling from his lips and wearing a faded blue toweling dressing gown to make himself a pot of tea. Then he would shuffle out again, knowing better than to drop the ash from his cigarette. To discourage smokers I never kept ashtrays on view.

We had four cars in the garage. I was then driving a Mercedes which Lou had given me to replace my old Volkswagen and Rod, whose penchant for cars was almost as ingrained as Sellers's, kept an A.C. Cobra, and Excalibur and a £26,000 Lamborghini Countach which he air freighted from Rome to Los Angeles at a cost of £2,000.

This then was our home and at this stage we were the envy of Hollywood. We had everything going for us.

Each day brought fresh happiness and we jokingly regarded Monday mornings as the weekly "anniversary" of our first meeting.

Whoever was the first to wake would sing "The Wedding Song" to the other. Rod may have started this little innovation, I don't know and I can't really remember, but it showed how much gratitude we felt for finding one another.

We made love at all hours of the night and day and we refused to be inconvenienced by guests.

Barbecue meals by the pool were always popular but we would not think twice about leaving our guests to chew on their spare ribs and their conjectures while we sought the refuge of our bedroom to make love maybe for the second or third time of the day, trying to set fresh records on the previous day's accomplishments in bed.

Our bedroom was a love nest in every sense of the phrase, blue ribbons softening the brass hardware to convey the cosiness of a child's cot.

Rod regarded every orgasm as a testimony of his love for me.

Greater love has no man!

— *fifteen* —

THERE was an underlying motive behind Rod's move to Los Angeles that was carefully concealed for a long period for fear it should harm his "patriotic" image.

Rod's accountants had advised his departure from Britain because of tax reasons. Already California was something of a colony of British tax exiles but Rod hated the idea of quitting his native land.

He did not want his loyal fans to think that he was turning his back on them or letting them down; as an artist he was sensitive and conscious of their feelings.

Besides, he was at the peak of his popularity in Britain while in America he was not then the superstar that he is today. Ironically, he found that in the States he was having to challenge the chart domination of his contemporary and rival, Elton John. They were deadly enemies and joyous friends.

It was Elton who advised Rod to turn down a major role in the pop opera *Tommy* only to walk into the vacant part himself.

Rod was flabbergasted. "He psyched me out of the part," he said, but laughing at his own error of judgment.

In so many ways Rod envied Elton who stayed in Britain, gritted his teeth in the face of crippling taxes and even became chairman of Watford Football Club.

Elton, like Rod, was a football fanatic but for Rod the green soccer parks were just a memory of what might have been.

When he wanted to see the England v. Scotland football international he didn't dare risk setting foot in London. So he decided to go into Dublin from Los Angeles
and watch the match on television. Not alone, I hasten
to add. Rod flew in his parents and other relatives to
share his ringside television seat in his Dublin hotel.

On another occasion I was traveling with Rod on a
promotional trip to Ireland when our plane was diverted
through London. Again Rod's residency, or rather the
question of it, was placed in some jeopardy. If he passed
through the immigration barrier to catch the waiting
domestic flight to Dublin it meant that he might be
detained, for tax demands were then disputed by him. It
was said that £750,000 was involved but Rod doubted
it. Nevertheless he was grateful for my help. As a
Swedish national I was able to pass through the barrier
and telephone his London lawyer to get advice on his
position which was precisely as we suspected. Once Rod
crossed through immigration control he could be
detained but remaining in the "transfer" section he was
safe as he had made no legal entry into the country. I
bought two tickets at the Dutch airlines desk for Am-
sterdam and we re-routed our trip to Ireland even
though this meant postponing engagements there for
twenty-four hours.

Rod was naturally rankled by the restrictions of being
a tax exile and the only strength he gained was in the
consolation that after one year's residency in Los
Angeles he could spend sixty days in Britain in suc-
ceeding years.

Rod served that year like a penal sentence and even
the Californian sunshine and all the trappings of his success could not make him wipe out the memory of
English pubs, sausages and football!

In one of my lone excursions from London to Los
Angeles I took in six four-pint cans of English bitter for
Rod to help him over any homesickness he might have
been feeling.

We were madly in love and Rod could not bear those
moments when we were apart and he would fly all over

the world just to be with me.

He once took a flight on Concorde from New York to Paris to catch up with me and we spent a romantic four days wandering the streets hand-in-hand, kissing under old lanterns and strolling by the river.

Rod, pampered by so many women, was still sentimental enough to pursue these romantic pastimes and at an earlier point we had driven overland to the South of France in his Excalibur, discovering quiet villages and vineyards on our way and at one interval making love beneath a stone-bridge at sunset. We were even marooned at sea on that particular expedition when our boat ran out of fuel and we drifted for nearly four hours before we were rescued, still in our swimwear and night rapidly descending upon us.

There was yet another occasion when Rod flew to surprise me in New York and actually located me in a pharmacy next to my hotel. He put his hands over my eyes and I thought for one fearful moment that I was about to be mugged, only to spin round into Rod's arms.

Like most men who figured in my life Rod was jealous of my past associations and I would never conduct a telephone conversation with Lou in front of him, although it was frequently necessary to talk to Lou because of Nicholai.

I was totally committed to Rod and I rejected the advances of many men while I was with him.

Before I had met Rod I worked on a pilot for the *Six Million Dollar Man* with Lee Majors. Lee, having taken the beautiful Farrah Fawcett as a bride, felt his macho image was a compelling influence on any woman.

I must have blunted his ego considerably during the shooting of that pilot and Lee was needled when I returned to Universal Studios later to tell him Rod Stewart was more my kind of man.

Good luck to Farrah but men in the mold of Lee Majors are not for me. I can't cope with them.

Rod may not have been the epitome of manhood but he had certain qualities that were appealing to me and when we were in the Philippines together I saw so many facets of his nature emerge.

I was shooting a film there, *High Velocity* with Ben Gazzara and Keenan Wynn and for once Rod had to take a back seat while I fulfilled the schedule.

It was very hot and humid and when I was working Rod browsed around our hotel, forming a strong bond of friendship with Nicholai whose second birthday we celebrated in Manila.

Nicholai's nanny Britt Inger had come with us and they shared a room opposite the one I occupied with Rod.

Unfortunately, the necessity of having air conditioning switched on in our rooms caused us all to develop sinus troubles and my own condition worsened in the blast of other air conditioning units in the film studios. The pain was agonizing and we had to summon a doctor in the middle of the night to give injections. But our stay in Manila was not without its funnier moments.

Whenever we dined out, Rod would book us into a restaurant as "Mr. and Mrs. Cockforth" which would always cause amusement when we were recognized, but at least it had the desired effect of shaking off the pursuing Press who rarely lost sight of us in their camera lens.

Late at night we danced in the discotheques of Manila with all the abandon of two young people in love, but soon after midnight the band would abruptly stop and pack away its instruments because of a political curfew. Our chauffeur was hard pressed some nights to get us back safely to our hotel to beat the curfew ban and invariably he would have to sleep in his car in the hotel's garage rather than risk driving home and finding himself the target of the militia.

By day we tried to explore as much of the Philippines as we could. We discovered, three hours' drive out of Manila, a rain forest where we could swim in the hot and cold mineral pools and on one occasion Rod dived in wearing a spare pair of my bikini briefs because he had forgotten to bring his own trunks.

Rod was never self-conscious about those kind of things. Very often he chose to wear my cotton panties on stage. Not only were they more comfortable for him, but they were seamless and invisible beneath his skin-tight trousers.

Unlike most of the male breed Rod was never embarrassed by the natural body functions. He would drift in and out of the bathroom, irrespective of what I was doing in there. When I was in sudden need of Tampax he organized a search at every pharmacy and market stall in the Philippines, offering black-market bribes for this apparently rare product in such a remote outpost.

The sight of Rod trying to explain the meaning of Tampax to a Filipino at a trading hut is one I shall not forget easily.

"What do you say it is, mister? A fish? No. Ah, you mean a car . . . No, mister, I cannot get this make," said the man, his face lined with bewilderment.

Some of the Filipinos thought we were asking for drugs and would turn tail.

Four days later Rod returned triumphant if seething with exasperation from his Tampax expedition on my behalf, having found a massive stock of them in the souvenir shop in the basement of our own hotel!

"Who would think of finding them in a souvenir shop along with the elephant tusks?" cried Rod in disgust.

Rod stayed two weeks in the Philippines with me during the six week film schedule and he then returned to Los Angeles where he laid down the tracks of his single "Sailing" which had been composed by the Sutherland Brothers.

The haunting, plaintive melody of the song brought tears to Rod's eyes; he thought it was one of the most beautiful tracks he had ever heard and "Sailing" was not only to become No. 1 in Britain but it also became the theme song for the British television series, *Warship*.

I thought it was a very pretty song, but I had always preferred his earlier hit "Maggie May."

To the delight of Rod's record bosses at Warner

Brothers, I agreed to accompany him on a promotional tour that whisked us across America and to the Continent.

We faced Press conferences one after another and never before had an unmarried couple put their private lives so much on the line.

The newsmen cared little about Rod's music.

Constantly we were asked, "When are you going to marry?" and "Are you going to have children?"

There were times when we felt like hiding from the non-stop inquisition. Once Rod tore up a reporter's notes but his temper really exploded in Chicago because I answered more questions than he felt necessary.

"When they ask about our private lives, tell them to get stuffed," yelled Rod, back in our suite. "It's none of their bloody business."

I was furious.

"How can you say that when you're throwing a Press conference?" I retorted. "Once you've invited them, they are entitled to ask any question they like. If you don't want people to ask about our lives together then you should never have agreed to the tour. Remember, the only reason I came was because of you."

Rod grabbed me by the shoulders and started screaming, "You do as you're damn well told," adding a profusion of expletives.

Wack! My face stung as his hand flew. I clenched my fist and sloshed him back as hard as I could. We were all over the bedroom, turning over table lamps and furniture. It was like a Western bar-room brawl and suddenly my black and silver lace dress was ripped from my body. At that point I burst into tears and collapsed onto the bed. Rod quivered with self-reproach and fell limply beside me, and began to cry himself.

"I'm sorry, Britt. Please forgive me," he said, knowing that I was feeling bruised and battered from his beating.

I could not hold it against him for long. I realized that we were the victims of constant Press harassment, invited or otherwise. We were like two people who had been dropped into an ocean-sized goldfish bowl.

Rod tried to make up for things the next day in New York. He bought me an exquisite new Ted Lapidus gown to replace the one he had ruined.

For Rod that was a gesture of overwhelming proportions.

He paid nearly 400 dollars for the dress and it took him some time to recover. The only other present he gave me through our entire relationship was a diamond bracelet.

If any truth existed of Scottish meanness, then Rod was its manifestation.

At first I tried not to overreact to his appalling stinginess. I felt that his cautious ways with money resulted from his working-class background.

My substantial funds, recovered after near bankruptcy, were eroded again during my days with Rod because I would rather pay for things myself than ask him for the money.

It was true he had bought our house on Carolwood. But the day to day running of the house fell to me and I could not charge all of the bills to Rod. He even protested bitterly if I didn't buy the groceries at the cheapest store in town!

I also paid Rod a hundred dollars a month for the upkeep of my two children while we lived in the household together and, of course, I took care of the nanny's wages.

Rod sulked if he felt I was spending too much money in the house and I recall how he primed Tony Toon to warn me that I would have to cut down on the domestic bills.

I sent Tony packing with the rebuke, "Tell Rod that if he stopped putting the bloody liquor bill on my household account then maybe I could manage a little better."

Rod could not protest. There was always a pack of musicians and hangers-on in the house and they all had to be fed and wined: I was not going to absorb those bills under any circumstances.

Rod liked to play the genial dinner host but he was at his most magnanimous if others were picking up the tab.

From time to time Warner Brothers would get reminded by Tony Toon that a dinner party was expected of them, whereupon an invitation would immediately follow.

Rod would order the most exotic food, including his favorite escargot, and he would ask for the most extravagant wines and liqueurs.

Often I would quietly wonder whether Warner Brothers deducted the cost of these grandiose affairs from Rod's record royalties. I could have understood it if they did.

Birthdays and seasonal festivities rarely prompted Rod to buy presents. In order for him not to feel any kind of embarrassment among his friends and relatives, I would have to buy the necessary gifts and sign the card in his name.

One Christmas I gave Rod a 2,000 dollar canvas, the original of a satirical picture produced in a rock'n roll Who's Who, showing him as drunk as a skunk being arrested by an English bobby.

The picture appealed to Rod's sense of humor and he loved it, but it didn't touch him sufficiently to open his purse strings to buy me a present in return. He was a little hard pressed even to utter "Happy Christmas darling."

When Rod was asked by the famous American columnist Earl Wilson about my noted absence from some New York occasion he replied, "The Missus? She's out spending *my* money." Some hope!

Rod didn't ever keep "ready" money on him. When he went out in the morning he would often cadge a ten dollar or even hundred dollar note from me or he would borrow in an emergency from his lurking shadow Tony Toon.

I am sure that Tony got his money back but Rod wouldn't think about repaying me, believing maybe the money came out of some kind of general till. A similar attitude existed towards the household bills. They would pile up in a bottom drawer and lie around for months.

It was not until we got a lawyer's letter threatening court action that Rod reluctantly coughed up.

Our telephone bill was always a headache. I would have to write and query the bill in order to "buy" time hoping that Rod would pay in the interim. But the ploy didn't always work. Once all three of our lines were cut off and we had to pay 240 dollars to get them plugged back in again.

The only time through our relationship that I can actually recall Rod going on a spending spree was on a trip to Paris, but even then he ran true to character. Every item he bought was something that he could personally wear or use.

That I was able to persuade him to buy some extra furnishings for our home was a miracle.

When his record company were throwing a party I hinted that he might like to buy me something exotic to go out in, but Rod said "No, it's not worth it" and to maintain appearances I ended up buying my own ensemble in the antique dress market.

I often wondered whether Rod's meanness was inherited from his parents whose aging years made them very sparing.

Perhaps I was too tolerant of his miserliness, but I was so much in love with him that it wasn't an issue on which I was prepared to make a stand. In some ways I regret I was his willing accomplice.

When Rod complained of tension and pressures, I suggested massage to relax him. Incongruous as it seemed, he was shy, but after his first session with my masseuse, he was extolling the benefits he felt from regular massage treatment. Because I was foolish enough to pick up the first tab, Rod clearly thought I was committed to settle the rest.

There were areas in which I actually saved him money by waiving the services of a valet and make-up girl when he was on tour.

I would spend hours darning and mending his stage

costumes, mutilated by his footlight gyrations and more especially by fans who would rip his clothes to shreds in their quest for souvenirs.

When his shirts and trousers needed pressing, as well as his scarves, Rod would toss them to me as I bent over an ironing board. It was as if I worked in a dry cleaner's steam room. I would also make him up both on tour and in private life.

I would pencil a thin black line round his nugget-brown eyes and dab in matching brown shadow above the eyes which I would highlight with mascara. The process was more elaborate for his stage appearances, and then I would add rouge and sealing powder. Ultimately he would resemble a marionette.

For social occasions we revived the fashion trends of the movie star days of the 'thirties and modeled ourselves on Fred Astaire and Ginger Rogers. We had been fascinated by all their old films frequently shown on television. I wore antique dresses of that period and Rod swaggered out in a tuxedo trailing one of his long scarves. I even managed to find an authentic 'thirties straw boater for him at Harold's Place, a store filled with memorabilia in Beverly Hills.

Early in our relationship Rod had regarded me as some kind of pristine goddess who could do no wrong: a living, breathing symbol that he alone worshipped.

Those around him were made to treat me with the highest respect. Once Rod sacked a roadie for swearing in my presence and he was only reinstated at my pleading.

Rod, always conscious of his humble beginnings, was grateful to me for filling his life with an appreciation of culture and the arts.

I was a walking encyclopedia on where to dress, where to dine and where to find antiquity.

I had shown Rod, my proletarian bard, a new style of living but he was never to shake himself free from the tawdrier facets of his environment.

— *sixteen* —

I HAD starred in many movies of a bizarre and lurid nature. But none can compare with my mindbending experiences out on the road with Rod.

Life, I discovered, can deteriorate to a primitive, medieval level when traveling with a rock band.

You lose all sense of time; sleep becomes a rare commodity and the values held most precious begin to crumble like dust.

Rod and The Faces' entourage ran to some thirty personnel encompassing musicians, technicians, engineers, lighting men and the roadies who looked after the baggage and equipment. There was something of a circus element about it.

The amplifying equipment, weighing several tons, was trundled from one city to another over thousands of miles and into different Continents over a period of several weeks.

Jet planes were chartered with the ease of a pedestrian hailing a cab; while travel agents would be harassed to find suitable accommodation for all members of the party and top class hotels for its stars.

By reputation rock bands aren't welcome in too many places and I was soon to find out the reasons for myself. Physical exhaustion coupled with the pressures of traveling have a frightening effect on the mental state of the individual.

Seeing some of Rod's men throw breakfast trays out of their hotel windows and ripping out telephone lines was only the beginning. I saw hotel rooms torn apart.

Once in Hawaii I was the unwitting cause of one such ritual. We were late in vacating a suite which was needed by the incoming Helen Reddy and her party.

Our plane was due out at 1:00 p.m. and I was frantically packing Rod's bags for him while he and the roadies were having a last minute beer on the beach.

Suddenly there was a rap on the door and when I answered it a small abusive man started ordering me to get out of the suite. He just terrified me and I was so scared that I called the switchboard to have Rod paged.

Rod and the roadies rushed back and they dealt with the matter in their own way. Rod hissed one word —"Destroy" and the roadies were unleashed like a pack of hounddogs.

They removed the legs from the bed, they took out the television tube, they detached the spray from the shower, they stuffed towels down the toilet, they unplugged the telephones and effectively defused the suite.

When, twenty minutes later, we moved out Rod was mouthing, "The next time they ask us to leave, maybe they'll be more courteous."

The extraordinary thing was that they were. Rod and I returned to the same hotel a few months later and they put flowers and fruit in our room and bottles of liquor. The earlier incident was not mentioned and whether it had all been smoothed over by Rod's manager Billy Gaff, I did not know.

When hotels claimed reimbursement for damaged property it was Billy who made amends. Sometimes we would have to fork out three or four thousand dollars by way of compensation.

The profits of Rod's tours were clipped heavily by incidents like these, but I saw greater sums paid out on the supply of cocaine, which became the natural substitute for food and booze in the small hours when hotel restaurants were closed.

Many members of Rod's entourage appeared to survive alone on a daily ration of drugs and like all nocturnal people they were sitting targets for the "pushers."

Rod was wary about the excessive use of cocaine, having once rescued a musician on the verge of dying from an overdose. Rod kept the stricken boy walking up and down all night long, not allowing him to sleep or pass into a coma.

In any event, Rod was still fanatical about fitness and he regarded drugs with suspicion and saw them as a threat.

"Pot" did not appeal to him, having never smoked. His one experiment with heroin caused him to vomit. The thought of plunging a needle into a vein was repugnant to him.

I stayed carefully on the sidelines to the late night revelries, only participating from time to time in a token way to show that I was not condemning anyone for their habits.

Drugs were a minor hazard on the road for me, against the problems caused by groupies.

Every band has its legion of groupies and Rod's outfit was besieged by them. They came in all nationalities and creeds.

Some of them were very beautiful girls. Others, as Rod often said, were "scrubbers," but the surprising batch were respectable married women, who wanted to live out their sexual fantasies with a pop star. Any star!

I was more bewildered by groupies than I could find myself jealous of them. They would lay siege on the stage door, or the hotel, and throw themselves at Rod, kissing and groping him as though he was some sort of sexual messiah.

Every exit made from a concert hall would be like running a gauntlet from almost as many groupies as genuine fans.

We eluded a posse on one occasion in West Virginia but one blond groupie managed to steal past security at our hotel and present herself at our door in the middle of the night. I thought it was one of the guards and when I opened the door she almost brushed past me.

Her eyes were glazed and she cried, "Where's Rod? I'm going to screw him." I slammed the door in her face and yanked out the telephone line so that we would not be disturbed anymore. All night long I had taken calls from fans telling me how much they loved Rod and when would I do the decent thing and get the hell out of his life? Some fans were more frightening. They threatened to give me cocaine with broken glass in it and if I didn't take coke then they would "doctor" my cold cream which would have a nasty effect on my face.

Rod's fan letters were equally incredible. Some girls would actually address their letters to me and ask me to describe Rod's anatomy to them in detail! "Draw IT for us," one letter urged. Other fans would tell Rod of the exciting sex life he was missing out on by being with me!

Fortunately groupies no longer had any place in Rod's life and he treated them disdainfully.

His real affection was reserved for the fans who appreciated his music and on stage Rod was totally professional. Every concert was like a première performance. Nothing could be out of place.

We were in America when one of the equipment trucks broke down before an open air gig in California. More than 50,000 fans were packed into the stadium but Rod refused to go on with substitute equipment that had been rented at the eleventh hour.

"The sound will be awful," he said, "we can't go on like that."

Billy Gaff was desperate. The fans were ready to tear the stadium to bits. Billy called in record boss Joe Smith who pleaded with Rod to change his mind. He told Rod, "You can't let the fans down. They've paid up to ten bucks to get in to see you. What will they think of you if you don't appear? It will be a thousand times worse out there."

Rod capitulated and any fears he had of bad sound reproduction were drowned in the overwhelming cheers of the fans.

Rod was always nervous before a performance. When Mick and Bianca Jagger dropped in on his trailer to

New York before a gig he was distinctly cold and off-hand for no reason. We were all friends and I could not understand his coolness.

But later in London, when Rod was appearing at the Olympia, the reason became more transparent. I realized that Rod was actually jealous of Jagger, who still held the throne as the world's No. 1 rock star.

Rod's long awaited return to London possibly marked the biggest triumph of his career. Every concert at Olympia was sold out months before and stars and celebrities found themselves in the same position as other fans, having to buy blackmarket tickets from the touts outside the doors.

But despite this Rod was plagued by his own insecurity and when Mick Jagger and Keith Richards asked for tickets he deliberately snubbed them. His secretary Doris Tyler was instructed to tell them, "There are no tickets available. We're sorry."

Mick said, "Okay, we understand. Then give us a couple of backstage passes and we'll drift in that way."

To my amazement Rod even refused them that request. It was breaking with all pop code ethics.

Artists were in the habit of crashing in on each other. Rod even prepared for that eventuality, just in case Mick and Keith dropped in without passes. So he ordered extra security guards at all doors and no one was allowed in without the authentic pass.

I don't think anyone in Rod's camp could understand his attitude. For the first time in his life Tony Toon was speechless. To try and reason with Rod when he was in that kind of mood was a fruitless exercise.

On stage Rod could hold his audiences in a state of euphoria. The only comment I made to him was that I would have been proud for any of my friends, or even rivals, to have seen me basking in that kind of aura.

I asked him, "Do you really have anything to fear from anybody else after this?"

Rod ignored my remark, even though I was transferring the rock'n roll throne to his head.

The massive security clampdown on Mick and Keith

continued, and two nights later even those holding valid passes were barred at the door.

I was stopped as I was escorting Rod's parents through.

"I am sorry Miss Ekland," apologized the guard, "but Mr. Stewart is refusing entry to everyone . . ."

I replied firmly. "You may refuse entry to me but do you really want the responsibility of saying 'No' to Mr. Stewart's parents?"

The security man shuffled uncomfortably as he gazed at Rod's mother who was sat upright in her wheel-chair.

"Okay, I'll go and get advice," grunted the guard.

Pete Buckland, the chief roadie returned with him and was full of apologies when allowing us entry.

"I'm sorry Britt. I don't know what is wrong with Rod. When he said keep everyone out he didn't see that applying to you and his folks but if you give a security man his instructions he's going to carry them out to the letter . . ."

I could easily have gone to Rod's dressing room and raised the roof but I chose not to. Rod liked to be left in private, with the band, an hour before any show, so that he was mentally prepared for his performance. The incident was best forgotten.

Rod remained unrepentant about snubbing Mick Jagger and Keith Richards and when we got to Australia he cold-shouldered Abba the Swedish group by refusing to let them use the giant video screen that was part of his equipment. They were appearing in concert only twenty-four hours after Rod but he wouldn't leave the screen in place for them and he ordered it to be dismantled.

Like all singers Rod suffered perpetual nightmares over the possible loss of his voice. It became more than a nightmare; it developed into a paranoia.

His gravel voice was strong, natural and resilient in texture, but Rod would conjure ill-thoughts as to its endurance.

When recording an album in Los Angeles, he came home clutching his throat. His face was a mask of anguish.

For a second I thought he was dying or something quite dreadful had happened in the studio to him.

"My voice, Britt," he croaked. "It's gone. I can't talk, I can't sing . . . this is it."

Over the next few hours he totally convinced himself that he had lost his voice forever. I summoned the doctor whose preliminary examination was followed with tests in the clinic the next morning.

The tests were negative and I suspected that Rod's "loss of voice" was as imaginary as Lou's illness had been. It existed purely in the mind, brought about by gathering tensions.

Rod blamed the Los Angeles smog, so producer Tom Dowd suggested that it might be wiser to cut the album in Colorado at the Caribou Ranch Studios where many stars, including Elton John, liked to record.

But nothing happened. Still Rod's voice failed to return so Tom thought we might try Miami. Into Florida we all flew but even the sunshine could not entice a warble from Rod's throat.

The exercise had cost thousands of dollars and the irony of the situation was that only when we were back in Los Angeles did Rod's voice finally spark into life and it was there the album was completed.

In fairness to Rod the demands on his voice were enormous and recording an album, or undertaking a concert tour, increased the threat of laryngitis. The symptoms were real enough.

In Europe the vocal cords again caused Rod a lot of worry and he canceled a Paris engagement, saying he would save his voice for London.

I wondered whether the real reason for the cancellation was not motivated by the fact that only half of the 8,000 seats in Paris had been pre-sold.

On the day of an important television show in London before a live audience he was lying in bed complaining that he had lost all feeling in his arms and legs.

"I can't move," he groaned. "I've had it . . ."

It caused an immediate crisis and management and television executives descended on us in a state of panic.

I called my doctor who provided what he termed the "reluctant" solution. He gave Rod a shot of cortisone which completely obliterated the pain he felt in his body. Two hours later Rod was on stage and as far as the audience was concerned he was in top form.

We faced a similar occurrence in Hollywood when Rod was due to make an appearance at the "Rocky" awards.

Rod took to his bed with a bout of flu and refused to move, despite the pleas of those around him.

Again I saw his sickness as purely psychosomatic, formed in the cauldron of so many pressures. I knew the signs. I had seen them manifest themselves similarly in, Sellers.

It was not always easy to sympathize with Rod and often, in order to jolt him out of his maladies, I suggested he might take an acupuncture cure!

Before the Australian tour I was feeling at a low ebb myself and a friend thought the best remedy would be to submit myself to the needles of a Chinese acupuncturist. I did and my nanny who popped in through the door during the ten-day treatment thought I resembled a hedgehog! I had needles sticking out from all parts of my body!

Rod was always such a bad patient. I once convinced him that he should have treatment for his spinal curvature and he was put into traction. But in the end Rod lost patience with it all. He terminated the sessions, despite my warnings that he would come to regret it in old age when the effects of the condition would grow worse.

Rod and The Faces went their separate ways just before Christmas 1975. The Faces put the split down to Rod's burning ego and some may have suspected that I had something to do with the decision, but I was not involved at all. It had been a matter of speculation in the trade Press for many months.

Rod had already recorded a solo album, "Atlantic Crossing," and this had naturally caused unconcealed bitterness among The Faces. It was clear to everyone that a split would come.

It was the timing of the announcement that really broke all ties. Rod reeled out the message through his mouthpiece Tony Toon just prior to a planned Australian tour and he attempted to switch the blame for the split on to the shoulders of Ronnie Wood, who was on "lease-loan" to the Rolling Stones. It was a subtle piece of fabrication but it didn't stick. Ian McLaglen and the other members of the group hit back with attacks on Rod, who was too busy mapping his own future then, to backtrack on the past.

Rod was already in the studios preparing his next album, and for the single, "Tonight's The Night," he surprised me by asking me to do a "voice over" in French in the final line of the lyrics.

At first I thought he actually wanted me to sing on the record.

"I can't sing, I've got a lousy voice," I told him honestly.

"You won't have to sing, you'll just talk to the music," said Rod, who indicated that he might invite singer Stevie Nicks of Fleetwood Mac to do it if I refused.

"Okay, I'll do it," I said, feeling suddenly susceptible.

The song was about a young virgin who was about to be deflowered: and I was to play the sobbing girl uttering "Mon Dieu" in French, by which Rod hoped he would crack the French market with his records.

The recording went without a hitch and I was left thinking that had I been able to sing I might have been more successful in music, always a passion with me, than on the boards as an actress.

The record was a huge success all over the world and the track helped sell Rod's simultaneous album "A Night on The Town."

Warner Brothers organized concerts, personal appearances and promotional exercises in America and in

Europe and we cut a video tape clip for television pop shows.

By now Rod was preening to the newspapers, "We've got more power as a rock'n roll twosome than Peter Wolf and Faye Dunaway, Paul and Linda McCartney, Mick and Bianca Jagger . . . we're the only two not married."

Our globe-trotting sales tour brought a family reunion for me in Stockholm where my brother Kalle then managed the city's most popular record shop. He had completely covered the store's windows with a display of Rod's album.

Rod had got a new band together in London. He had managed to sign guitarist Jimmy Cregan, bass player Phil Chen and lead guitarist Gary Grainger who hung out with a small band. These were to be his key men in the future.

As an artist Rod was maturing. I encouraged him to write his own material as I felt he could do much more with his creative talents and Rod was perceptive enough to see the benefits with the promise of larger royalties.

When he was composing a new song he would hum odd notes into a cassette recorder and he would jot down lyrics on a notepad, occasionally asking me to pair a rhyming word. Most of the songs from "A Night on the Town" were his; so were three songs from the earlier album "Atlantic Crossing."

His lyrics were earthy and gutsy, if lacking romanticism. One lyric to a song, "Three Times Loser" was about a guy who had contracted V.D. I asked him what had inspired such a tawdry lyric and he said, "It's got nothing to do with any personal experience, if that's what you're thinking." I was relieved.

I used to call Rod my proletarian bard because I saw him as a street urchin writing about simple, everyday things. That part of his life Rod had never left behind and now it was to become part of his poetry.

At least Rod was thinking now: thinking and hustling in the same way that I had once seen Lou involved. Business deals and future projects began to occupy

Rod's mind as much as his music.

Rod wanted his own record label and with patriotic worthiness he intended calling the company "Tartan" but found that a brewery was already functioning under that name.

Finally he settled for "Riva," having seen a speed-boat of that design on holiday in the South of France when I identified it as a model that Sellers once owned.

I don't know what Warner Brothers felt about the birth of Rod's U.K. launched "Riva Records," but I do know they were over the moon about "Tonight's the Night." It brought a harvest of gold discs from all parts of the world and a Warners' executive declared that my part in the publicity campaign, if not on the record, clinched it for them. And for Rod.

I didn't get a dime from the multi-million dollar royalties and I didn't ask for one. I did it all for love. Oh—and a sniff of coke that Rod gave me at the re-cording session to ease my nerves!

— *seventeen* —

MY agent Maggie Abbott was giving up on me. Every film she offered I turned down without excuse. I was so much in love with Rod that I just wanted to be with him.

"Britt, you never change," she lamented one day, "you blew out two marvelous films when you were with Sellers. You missed a hell of a chance when you got tied up with Bino. And now look at you . . . it's the same old story. Why do you always have to fall in love?"

I could feel some measure of sympathy for Maggie. She had just reluctantly cabled Vittorio Gassman in Italy to break the sad news to him that I was rejecting a major rôle in one of his movies.

Maggie was nonplussed at my decision.

"I can't think of any other actress in the world who would be insane enough to stand up Vittorio Gassman. It would have been a wonderful opportunity. You would have been working with a genius," she said despairingly.

I nodded. "Yes, I know." But I remained tight lipped. I knew exactly what Maggie was feeling. What was the point of her pushing my career if I was not going to co-operate with her?

Besides, as an agent she could barely make a decent living out of me. It was as well that she looked after the affairs of other artists who were infinitely more receptive to her good advice than I was.

Several months passed before Maggie decided to

make another plea for me to return to work. There was a huge German-financed movie about the slave trade of the Victorian period all set to roll in Rhodesia. It was titled *Slavers* and Ray Milland, Ron Ely, Trevor Howard and Cameron Mitchell were all set for the cast.

The producers were in Los Angeles and were keen to sign me. The timing was perfect. Rod and the band were about to leave on another concert tour, which normally I would have joined.

But Maggie put her foot down.

"Why don't you let Rod get on with his work while you get down to some of your own?" she remonstrated.

Rod thought it was a good idea. I would be away in Rhodesia nine weeks but I could possibly still make the tail-end of his tour.

I was not at all sure that I would clinch the rôle. Not after dyeing my long lank hair with henna. My hair had turned out a brilliant orange and Rod was goading me, "Mind someone doesn't mistake you for a carrot."

I would recoil from the mirror in horror whenever I caught a glimpse of myself. I couldn't step outside the door without wearing a turban.

When I went to see the two producers of the movie one of them said, "But you will report as a blonde for the movie, won't you, Miss Ekland?"

"Yes," I nodded weakly.

By now I knew the devastating effect of henna. It just couldn't be washed out like a dip. I spent three agonizing days with a Los Angeles hairdresser. As huge blisters appeared on my scalp he attempted to bleach my hair back to some semblance of its normal color tress by tress. A day or two later my hair began to fall out and his next advice was to chop the length of my hair by several inches. It still came down to my shoulders.

During the week of costume fittings for the movie I was scared that I might lose my hair altogether, but as the blisters healed so the pain and discomfort disappeared.

From then on I treated henna with considerable

respect and when Rod later dyed his hair red—I'm sure he looked on me as the guinea pig—he dipped it with harmless peroxide.

It was a long, tiring journey to Rhodesia. I had to fly through via London and Johannesburg, completing the journey to Fort Victoria in a small monoplane.

I was to provide the romantic interest in the plot and Ron Ely, the barrel chested beefcake of the movie, believed we might escalate things into real life.

I leveled with him. "I'm in love with someone else," I told him and it wasn't difficult for him to guess with whom. I had taken a stack of Rod's tapes to Rhodesia and I played them all of the time.

Ron, a former American athlete who played Tarzan in the television series, put my loyalty to the test at dinner with me most evenings after the day's filming.

But in the end he said, "That little pop guy of yours must have something very special."

"Yes," I replied, "he has."

Ron took it well. He was a typical male chauvinist who enjoyed dictating the odds but he conceded that he had met his match in me.

Because of the sanctions being applied by various governments against Rhodesia, the international telephone lines were in chaos and I waited days on end to speak with Rod. And when he did come through I said to him, "Why don't you send me a romantic message? I miss you so much out here."

The romantic message came by return on Telex. It said, "Dear Britt. Here is the romantic message you wanted. Tired of wanking. Please come home, Soddy."

Soddy was my pet name for Rod. There were times when he was such a sod even in his most charming moods. Rod coined a similar term of endearment for me. He would call me Poop or Poopy, which had all sorts of unsavory connotations but as far as I was concerned he meant it in its most affectionate sense.

I missed Rod like mad. I slept alone in a thatched hut in the grounds of a motel in the isolated Rhodesian veldt.

The hut was infested with bugs and creepy insects and every night I had to spray the room and take cover beneath the canopy of my mosquito net.

An appalling incident occurred during filming that was to remind us of the savagery that lurked in the bush. One of the lions that had been used in some of the scenes had to be shot, after it had attacked and killed its keeper.

When I posed for publicity pictures with a cheetah I found it hard to believe he was the cuddly, friendly creature he was made out to be.

One night Rod telephoned unexpectedly. I woke drowsily to his call. It sounded as though he was at a party but then I recognized the babbling voices of his band. They were in high spirits and above the noise I could hear Rod screeching, "We've done it, Poopy. We're No. 1 in America with 'Tonight's the Night'."

With that, he and the boys rendered their boozy version of the song on the telephone.

I couldn't sleep when I put down the receiver. I was too excited and I was up long before the Rhodesian dawn.

The film was completed on schedule and I left for London to catch up with Rod. Our reunion was sadly brief. I had to return to Africa almost immediately.

Many years before I had worked on *Night Hair Child* for producer Harry Alan Towers who had threatened to pull stills from the final print because I had refused to pose in the nude. While I was in Rhodesia he had contacted my agent asking me if I would star in *King Solomon's Treasures* being shot in neighboring Swaziland with David McCallum and Patrick McNee playing the leads. I turned it down but Harry Alan Towers cabled back asking me what I wanted.

In view of our previous experience I laid down some very demanding conditions, stipulating first class air fares and hotels, a twenty-four hour chauffeur driven car, expenses and a definite stop date. Harry sent a cable back saying "Okay." So I signed. I had struck a hard bargain, but I had no regrets.

Rod agreed I would have been crazy to turn it down. The deal, for ten days' work, was worth more than 50,000 dollars to me.

"We can wait another ten days before resuming normal service, Poopy," he laughed.

I took Victoria and Nicholai with me and we stayed in Johannesburg, where some wealthy friends conveniently ran a helicopter shuttle service for me to the film location. I must say it made things very easy for me. We would even go out by helicopter to dinner parties.

My African adventure over, I bought Rod, always ready to hoist the Scottish pennant of the "Lion Rampant," a stuffed lion's head and skin.

At 1,200 dollars it was quite a specimen with the lion's teeth bared and its claws open. Even its mane was perfectly intact.

I had the skin flown back to London in a huge box and when he opened it Rod's eyes were filled with disbelief.

"It's like having another member of the family in the house," he remarked, spreading the lion out on the carpet of the rented flat in Portland Place which we had taken over from Rudolf Nureyev.

Somehow it was. Serving a tray of tea without tripping over the lion's head became quite an art.

— *eighteen* —

WE were flying into Stockholm. Fresh winter snow sprinkled the ground and I turned to peer out of the cabin window of our descending jet.

I felt Rod's hand slide into mine. His voice was strangely soft.

"It's about time I made an honest woman of you, Poopy," he whispered, squeezing my hand.

Marriage to Rod had always hinged on my willingness to have his children. Until then I saw no reason to acquire a legal certificate. Our love for one another was a total commitment in itself.

What I was not prepared to do was to have any more children unless I was married. For *their* sake, as well as my own. A third child by a different father, without marriage, was beyond comprehension. And to get pregnant just to make him marry me would have been a blemish to our love.

Rod understood my position and now aboard the jet he was saying "Let's get married." I snuggled closer to him in his seat, my thoughts wistfully drifting to our future. Rod was already telling newspapers, "I would like to have a child with Britt."

I had no qualms about marrying him. I was sure Rod would make a good husband and father. His whole background was a family one and Rod was still very close to his folks and to his brothers and sisters.

Every year there was a family reunion and I became

part of his family. I will always cherish the Christmas spent at the semi-detached Cambridge home of Rod's elder brother Don.

There must have been at least twelve of us who sat down to the traditional turkey and plum pudding lunch. Most of us stayed in the small, cluttered house over the holiday: Rod and I slid into a single bed but it was the only one available and we did not mind.

We had soaked up the luxury of some of the best hotels in the world, but none had ever caught the atmosphere of this simple, ordinary family home at Yuletide.

Everyone was so warm and friendly. Rod's family treated me as one of them. What was more, they adored Victoria and Nicholai and gave them lovely presents. I was so moved by their kindness and affection.

That is why I knew that marriage to Rod would work out. These were his family roots and he wanted to spread his Scottish lineage even further.

This, then, was the meaning of his sudden proposal on the jet into Stockholm.

There was no need to tell Rod that I was ready to be his wife. He knew that. I was already in that rôle.

I kept home for him in America: a home shining with our love and all the treasures and furnishings we had chosen together.

Now I realized that we were entering a new phase of our relationship where Rod wanted to begin a family and I was ready to wear his wedding ring.

There was no hurry. No urgency. We would talk of it again when we were back from our travels. I was deliriously happy, prepared to abandon my career entirely.

People had marveled at the durability of our relationship, believing that a pop idol and a film star together were the model of a relationship too fickle to be sustained. Somehow we survived. We had been scrutinized, verified, analyzed and relentlessly judged by the standards and values of millions of people as far apart as America and Egypt, Australia and England, Japan and Brazil.

The perils were ever constant. Much earlier in our relationship the pressures from the media, particularly the trade Press, had put Rod into a tight corner. They accused him of being dominated and influenced by a "famous film star" and said that he was sacrificing his career for her.

Rod retaliated in an uncharacteristic way, by trying to illustrate that I didn't hold any influence or place in his life. He gave an interview to a British newspaper saying that he had no intention of ever marrying me.

"She isn't the right woman for me," he pronounced in the columns. "I've no plans to marry her."

They were cutting, horrific words and I collapsed into a heap of tears when I read them. I tossed the newspaper in his face and screamed at him, "How dare you say those kind of things when we've just built this home together. If you feel like this why go on with our relationship?"

Rod bit his lip like a schoolboy being scolded for a misdemeanor and tried to explain.

"I didn't really mean it, Britt," he lamented. "It's just how I feel at this moment. Maybe tomorrow I'll change my mind and we will marry. Who knows . . . ?"

The guilt hung over Rod's head all day and the luckless Tony Toon was called in to arrange a further interview with the London *Daily Mirror* in which he was to retract every single word.

"I should not have said these foolish things," said Rod. "Britt is the only woman in the world for me and one day we will marry . . ."

Unlike any other couple in love, we had no choice but conduct our lives in the full gaze of the Press. Pens were always poised to write, "They've split."

Sometimes it hurt. Especially the distortions. Nigel Dempster, the London *Daily Mail* gossip writer, once declared our romance was over on the morning we were kissing and holding hands at London Airport.

But an episode that involved Susan George the British actress, fed them with the kind of ammunition that newspapers breed on.

We were at a dinner party in Los Angeles after a Queen concert. I invited Susan as she was on her own to join our table and for an hour or two she was talking to Rod, while I was chatting with Freddie Mercury and the other Queen musicians.

I wanted to go home but I could see that Rod didn't feel like moving. He was totally immersed in conversation with Susan.

I didn't want to break things up, so I whispered to him that I was taking the car home and I quietly made my exit.

On the way home I fretted that Rod had not stirred from his seat to come with me. Maybe he fancied Susan. I fretted. She had big boobs and most of Rod's earlier women had big boobs. What if he slept with her? My head was spinning in all directions. It could only be the champagne.

Two hours later Rod arrived home. Susan had given him a lift. I knew as soon as the bedroom door opened we were going to have a row. Obviously Rod felt that aggression was the best form of defense. "Why did you ditch me there like that?" he yelled at me.

"You saw me go. You didn't have to stay with Susan George all night long," I retorted.

We started fighting one another and Rod, now seeing my fury, was in retreat. We scrambled across the bed exchanging blows. Suddenly I fell, hitting my head on the bed rail. I screamed with pain. I'd collected a gorgeous black eye and the repentant Rod disappeared to get some ice cubes to dress it.

At that point we called a truce and Rod was bursting with apologies. We made love and the incident was closed.

However, the next morning the newspapers gave their version of the story. They said I had thrown a glass of champagne over Rod and stalked out after accusing him of having an affair with Susan George.

Rod summoned our feedbox, Tony Toon, but he denied responsibility for leaking the story.

"It must have been put out by someone else," said Tony.

Dropping Susan's name into the melting pot delighted the gossip columnists. They later noted she was present at a London concert of Rod's while I was abroad filming and then came the curious story of how I got a locksmith to break down the door of the Portland Place flat with the sole intention of hoping to discover Rod and Susan together. I must confess it was a spectacular piece of imagination.

It was true that I had paid a locksmith £40 to gain access to the flat I shared with Rod. But as he was in Scotland with the keys and I had flown wearily into London from Munich I had no other way of getting in. I wasn't going to spend a winter's night out on the pavement.

In the coming weeks I began to meditate on the future of our relationship. Maybe we should marry, if only to stop the insinuations. But Rod only fleetingly mentioned the subject again. All his energies and time were devoted to his music and his band.

We planned a holiday aboard the *QE2*—it had always been Rod's dream. The cruise brought us closer together than ever before. Older passengers aboard must have regarded us as honeymooners. Our love for one another just shone from our eyes.

We occupied a suite on the top deck and when a steward showed us into it Rod's face gave away his feelings. There was no bed. He turned to the steward and asked, "Where do we sleep?" The steward pressed a button and the bed descended out of the wall. It was all very ingenious, except that one night the bed fell on to my foot and crushed one of my toes!

We had bought a whole new range of 'thirties clothes to wear aboard and the trip seemed to inspire Rod with his music. He wrote the lyrics for two more songs.

At nights, after dinner, he walked the decks in his red silk lined black velvet cape, reliving in his mind the whole *Titanic* disaster. He would even claim to hear "voices" as he leaned over the ship's rail. I already knew that Rod was intrigued by the *Titanic* by the collection of books in our home on the saga.

Throughout the entire voyage, Rod was amazingly romantic, and I was sure that when we returned we would make plans for our wedding. But nothing happened.

Maggie was of the opinion that my relationship with Rod was futile.

"Britt, it is leading nowhere," she said crossly. "It's stupid to go on the way it is now. In the end you will tire of one another and my feeling is that you are already getting a little fed up with him."

I guessed that Maggie was right. It was not that I was growing tired of Rod, but I was dejected by his apparent unwillingness to lay down positive plans for our future together.

If Rod really wanted marriage and a family, then I was perfectly prepared to settle down with him.

Instead, Rod was to become more distant. A lot of moodiness crept into our relationship, but on these occasions I would not pander to him in the way I had done with Sellers. I just kept silent or went out to have tea with my girl friends. I thought maybe that we should just take a rest from one another, instead of living in each other's pockets.

It was the summer of 1977 and I thought of my home in Sweden and of the little timbered seafront house at Smadalarö that I had bought from my grandparent's estate.

I mentioned to Rod that I might take a holiday there with the children at a time when he would be virtually imprisoned in the studios recording a new album.

He agreed.

"It's what you need, Poopy," he said, "the holiday will do you good."

I went through London on my way to Sweden and bought some beautiful wallpaper to redecorate my house. I also ordered some new furnishings.

The local Swedish people greeted my arrival warmly. It was as though I had never left them, but I don't imagine it dawned on them that I had not been to the house for ten years. The house had been taken care of by my family.

The summer was hot and sunny. I walked barefoot along the beach every morning with Nicholai and Victoria. I did the housework and cooking myself and I slept at regular hours. It was as if I had put the clock back on life itself. Everything was so peaceful and serene.

Sometimes I felt a twinge of guilt, because I didn't think of Rod as much as I should have done. When he rang it was as though I was talking to a stranger, not the man I still thought would become my husband.

I returned to Los Angeles at the end of July. Victoria had to go to see her father. Nicholai was due back with Lou.

I flew in tanned, refreshed and invigorated. Like a Nordic princess. An amusing situation greeted me. Both Rod and Lou were at the airport.

Lou had driven over to collect Nicholai in his yellow Ferrari and Rod had traveled across in his red Lamborghini to pick me up.

I came through immigration control and saw the two faces gazing over the barrier in my direction. I could not really go to one first without offending the other but I had no choice.

I decided to hand Nicholai to Lou, exchanging a word or two in the process, before spinning round into the arms of Rod who pressed his lips against mine in our first embrace for two months.

Lou drove off to Malibu while Rod and I headed for home at Carolwood. It was good to be back and Rod was bursting with news about the double album he still hadn't finished, about the places and people he had seen and of the changes he had made to the house.

The new swimming pool canopy I had designed and ordered was apparently now fluttering over the patio and it was small things like this that made me feel that perhaps I had been too long away from Rod and our home.

He looked tired and drained, as if he had been working too hard, and in our first few days together I noticed a decline in his virility. Normally we made love every night of the week. Now he pleaded tiredness and preferred to sleep.

Yet I could not really detect a lessening of his affections for me.

We went out to dinner with Billy Gaff and a bunch of friends one night to St. Germaine's, one of the posh restaurants in Los Angeles. In the middle of the meal Rod leaned over to me and whispered, "I've written a song for you Poopy . . ."

"Have you?" I said, warming to him. "Let me hear it." No one took any notice as Rod softly sang some words into my ear that were quite familiar to me because he had so often used them in his endearments in the past.

He sang, "You're in my heart, you're in my soul . . . you'll be my breath till I grow old . . . you're my lover . . . you're my friend . . ."

My eyes filled with tears. It was the loveliest song I had ever heard.

I wanted to go to the studio to hear the cut version but Rod wouldn't let me. He said he didn't want to spoil the surprise of how the song would work out once he had completed mixing the tracks.

I couldn't argue.

Rod drove off to the studios most afternoons, returning around six o'clock and then would head back for the night session.

I saw little of him during this period, but I did not complain. I was asked to appear on an American television program "Us Against The World" in which two sets of celebrities compete against each other in various water and athletic events.

I decided to get into peak trim for the contest and spent my days training in the gym and swimming in the pool.

— *nineteen* —

MY old friend George Hamilton sauntered into the Hollywood party being thrown by Alan Carr, the engagingly quixotic co-producer of *Grease* and many other films.

I smiled. For gripping George's arm was his wife Alana—the girl he had gone home to marry after our fling in the South of France.

Only now, despite their party presence together, they were in the throes of divorce. They didn't seem embarrassed but then in Tinsel Town divorce is purely an academic exercise.

In fact George was in high spirits. They had been out celebrating his birthday with none other than Leslie Bricusse—who had originally introduced us—and Leslie's wife Evie.

The party was at its height. When Alan Carr throws a shindig, it's like the ball of the year. Lobster, caviare and champagne become incidental items on a budget that must exceed those that lesser producers might attempt to make a movie on.

All evening I had been making apologies for Rod's absence. Of course, he was not supposed to be there with me; he was recording.

To get over my misery I decided to dress up in an ankle length white lacy gown. I looked terribly angelic, or so Maggie said when we drove over to Alan's breathtaking house at Malibu.

When George and Alana Hamilton came through the

door, we all kissed and greeted one another. George clearly wasn't going to be hemmed down by Alana and he took the first opportunity to sidetrack her.

He drew me aside. I thought, "Here comes the old charm" hearing on the grapevine that he was already fancy free and impatiently counting the days to his divorce. But I was totally unprepared for what he was going to say.

"Fancy Rod going out with Liz . . ." he said grinning away. "I never thought you two would bust up . . ."

I was totally bemused.

"But we haven't busted up, George," I said.

He shrugged.

"Sorry Britt. Then I must have got it all wrong. But I heard that Liz was driving his car and staying up at the house. In fact I saw 'em together only last week . . ."

"Liz who . . . ?" I asked.

"Liz Treadwell. Until a couple of months ago she was my girl friend and I just thought it was kind of funny that my ex-girl friend should be going with your ex-guy that's all. I wouldn't have mentioned otherwise. I really thought you knew, Britt. Everyone else in town does."

I had never heard of Liz Treadwell before and as George was talking I felt myself growing colder and colder.

I put down my glass of champagne. It tasted bitter.

When I got home the house was empty. It was just after 1:30 in the morning. I picked up the telephone to call Rod at the studio. I was now burning with torment. I had to know the truth. I dialed the number but then slammed the receiver down. No, I would wait for him to come home.

I did not undress. I flopped on the bed in my evening gown. The minutes dragged like hours but I could not sleep. My ears were alert for any noise from the drive. I thought I would hear Rod's car come through the gates.

I got up and started walking round the house. Every suspicion that lurked in my mind became a fresh nightmare to me.

Rod had gone to New York just a few days before to

sign for a film with Elton John. Why had he not asked
me to go with him? Why had I never been able to go to
the studio since my return from Sweden?

I could not satisfy myself with any kind of answer.

Why hadn't Rod made love with me every night?

Was it because he was sleeping with this woman Liz?

So my anxieties piled up like a pyramid.

It was now daylight and I crossed the patio to the
staff cottage that Tony Toon occupied. I banged hard
on the front door and finally roused him.

"Where is Rod?" I demanded to know. "What's
happened to him? He did not come home last night and
I'm worried. He didn't even call . . ."

Tony drowsily scratched his thinning pate.

"He's okay," he said. "Things went on late and they
all went off to the Hilton afterwards for drinks."

"They all got a bit pissed that's all, and I think Rod
put his head down there for the night."

I expressed my displeasure.

"Well Tony," I snapped. "He's never done that
before. So you had better find him fast. I have been
worried all night about him. There might have been an
accident. Someone should tell me."

Little more than an hour later Rod's car crunched up
the drive. Rod got out with Peter Buckland, his tour
manager.

I waited for them in the living room and Rod wan-
dered through looking suitably sheepish and feigning his
little boy lost act.

"I'm sorry Britt. I got drunk and fell asleep . . . we
kipped down at the Hilton," he said, word perfect from
Tony Toon's briefing.

Pete hovered nervously in the background.

"Okay," I sighed resignedly. "But you really might
have got someone to ring me, Rod. I'm feeling like a
wreck. I've been up all night waiting for you."

There were more apologies before Rod turned with
Pete to go down to the swimming pool. It was a
beautiful sunny day and they obviously intended to laze
out on the patio.

They had only gone four or five paces when I summoned Rod back.

"Oh, Rod, I would like to talk to you about something else," I said, my stilted words conveying it was a private matter.

We went up to the other patio at the back of the house and Rod was distinctly unnerved. His chin rested on his chest, his shoulders were drooped. I did not keep him in agony for too long.

"Please tell me about Liz Treadwell," I invited him quietly. "I hear that you have been having an affair with her and that she has been living in this house and driving your car . . ."

Rod slumped into a terrace chair.

"How did you find out?" he said.

I ignored his question. My heart was pounding.

"Have you slept with her?" I asked.

He nodded guiltily.

Neither of us spoke for several minutes.

Then he took a deep breath, as if preparing to say something.

"I'm sorry, Britt. It all happened while you were away in Sweden. You know what it is like . . ."

I had tried to remain calm and collected but I could not restrain myself any longer.

"What about the pact we made, Rod?" I said, my anger rising. "We both promised we would never sleep with anyone else. You said you would never have that kind of need."

Rod's sallow face was pale with shame, his eyes and hands were twitching.

"Do you love her, Rod?" I asked.

He shook his head. "I don't know," he said.

"Do you love me?"

"Yes," he nodded.

"Then you've got to make a choice. You can't have us both," I said.

"I can't make a choice," he murmured.

"Then you'll have to, Rod," I said.

Rod looked up.

"Who told you, Britt? Who did you hear it from?" he said.

"George Hamilton. I bumped into him at last night's party."

Rod's lips tightened.

"Why doesn't he mind his own bloody business?"

I defended George.

"But Rod, it was perfectly natural that he should tell me. He was making out with Liz Treadwell long before you."

On the terrace by the pool Pete Buckland was sunbathing. I knew that more of Rod's cronies would be arriving soon.

I had to resolve the matter there and then.

"Rod," I said. "I am going to give you a week in which to make up your mind as to what you want to do."

"Okay," he said slowly. "Maybe I should move out. We've taken a house on Mulholland for the band. They've got plenty of spare bedrooms so I can move in on there."

"I think that might be a good idea," I said.

Rod took some of his things from his wardrobe and tossed them into a suitcase. I heard the car engine roar into life. He was gone.

I broke down and cried. I felt hurt, cheated, betrayed. Our whole future together, our hopes, our dreams, were shattered. My eyes tearfully surveyed the house we had virtually built together: the collection of art nouveau, the antiques and furnishings we had brought back from the remotest parts of the world. What would happen to us now?

In my diary I unfolded my anguish . . . "My own private earthquake" . . . "Lies and deception" . . . "Snakepit" . . . "Hell not far away" . . . and "Alone at home with a hole through my heart."

I telephoned Maggie seeking consolation, but in the process I inevitably pieced together Rod's trail of infidelity through the summer. My friends, I concluded, had been keeping things secret from me for too long.

Liz Treadwell, a blond Californian beach girl, had not been the only light to shine in Rod's life during my absence in Sweden. He had taken out a succession of girls.

I was totally dejected. But no more so when learning that Rod's relationship with Liz Treadwell was continuing and that she was living with him in the Mulholland house that he had told me had been rented for the band.

I also learned that she had accompanied him on his trip to New York.

My love and respect for Rod crumbled like parched earth beneath the feet. There was nothing left, except for a burnt out shell.

I lunched with George Hamilton who saw the mental anguish I was suffering and he sent me to his shrink.

"You are going to need help to get over this, Britt," he said.

Pouring my heart out to the shrink led not to salvation but into a territory of deeper stress.

My psychiatrist's real qualifications were as a nutritionist and he put me on a liquid protein diet and fed me vitamin pills.

That wasn't all. His son was a lawyer who suggested I should remind Rod of his obligations with a 12,500,000 dollar lawsuit.

As I had formed a professional as well as personal partnership with Rod, he felt I was entitled to half the proceeds that had resulted from our joint efforts.

Besides, under Californian law the question of a woman in a live-in relationship claiming half the community assets was under debate.

By now I was like a piece of pulp. I was in a state of confusion and unrest.

I would sign any document that was thrust in front of me.

I had no idea of what I was doing. Day after day I had listened to the shrink and his lawyer son and I was convinced of my rights.

Thank God, something inside me prevented me from

doing something drastic to myself.

Maggie thought I had taken leave of my senses and wouldn't talk to me; while the shrink advised me not to communicate with any of my old friends because I could not trust them.

It was as if I had been programmed. On the night the writ was served on Rod, I actually drove a private detective in my car to the studio.

When Rod appeared from the studio door, the detective intercepted him and handed him the court document. A flashbulb popped: a lurking photographer had got a better picture than the one he had anticipated.

I guessed she was there with him but we could not see her.

It didn't matter. As the detective said on the way back into the center, our objective had been achieved.

Billy Gaff called to see me the next morning. It was like a sovereign sending an emissary to straighten things out. In normal circumstances I might have expected dogsbody Tony Toon but I suppose that a writ for 12,500,000 dollars necessitated a top brass assignment.

I poured Billy some tea and we sat in the lounge.

"Britt, you can't do this to Rod," said Billy. "You've got to drop it. You don't have a leg to stand on. You're being a silly girl."

I suddenly grew angry.

"Billy, don't call me a silly girl," I said. "I gave up my entire life for Rod. I sold my London flat. I moved all my belongings here. We built this home together. He asked me to marry him and now you're saying that I should get lost . . . ?"

Billy clasped his hands.

"Look Britt, he knows that he has done wrong. We've all told him that he has been a fool, but the fact is he *still* loves you. It's all finished with the other girl. She didn't mean a thing to him. Look—can't we get you back together? He's willing to come down here now and move right back in with you and you can start with a clean sheet. If only you can forgive him. Come on, Britt, you know what he's like. He didn't do this to hurt you deliberately. He just got carried away . . .''

I began to soften. Billy was persuasive. Why did I have this complex about infidelity?

I wanted to be the understanding woman and act rationally. Maybe I could bend the rules and give him a second chance.

Rod came back to the house that afternoon. We were like two different people. The atmosphere was almost formal and it was as if we were skating on ice, hoping to keep away from the cracks.

"Why did you drop that writ on me?" Rod finally rustled up the courage to ask.

"Because you hurt me and told me lies," I said.

We kissed but there was no fire, no passion. And we slept together for three nights but we lay coldly with our backs to one another.

The second morning a white card tumbled out of Rod's wallet onto the bed cover. The number scrawled on it seemed vaguely familiar but I could not think why.

I passed on the information to my nutritionist whose network of contacts traced the number to the Waldorf Astoria in New York and discovered that Liz Treadwell was staying in the hotel in a suite reserved by one of Rod's associate companies.

So their affair was not over. Another ugly scene broke out between us.

At the time my father had flown down from Canada because I felt the need of his support in my court case against Rod. A preliminary hearing was set before Judge Edward Rafeedi who refused to make any temporary orders until the case could be determined in full.

It was a setback but my lawyers were optimistic about gaining an overall victory, basing their case on my live-in agreement with Rod that we should pool the earnings and assets that derived from our relationship. My backing on his promotion catapulted him to superstardom, my lawyers said.

Rod, in his pronouncements to newspapers, had certainly given that impression. He was quoted in the London *Daily Mirror* as saying, "Sometimes—with respect to Billy Gaff who manages me brilliantly—I wonder why Britt's not my manager. She's so aware of the business I'm in and I've never had a partner like that before.'' He told America's *People* magazine, ''Britt came along and said I was wasting my talent. She gave me a kick in the ass.''

It was my belief that we should share everything together. Our lives, our emotions, our belongings and our futures.

I think in his heart Rod knew that too. But he entered a defense to my court action, denying that we had a ''professional partnership'' and what was more adding that I was a lousy cook and that I had merely tagged along ''for the ride'' on his world tours.

It was all very hurtful but I guessed that Rod knew the truth. He was still anxious to patch things up and Billy and Maggie acted as mediators.

I dined out with Rod at Pip's and we danced, but at the end of the evening Rod dropped me at the door of Carolwood like a boy going out on his first date. He was afraid of upsetting Liz but he didn't want to tell me that.

I was still not eating. I had hardly touched a thing for six weeks and I was down to 96 pounds—twenty pounds less than my usual weight. My shrink-cum-nutritionist said I was suffering from anorexia nervosa and he prescribed a different set of vitamin pills for me.

It was my 35th birthday and fifty pink roses and a bottle of Guinness arrive at the door, together with a card that read, ''Drink this and fatten yourself up, girl—Rod.''

Rod was again on tour with the band and insiders were telling me that his affair with Liz Treadwell had finally blown apart.

I might have guessed myself when the telephone started buzzing again with calls from Rod telling me he loved me, that he had made a mistake and expressing his willingness to resume our relationship the moment he got back into town.

''I can never leave you, Poopy,'' he said.

I began to believe him. I even waited in at nights for his calls. I also started eating again and I ordered my lawyers to put a "hold" on the court action.

One night Rod rang and said he was coming home and could I cook him dinner? He was in the Midwest somewhere and he was going to charter a plane.

I felt butterflies break out in my stomach. I was so excited. I got the house looking like a new pin. I cooked liver, one of his favorite dishes, and I checked that all the wines he liked were in the fridge including Sauterne for which he had a particular passion. I set a table with candles and flowers.

When Rod came in our love instantly re-ignited, dissolving all the hate, hurt and revenge that had filled our veins for two months.

We made love with all the fervor, the passion and the tenderness of our first night together.

Suddenly the storm clouds had gone. We were together again, talking like a couple of kids in the small hours as we re-planned our future.

"There will never be anyone else. Not now, Poopy," said Rod.

Soon after dawn he had to go. He had to catch the charter plane for Chicago.

"But don't worry, Poopy. I will be back," he said affectionately nipping my ear.

Two weeks later I had to go to Sarasota, Florida to work on the television film *The Great Wallendas*, based on the lives of the famous circus family. Rod had called twice but now there was silence.

Friends on the set hid the newspapers from me, but a couple of rags fell into my hands. The gossip columns were full of Rod and fresh affairs. I called Los Angeles and my shrink had already verified the reports. They were true, he said.

Again, I felt sickened. How could I go on trusting Rod the way I did? Didn't his word count for anything?

I could not believe that he was still that immature.

Just for once I had to be brave. My role as Jenny

Wallenda was an important one. I had trained and worked hard for it. I could not let my private hell interfere on the film set, but somehow I must have communicated my sorrow without realizing it.

Bubba, a twenty-two-year-old American boy who was a high wire artist, befriended me. He was very shy and he found it hard to approach me because I was one of the stars of the film.

But stumbling over his words he told me one day, "When I am on the high wire I look down into your face and I know that you are very sad . . . Is there anything I can do?"

I was touched.

"What is your name?" I asked him. From that moment on we were friends.

Bubba was so poor that he could not even afford to buy me a meal. I would sit with him in a backstreet coffee bar and listen to him tell the story of his life with the circus. It was fascinating.

I fell in love with him, if it is possible to love two men at the same time. Bubba was a good looking boy, and he was so full of spirit and adventure.

It was so funny. He knew all of the circus antics and he would shed his clothes and walk around the bedroom on his hands.

I had taken a condominium facing the sea and in Bubba I found a fresh will to live.

I also found strength to face Billy Gaff, once more playing his role as Rod's emissary on a fleeting visit to Sarasota.

"Rod is willing to settle out of court," said Billy coming quickly to the point. "You can have 200,000 dollars now and get it all over and done with."

I tried not to grimace but I knew my lawyers were seeking 12,500,000. They could not have been asking for an amount like that without reasonable grounds.

But I wasn't interested in the money. Billy's jaw sagged when I told him.

"If I take one penny off Rod I won't see him again,"

I said "I loved Rod—and I still do. It's not money I want. It's him."

Billy talked of a "fresh" agreement and I outlined the details of the way I felt that agreement should be. He flew back to New York. Later he telephoned me to say that Rod had agreed with it and the lawyers would be instructed to set it up.

My parting with Bubba came on completion of *The Great Wallendas*. It was a sad moment and my throat ran dry. He could not bring himself to say "goodbye." He telephoned me from a booth and he cried his farewell.

At that point I should have known that any possible hopes of a reconciliation with Rod would only cause me further heartache, but I allowed myself to be persuaded into it.

Unfortunately, Rod's attempts to put things back on an even keel had a superficial ring about them.

He was under the impression that I would accept any form of behavior that he cared to throw at me. I wasn't going to be subjected to the role of a housekeeper, as he had once manipulated poor Dee Harrington into being.

Rod, although crying his need to repair our relationship at Carolwood, would openly flout any commitment he made.

There were three concerts at the Forum in Los Angeles. He only allowed me to go to the third and the whole evening was ruined by a floosie he brought into the house and perched at our cocktail bar in the lounge before we had even left for the gig.

Rod said the girl was a friend of his secretary, Doris Tyler, but of course she wasn't. I was humiliated.

I strongly suspected that she wasn't the only floosie that Rod was associating with. There were nights when he would not appear home and I knew that he had gone to parties at Billy Gaff's house.

Rod was back into the whole groupie thing and he really thought that I would accept it all without so much as raising an eyebrow. One night he came home so drunk that Tony Toon had to drag him across the floor on to the bed.

Even when he stayed home Rod acted in a strange, unrecognizable way. He had dyed his hair white and his personality had changed to an aggressive one. Late at night he would bring in a bunch of mates and I was worried about the amount of cocaine I knew was being brought into the house. I warned him about it, but he took no notice. It was as if he didn't care any more.

In his glazed, pitiful eyes he no longer held me as the goddess he once worshipped. I was just as much a chattel as any one of the footballs he could kick around.

I was looking like a ghost and my weight fell by another five pounds. I got sties on my eyes. I could not think or act rationally . . . I even began to snort cocaine, from the very packages of cocaine I had warned Rod about.

All I wanted to do was to escape. I had a total nervous breakdown. Maggie Abbott urged me to change psychiatrists and I consulted Aaron Stern, a famous Beverly Hills physician. The fees were a hundred dollars a session and I went every day for a whole month but my sanity was worth it. At last I was able to look at my children and realize how much they relied on me and how much they trusted me. I knew I had to get myself back together—for their sake. There was hope if nothing else.

Maybe Rod's conscience troubled him. Knowing how much Victoria had always missed her pony "Buttercup" he made the remarkable gesture of buying her a cognac-colored Arab stallion she named "Rosie Lee" and he bought her the saddling and paid for a whole year's stabling. It meant an outlay to Rod of some 5,000 dollars. Never had I known him to be so generous.

It hurt Rod so much that he left it to Billy Gaff to hand the horse over to Victoria.

As a token of Victoria's thanks I bought a rare ceramic vase for Rod which I knew he would appreciate, having now realized the worth of our art nouveau collection.

When Rod went on tour, a certain measure of peace prevailed in the house but our relationship was still in a transitional state of agony.

There were calls from London and then from Rio de Janeiro suggesting I should fly out to talk over our future. Rod even sent air tickets for me to go to Rio but he did not ring through to confirm the final arrangements and when he eventually phoned I told him, "Go fuck yourself."

I thought that might be the end of it but one night Rod flew back and walked casually into the house when I was throwing a dinner party to mark the television screening of *The Great Wallendas*.

I almost fainted when he said he had flown in from London especially to see my television appearance.

Again, we could have made a fresh start and I remember on Valentine's night we were very much in love and we went out to dinner at Le Dome together.

But it was not long before Rod blotted his copybook once more.

Somewhere in the middle of it all Bianca Jagger rang and asked for Rod. I recognized her voice when she said, "Is he coming to Spain?" I hung up. I didn't care what her motives were.

I had finally reached the point where I could not physically or mentally cope with the situation. Here I was. Alone with two children and nowhere to go. My flat in London sold and most of my furnishings left with Rod. What was I to do?

I telephoned Lou and asked if he could help.

Poor Lou. Whenever I was in trouble I always telephoned him. But I didn't have anyone else to turn to.

Lou had never let me down and he didn't then.

He put the Stone Canyon house at my disposal. By now it was in need of repair as it had become something of a hostel for Lou's visiting friends.

However, Lou was the first to realize the house needed renovation and when I moved in he gave me the go-ahead to carry out repairs and redecoration. He also loaned me 1,000 dollars so that I could take the children to Hawaii for a few days' rest, away from the turmoil. His kindness was my salvation.

But the day I actually moved out of Carolwood my heart filled with sorrow and a deep sense of loss. I loved that house so much and when Rod once threatened to go on to Bermuda for tax reasons I told him, "I can't leave Carolwood. I want to live out my life here."

Rod could not understand it. "It's only paint and wallpaper, bricks and mortar," he said, "we can always start again. We can build another home."

I felt hurt because Rod didn't have the same sentimental thoughts about the house that I did. I could never start again. I thought Carolwood was the loveliest house in the world—and I still do. There will never be another house like Carolwood. And we had made it our home together.

Now I was finally leaving and I fought back my tears.

I had engaged a packing firm to box up my clothes and those of the children, and some of the china, art books and odd things that belonged to me.

Rod lingered around the house that morning and he asked, "Are you really going?" I tried not to look at him for fear I would burst into tears.

"There's no option is there?"

Rod didn't answer.

He took sanctuary in his room.

There were no goodbyes.

— *twenty* —

In my passport I am named as "Mrs. Britt Sellers also known as Britt Ekland." My nationality is shown as Swedish, and that is still a matter of pride for me today.

I could have taken English citizenship but I have no wish to escape from my roots which are still embedded in Stockholm where the rest of my family live today.

As a family we have kept reasonably close. Of course we have had our differences. Is there a family that can really say otherwise?

My mother spends regular holidays with me, taking delight in her grandchildren and I am still in touch with my father and my three brothers.

My eldest brother, Bo, is an accountant specializing in tax matters and he handles my affairs in Stockholm. He is very happily married and he and his wife Maria and their two children were selected by the German magazine *Stern* as representing the "perfect Swedish family."

My youngest brother Kalle still owns Stockholm's main pop record store, but of my three brothers I was closest to Bengt. He once studied architecture, but he then followed me into the acting profession, which was, in the circumstances, a precarious thing to do.

Visconti thought that Bengt with his incredibly striking features—he is tall, dark and blue eyed—would make a leading man of the Alain Delon stamp.

Unfortunately, the film that Visconti planned for Bengt fell through.

However, Bengt appeared in several other movies, including one of mine, *The Cannibals*, in which he actually played my brother.

I also got him a part in an episode of Robert Wagner's television series *To Catch a Thief* and in Sweden he worked with the eminent director Ingmar Bergman, something which remains an unfulfilled ambition of mine.

With only three years separating us in age we were often mistaken as twins and Bengt stayed with me in Rome and in London for long periods.

I did everything possible to encourage his career, but unfortunately Bengt could not cope with the frustrations of the profession such as the long periods that one must inevitably wait before a suitable part becomes available.

When television and film work wasn't readily available Bengt worked as a male model or he took other odd engagements and I got him a job as a dispatch rider at the time Patrick Lichfield started a special postal collection service during an official Post Office strike in England.

Finally Bengt quit acting in a fit of despair and his life went through a particularly bad phase. His marriage, like his career, also broke down and when I next saw Bengt he was back in Sweden burying his woes by immersing himself in the pages of books on Marxism.

I am afraid that he blamed me for his failures and protested that I had disorientated his entire life by having subjected him to the ''jet set'' environment.

Bengt eventually got over this unhappy episode and began more serious studies which took him into teaching where he is now settled. But, I must admit that Bengt's dissatisfaction was very painful for me.

A far more distressing area of my life, however, has been even more acutely closer to home. It has concerned the constant harassment that I have suffered from Sellers.

Our divorce wasn't easy to explain to Victoria and I think she only began to understand its real meaning

when she was eight or nine. Other children, whose parents were also divorced, helped her to grasp the situation.

Victoria grew up with me and I gave her father every reasonable access, but there were countless occasions when he was unable to see her.

Eventually Victoria went into a boarding school but she left after only one term because she became desperately unhappy and the headmistress had to agree that she was homesick.

Victoria is a sensitive, and bright girl who needs a great deal of love and affection at all times.

She is unaware of the fact that thousands of dollars were spent on lawyers and litigation in a continual tug-of-war over her future.

All through her young life Victoria kept a special place in her heart for her father, seeing no wrong in him, and I never tried to alter those thoughts because I wanted her to respect him. It was unimportant what we, her parents, thought of one another.

Victoria, having seen all her father's films and knowing of his fame, was in awe of him and she overlooked the periods when he was not talking to her.

If she suspected something was amiss then I would say to her, "Never mind. I expect your father is not too well." Or I made up some other excuse so that she would not think badly of him.

As a mother I probably have many faults. I am not the kind of mother who has been able to read bedtime stories or to sit at a kitchen table with a tube of glue and make animal cardboard cutouts.

Nevertheless, I am totally dedicated. The essential needs of my children have been my first concern.

Victoria is fourteen now. I try not to see any of Sellers in her, although I must confess there is a physical resemblance.

She has his dark, almost black eyes, black eyebrows and eyelashes, and very dark brown hair and olive skin but fortunately her other features are closer to mine.

She has a heart-shaped face and certainly her nose is similar to mine.

Very soon now, thank goodness, she will be able to make her own decisions about her future.

She will be able to accept or reject the guidance that I have felt is necessary to impart.

Maybe she will then see her childhood in the true perspective that is presently obscure to her.

I have told Victoria to keep in touch with Michael and Sarah, the children of Sellers's marriage to Anne, in an effort to keep some semblance of family life.

At school, Victoria is showing promise at art and her future could well be in this field. Should she express a desire to become an actress I shall not stand in her way but I shall try and cushion her from the mistakes and pitfalls that we must all experience in those early years.

Victoria actually made her screen "debut" when she was eighteen months old in a shot for the television film _The Trials of O'Brien_ which I made in New York with Peter Falk. She was also seen in a sequence in the James Bond film _The Man With The Golden Gun_, walking casually through the swingdoors of a hotel in Bangkok. She was then nine years old and she found it all very funny.

Any child of a marriage between two artists is certain to be subjected in some measure to the influences of the profession—whatever we may have done to protect them.

Victoria is now in Los Angeles where she attends school with Tony Curtis's daughter Alexandra.

I filmed _Casanova and Co._ with Tony in Venice a couple of years ago and I know that he and his wife are concerned in the same way about Alexandra's future.

Inevitably it will be our children who will make the final decisions but we shall guide them as far as it is possible to do so.

As for Nicholai, he is only five. Victoria loves him and she is like a second mother to him. He is smart, sporty and very loving. I know every mother believes her son to be handsome but I don't care to think of any child being so good looking as Nicholai. He's so perfect.

Lou is the most devoted of fathers to him and plays an active part in his day-to-day life.

It fills me with relief that Nicholai has a father who loves and cares for him in precisely the way that I do and that all decisions we make are made in accord.

When I consider my own future it must necessarily be formed round the needs of my children, as they remain of prime importance to me.

As I have said earlier, any man who comes into my life must first accept my children.

It is always possible that I will marry again and have more children. I am still in search of that emotional sustenance but there is no mad rush.

If I were to introduce a new man into the home, I would go to painstaking lengths to ensure his gradual acceptance by my children.

Not once have I subjected either of them to seeing me in bed with any of my lovers. They *never* will.

Victoria has probably seen me fall in and out of love without realizing it. I have always hidden my feelings from her.

She formed a close and warm regard for Lou because he treated her—and still does—with the same kindness and consideration that he shows Nicholai.

She also got along very well with Rod and at school she found that Sellers wasn't nearly so much of a hero as a super rock idol like Rod who sent her companions green with envy.

I am sure that Rod held an awful lot of affection for Victoria and Nicholai, although he may not have recognized it at the time. He once said in a magazine interview, "Britt's children are a pain in the arse sometimes. I was thrown in the deep end with them and I'm not a great lover of kids anyway. But I think they really dig me because I'm not like a father figure to them. I'm more like a stupid, big brother."

I still think Rod would have made a good father, as he has found out himself.

When I spoke to his parents, at the time of our breakup, I know that they were crestfallen because more than most things they would dearly love to see Rod settle down and have a family. Rod told *Cosmopolitan*: "Britt and I should have got married. I was so in love with her, especially that first year."

Since our parting we have met twice, on both occasions quite accidentally.

I was having drinks with some friends on my birthday last year at Lou's private club "On the Rox" in Los Angeles when Rod was holding court at an adjoining table.

Rod invited me and my friends back to the Carolwood house for a night-cap and everything was friendly and amicable.

When we got there he implored me to have a look over the house.

Very little had changed, except the bedroom that had once been occupied by Victoria had been stripped and given a new white satin finish.

Rod was then involved with Alana Hamilton, ex-wife of George Hamilton; she later became his wife.

I said to Alana, "So you are the new mistress?" but she made light of it. "I don't think so," she said.

The Press was very anxious to witness my first public confrontation with Rod, but a New Year's Eve kiss in London when we found ourselves in the same night club was greatly exaggerated.

David Wigg of the London *Daily Express* must have put a stop watch on the encounter, saying that it was only terminated by Alana pouring champagne over me. Totally untrue but then again very imaginative.

By then Rod knew that I had employed his former secretary Doris Tyler as my personal assistant. After one of his concert tours, she faced the prospect of redundancy but as she had always helped me with my affairs during my days with Rod, I could not see her put out of work.

In a way we also experienced similar heartache. Doris and her husband Richard, who designed Rod's stage costumes, were divorcing and Doris was striving to bring up her son Sheridan. I felt a considerable empathy with her situation and Doris and her son now live with me and the Ekland family has grown.

In the spring of 1979 Rod married Alana when it was said she was four months pregnant. I sent a good luck telegram.

As to my own personal life, I have been more than cautious in forming any new romantic attachments.

I could have easily ventured another season with George Hamilton, who swept me out to parties in the homes of Sammy Davis, Jr. and producer Robert Evans. But the magic was gone.

More than anything else I valued my time to explore my new freedom and I dated mostly younger men who showed no desire to settle down.

I try to lead a private life and feel that in L.A. I have succeeded.

Although, I have come to build an affection for the public glare. How can I truly be hostile to it, when I am in show business? We crave for attention if the truth is known, and we survive on it.

But I have made one pledge in my personal affairs.

Never to sacrifice my career again for a man.

— *twenty-one* —

LIFE as a star has brought its rare moments. An English sculptor, John Cotter, produced a facsimile of my lips and offered replicas in bronze, aluminum, plastic and rubber, scented in "Musk" and underlaid with "rose petals."

"Shut your eyes and imagine it's Britt Ekland you're kissing" ran his sales slogan when offering "the last few pairs" at £42 a set!

Britain's drinkers named me among the Top Six faces they wished to see on their beer mats and Swedish pools winner Nils Sandberg, scooping £119,000 on Vernon's coupons, offered to make me his fourth wife.

It was a flattering proposal from a great grandfather and as difficult to reject as any of those I receive among the 20,000 fan letters I get each year!

My two friends David Niven and Sammy Davis, Jr. also have a winning way with them. David says that had he not married Hjordis then I would have been the only other Swede he would have considered taking as his wife, while Sammy once married to a lady named May Britt jokingly insists he got our names confused at the time . . .

These facets of a star's life can be quite piquant. I have always believed that if one is a star one must live like a star and I travel 150,000 miles a year in the quest of my career.

I've enjoyed being part of the razzmatazz that essentially belongs to show business.

I've worn sequined suits, top hats and tails as happily as Yves St. Laurent gowns at parties, premières and glittering gala occasions.

I keep a collection of more than 500 pairs of shoes, possibly a throwback to the "black" and "brown" footwear days of childhood, but the real cause is more likely to be Freudian. Survival is the motivating purpose of every step I take!

Neither death nor age worry me. I think of death as being no more discomforting than a long and perhaps deserved sleep. I haven't yet considered life after death as I'm still too preoccupied with this one.

Gray hair, wrinkles and varicose veins that may blemish the body with the passing years I shall accept and come to terms with. I intend to grow old gracefully.

My whole ambitions for the future, outside the prospects of marriage, still revolve around my deeply cherished ambitions to gain absolute recognition as one of the world's leading actresses, if only to vindicate the award I got in 1966 from the Motion Picture Exhibitors who voted me then as one of the "Top Ten Stars of Tomorrow."

Striving towards this objective I have totally immersed myself in my work over the past two years, and in the process I have found the exercise a useful therapy in healing all the emotional scars of my past.

Most of the spring of 1978 was devoted to filming a new television series in Sweden about a shipping tycoon's family. The British actress Hilary Tindall played a co-starring role in the series, simply titled "The Shipowners."

In America I shot two segments of the outer-space television marathon "Battlestar Galactica" for NBC, and taking part in my second "Us Against The World" celebrity sports match I actually finished on the winning side. An omen that showed perhaps that things were definitely on the up!

I flew to Australia. Equity wouldn't let me pick up 100,000 dollars from commercials booked for me, but no matter, I did present the Australian film awards in Perth.

I also traveled to Rome to film an episode of the English television series The Return of the Saint, and at the close of the year I was in London starring in my first stage play since drama school days.

I was naturally apprehensive about the play, a comedy about a young wife who seeks the advice of her ex-husband in choosing his successor.

The play, *Mate*, had a successful provincial run but I am afraid it was not sufficiently strong enough to sustain its West End season and I wrote to the producer Walter Jokel and told him so. He ignored my advice and the play flopped after three weeks.

I also missed the last three performances, after slipping a disc while on stage. For the next six weeks I wore a neck brace and underwent painful traction treatment.

There are many people I still want to work with in the profession. There are a handful of directors whose creativity I greatly admire.

The 'eighties are here. It's a new era and I vow the world hasn't heard the last of Britt Ekland.

This is only the beginning.

And I wasn't born to be a loser!

— *appendix* —
FILMOGRAPHY

FILMOGRAPHY

Year	Film	Studio	Director	Co-stars
1963	To Bed or Not to Bed	Italian	Igi Polodori	Alberto Sordi
1963	Il Commandante	Italian		Toto
1965	After the Fox	United Artists	Vittorio de Sica	Peter Sellers
				Victor Mature
1966	The Double Man	Warner Bros.	Franklin Shaffner	Yul Brynner
1966	The Bobo	Warner Bros.	Robert Parrish	Peter Sellers
1967	The Night They Raided Minsky's	United Artists	William Friedkin	Jason Robards
				Elliott Gould
				Norman Wisdom
1968	Machine Gun McCain	Euro Int	Guilliano Montaldo	John Cassavetes
				Peter Falk
1968	Stiletto	Avco Embassy	Bernard Kowalski	Alex Cord
1969	The Cannibals	Euro Int	Liliana Cavani	Pierre Clementi
1969	Tintomara	Athena	Hans Abramson	
1970	Percy	Anglo-EMI	Ralph Thomas	Hywel Bennett
				Elke Sommer
				Julia Foster

Year	Title	Company	Director	Cast
1970	*Get Carter*	MGM	Michael Hodges	Michael Caine
1970	*Time For Loving*	Hemdale	Christopher Miles	Mel Ferrer
				Joanna Shimkus
				Susan Hampshire
1971	*Night Hair Child*	Rank	James Kelly	Hardy Kruger
				Lili Palmer
				Harry Andrews
				Mark Lester
1971	*Endless Night*	British Lion	Sidney Gilliat	Hayley Mills
				Hywel Bennett
				George Sanders
1972	*Baxter*	Anglo-EMI	Lionel Jeffries	Jean Pierre Cassel
				Patricia Neal
				Scott Jacoby
1972	*Asylum*	CIC	Roy Ward Baker	Peter Cushing
				Charlotte Rampling
1972	*The Wicker Man*	British Lion	Robin Hardy	Edward Woodward
				Diane Cilento
1974	*The Ultimate Thrill*	Independent	Robert Butler	Roger Moore
1974	*The Man with the Golden Gun*	United Artists	Guy Hamilton	Christopher Lee
				Maud Adams

1974	*Royal Flash*	20th Century-Fox	Dick Lester	Malcolm McDowell
				Alan Bates
1975	*High Velocity*	Independent	Rene Kramer	Ben Gazzara
1976	*Casanova, Italian Style*	German		Tony Curtis
1977	*Slavers*	Lord Films	Jurgon Gosler	Trevor Howard
				Ron Ely
				Ray Milland
1977	*King Solomon's Treasures*	Anglo-Canadian	Aluin Rukoff	Patrick McNee
				David McCallum
1979	*The Hostage Tower*	Independent	Claudio Gazman	Peter Fonda
				Merl Adams

Glittering lives of famous people!
Bestsellers from Berkley

★ ★

__**BRANDO FOR BREAKFAST** 04698-2—$2.75
Anna Kashfi Brando and E.P. Stein
__**CONVERSATIONS WITH JOAN CRAWFORD** 05046-7—$2.50
Roy Newquist
__**HOLLYWOOD IN A SUITCASE** 05091-2—$2.95
Sammy Davis, Jr.
__**LADD: A HOLLYWOOD TRAGEDY.** 04531-5—$2.75
Beverly Linet
__**SUSAN HAYWARD: PORTRAIT OF A SURVIVOR** 05030-0—$2.95
Beverly Linet
__**MISS TALLULAH BANKHEAD** 04574-9—$2.75
Lee Israel
__**MOMMIE DEAREST** 05242-7—$3 2 5
Christina Crawford
__**MOTHER GODDAM** 05394-6—$2.95
Whitney Stine with Bette Davis
__**MY WICKED, WICKED WAYS** 04686-9—$2.75
Errol Flynn
__**NO BED OF ROSES** 05028-9—$2.75
Joan Fontaine
__**SELF—PORTRAIT** 04485-8—$2.75
Gene Tierney with Mickey Herskowitz
__**SHOW PEOPLE** 04750-4—$2.95
Kenneth Tynan
__**FRANCES FARMER: SHADOWLAND** $2.75
William Arnold
__**TRUE BRITT** $2.95
Britt Ekland

Berkley Book Mailing Service
P.O. Box 690
Rockville Centre. NY 11570